Veterans Benefits Guide

by Angie Papple Johnston

Author of *Military Transition For Dummies*

for
dummies®
A Wiley Brand

Veterans Benefits Guide For Dummies®

Published by: **John Wiley & Sons, Inc.,** 111 River Street, Hoboken, NJ 07030-5774, www.wiley.com

Copyright © 2023 by John Wiley & Sons, Inc., Hoboken, New Jersey

Published simultaneously in Canada

For general information on our other products and services, please contact our Customer Care Department within the U.S. at 877-762-2974, outside the U.S. at 317-572-3993, or fax 317-572-4002. For technical support, please visit https://hub.wiley.com/community/support/dummies.

Wiley publishes in a variety of print and electronic formats and by print-on-demand. Some material included with standard print versions of this book may not be included in e-books or in print-on-demand. If this book refers to media such as a CD or DVD that is not included in the version you purchased, you may download this material at http://booksupport.wiley.com. For more information about Wiley products, visit www.wiley.com.

Library of Congress Control Number: 2022945874

ISBN: 978-1-119-90761-9 (pbk); ISBN: 978-1-119-90762-6 (ebk); ISBN: 978-1-119-90763-3 (ebk)

SKY10036100_092122

Contents at a Glance

Table of Contents

Introduction

Somewhere in the neighborhood of 200,000 people leave military service each year. If you're reading this book, there's a pretty good chance that you're on your way out, military service is already in your rearview mirror, or someone you care about once swore an oath to support and defend the Constitution of the United States.

As a veteran of the United States Armed Forces, you're entitled to a wide range of benefits designed to help you get — and stay on — your feet. Some of those benefits come directly from Uncle Sam by way of your branch, the Department of Veterans Affairs, and other government agencies, and others are from civilian organizations that want to pitch in to help veterans succeed.

Regardless of where these myriad benefits come from, the fact is that you've earned them. But nothing is as easy as it seems: Sometimes these benefits are tough to find. The Veterans Administration (VA) and other government agencies aren't exactly known for their efficiency, and sometimes great veterans benefits get lost in the shuffle. They're buried under mountains of paperwork, accidentally hidden on hard-to-navigate websites, or simply not publicized at all, so many veterans don't even know what they qualify for without sitting down with a VA rep or Veterans Service Officer (commonly called a VSO). And that doesn't even cover benefits you can get from civilian organizations and agencies!

That's where *Veterans Benefits Guide For Dummies* comes in.

About This Book

Let me get this out of the way first: This book doesn't contain any classified information on veterans benefits. In fact, if you knew where to look, you could probably find sufficient information on at least some of the benefits I outline in this book. Most of them are tucked away somewhere on the VA's or Department of Defense's many websites, in the text of federal and state laws, and buried in other publications. In other words, they're all over the place.

This handy guide consolidates all of them, so it's your complete guide to veterans benefits that come from multiple government and civilian organizations. (Just remember: These benefits are subject to change, so if you find one that interests you, go straight to the organization that offers it to get the most current information.) You can use this book to save time and avoid the headaches associated with finding and applying for your earned benefits. It explains all your benefits in ways that won't stress you out or leave you scratching your head in confusion. This book even tells you who qualifies for which benefits based on discharge status, time periods served, and family status (that's right — your spouse and kids can earn some, too). I even point out a number of benefits you can get from your state government and private organizations so you have the most well-rounded picture of what you're entitled to.

This book answers big questions, such as

>> Can I get medical care or mental healthcare if I didn't retire from service? Where can I go and what can I do if I'm in a crisis?

>> How do military pensions and VA disability payments work?

>> How will the government help me find a job?

>> How do I use my VA loan, and what can I use it for?

>> How do I use my GI Bill, and how much money will Uncle Sam pay me to go to school? What other programs can pay for my tuition?

>> What benefits can I get if I don't have an honorable discharge?

>> Can incarcerated or homeless veterans get any special help?

>> What burial benefits are available to veterans and survivors?

>> Can my dependents use benefits I earned, or do they get their own?

>> What fun benefits are available to vets when it comes to travel, shopping, and other recreational activities?

Foolish Assumptions

I know what happens when you assume, but I went ahead and thought a lot about you before writing this book. I figure the following about you:

>> You're getting ready to separate from the military, you've already separated, or you care enough about a particular veteran to help them get the benefits they've earned.

>> You want to position yourself (or someone else) for success in the civilian sector.

>> You have questions about specific benefits and how to get them.

Icons Used in This Book

Throughout this book, you find icons to help you pick up what I'm laying down. Here's a rundown of what they mean:

TIP

This icon alerts you to helpful hints that can save you time and avoid frustration.

REMEMBER

This icon points out important information you should keep in mind.

WARNING

This icon flags actions and ideas that could cause you problems. Often, warnings accompany common mistakes or misconceptions people have about applying for or receiving benefits.

TECHNICAL STUFF

This icon points out information that is interesting, enlightening, or in-depth but that isn't necessary for you to read. (But you should read it anyway!)

EXAMPLE

This icon points out real-world examples of documents, situations, and other issues you may encounter on your quest for veterans benefits.

Beyond the Book

You didn't think that all you were getting was this book, did you? No way! This book comes with a free, access-anywhere Cheat Sheet that includes tips to help you get the benefits you've earned, guidance on the GI Bill and the VA loan benefit, and a few tips and tricks on getting the most out of your previous military service. To get the Cheat Sheet, head to www.dummies.com and type "Veterans Benefits Guide For Dummies Cheat Sheet" in the search box. The website has dozens of articles for extra guidance.

Where to Go from Here

Not all the benefits in this book apply to you. In fact, you may not care about some of them at all. For instance, if you already have a master's degree, you may not want to bother with the chapter that explains how to use your GI Bill; if you don't have a retiree ID card, you can skip the section about shopping on your nearest military installation. You can flip around this book to your heart's content — it's laid out in a way that enables you to fast-forward or rewind to the topics you need most.

Not sure where to start? The beginning is as good a place as any. You can also flip through the Table of Contents or Index, find a topic that interests you, and head to that chapter.

If you're a veteran in crisis, there is *immediate* help available. You can walk into a VA hospital 24 hours a day, 7 days a week, or go to a Vet Center on a VA campus near you during regular business hours (usually Monday through Friday). You can also call 800-273-8255 and press 1, text 838255, or visit www.VeteransCrisisLine.net to connect with someone immediately at any time of day.

1

Writing Your Next Chapter

Get ready for post-military life by gathering documentation and getting an early look at your earned benefits.

Figure out how your discharge status affects your benefit eligibility and find out how to apply for a discharge upgrade if necessary.

Discover the fastest, easiest ways to file VA claims and make appeals if necessary.

Chapter **1**

Gearing Up for That DD-214 Life

The military discharges about 200,000 people every year, and most are entitled to at least some veterans benefits. Those benefits include disability payments, free or low-cost medical and mental healthcare, travel discounts, home-buying benefits, tuition-free school attendance (plus government payments to pay your rent while you're earning a degree), job training and preparation programs, and burial benefits. In many cases, dependents get benefits, too.

Make no mistake: The military got what it wanted from you, whether that was by way of deployment to a foreign country, by working you from sunup to sundown Monday through Friday (and plenty of weekends), or through your literal blood, sweat, and tears. Sure, you got paid (and maybe you even enjoyed yourself — I did), but many of the benefits that I outline in this book are things that Uncle Sam still owes you. Now, it's time to cash them in.

Unfortunately, the government isn't going to chase you down and hand you everything you deserve; instead, you have to apply for the benefits you want. To do that, you have to know what's available, what you're eligible for, and how to access what you've earned. If you're still in the military, you can get a head start by using the benefits still available to you. Then you can prepare to find and access your post-separation benefits, which is what this chapter is all about. It helps you prepare to leave military service with tapping into your future benefits in mind.

Minding Your Medical Records

Your medical records are going to be a very important part of your life for the foreseeable future if you're aiming for a disability claim. Even if you don't think there's anything wrong with you after military service, you still need to keep tabs on all the files that military doctors have compiled on you throughout your career. From the smallest visit to sick call for ibuprofen and wise guidance such as "Rub some dirt on it" to your final physical, you need these records on-hand whether you served 3 years or 30. The following sections explain how to get your health, dental, and mental health records in military healthcare.

Capturing copies of health records

Before you leave the military, you're required to get a final physical. Sometimes called a *separation physical*, this quick checkup is an out-processing requirement. During this visit with your primary care provider, you get one last opportunity to document whatever ails you. Whether your ears haven't stopped ringing since 2015, your back hurts when you catch a whiff of military-issued gear, or your knee swells up ten minutes before it rains because of the time you jumped off the back of a 5-ton in full kit, you need to let your provider know — even if the information is already in your file from previous visits. Don't be afraid to bring up minor complaints; the VA's piles of benefit applications are full of claims for medical problems that started small and became worse over time.

You can get a copy of your entire medical file (excluding dental and behavioral health, which I cover in the following sections) after your separation physical. Simply head to the reception desk at your provider's office and ask for it. Some installations still give paper copies, though others will either burn you a CD (seriously) or send you an email with everything you need. Make sure your file includes the final report from your separation physical and that all your records are updated electronically.

WARNING

You alone are responsible for making sure your medical information is correct and complete. If something is missing from your file, talk to your provider before you pick up your discharge documents. It's entirely possible that important information got lost along the way, so check all your medical records before you leave military service; after you're out, you won't be able to get an appointment with your military doctor to clarify anything.

TIP

Get the most out of TRICARE by having your family schedule medical checkups, school and sports physicals, and other appointments while you're all still insured. (Chapter 6 discusses the ins and outs of TRICARE.)

Sinking your teeth into dental records

In order to clear your installation and put the military in your rearview mirror, you have to visit the dentist one last time. (Not for the last time ever, though. You may be entitled to dental coverage, which I drill into in more detail in Chapters 5 and 6.) You need your dental records to show your next dentist what the military did throughout your time in service. You never know, you may also need them to file a claim with the VA in the future.

Just like the doctor's office, ask the front desk at the dental clinic for a complete copy of your records, including your X-rays.

TIP

If you know you're getting out of the military, schedule one last cleaning and checkup with your military dentist. That'll buy you six months on the outside before you have to find a new dentist. Have your family schedule appointments, too, while they're still covered by your insurance. X-rays for everyone are expensive in the civilian world.

Scoring your mental health records

If you've ever been treated for any mental health condition, including posttraumatic stress, addiction, or substance abuse, or if you've received counseling services, you need copies of your behavioral health records. (They won't have any records for you if you've never been seen.) You may be entitled to VA benefits based on the mental health treatments you received. You can get these records when you clear behavioral health.

TIP

If you know you need mental healthcare services, begin care while you're still in the service. In addition to getting yourself the treatment you need, doing so provides the added benefit of showing a history of care for your condition. That may make it easier to prove a claim with the VA after you leave military service.

Using Your Branch's Transition Program

Each military branch has its own transition program, and you're required to use yours if you plan on leaving military service. Here's the bottom line: A lot of people think they won't get much out of a transition program, so they take the day off work, sign in, and mentally check out. Those people are making a huge mistake.

Transition programs have come a long way in the last few years, and they provide all the information they can to help you get off to a good start. You get free information on a handful of VA benefits, coaching on how to access them, help with civilian and government resumes, and even a nudge in the right direction for apprenticeship programs, your GI Bill, and a wide range of other perks. The good people who run your transition program will also be there to answer all your questions about separation, and they'll give you tons of resources to use along the way.

Here's a quick look at each branch's transition assistance program:

» **The Army's Soldier For Life Transition Assistance Program (SFL-TAP):** SFL-TAP is for soldiers who have at least 180 days of continuous active-duty service. Just about every active-duty Army installation has an SFL-TAP center.

» **The Air Force Transition Assistance Program:** This program is run by the Air Force Personnel Center; you can attend your courses locally at your Airman and Family Readiness Center.

» **The Navy Transition Program:** Formerly called Transition GPS, now it's just plain TAP. Sailors can get access to valuable TAP services at the nearest Fleet and Family Support Center.

» **The Marine Corps Transition Readiness Program (TRP):** The TRP is divided into three components:

- Transition Readiness
- The Marine for Life Cycle
- Career Services and Advising

Head to the Marine Corps Community Services center to get into your classes.

» **The Coast Guard Transition Program:** This program is headed by the U.S. Coast Guard's Office of Work-Life. Schedule your seminars by getting in touch with your Transition/Relocation Manager.

Though these transition programs go by different names, they all offer many of the same benefits. In fact, the Department of Defense (DOD) oversees the entire transition program. The DOD requires every separating servicemember to undergo a mandatory pre-separation assessment and individual counseling; then, servicemembers have to attend a one-day pre-separation seminar. Finally, a three-day TAP core curriculum program helps put you on the path you choose (the program offers an employment track, an education track, a vocational track, and an entrepreneurship track). Spouses may sometimes attend on a space-available basis.

REMEMBER

Every servicemember — including those who are being involuntarily separated from the military — is entitled to use transition assistance programs. However, some parts of the program may be unavailable to you if you're going to receive an other-than-honorable, bad conduct, or dishonorable discharge (refer to Chapter 2 for more about these discharges).

You can start attending your transition assistance program a year before you separate; if you're retiring, you can access it two years out. In my humble opinion, reading *Military Transition For Dummies* by yours truly (John Wiley & Sons, Inc.) before, during, and after your transition is the best way to ensure you land on your feet.

Taking Control of Your Current Benefits

While you're still in the military, you have access to a wealth of freebies that can help you get off to a great start. You have access to a number of benefits that you won't have after you separate, so you should take advantage of the services in this section.

Being thrifty with your TSP

The Thrift Savings Plan (TSP) is a government-sponsored savings and investment plan. It offers savings and tax benefits that are similar to 401(k) plans. The catch: You can't continue to contribute to your TSP account after you leave military service.

However, if you pick up another government job, you become eligible to start a new TSP account; you can then put your money from your military TSP into your government service TSP. Confused yet? The bottom line is that I suggest you talk to a financial adviser who may tell you to put as much money as possible into your TSP while you still can. In any case, you can take out your money (and the interest it's earned) whenever you want. You can get free financial advice through Military OneStop.

Getting help writing your will (and more)

The lawyers in your branch's legal department (the Judge Advocate General [JAG], office for the Army, Air Force, Navy, and Coast Guard; the Judge Advocate Division [JAD] for the Marine Corps) can help you with a wide range of legal issues before you separate from service, including these:

>> Wills and general estate planning advice

>> Leases, landlord-tenant relations, and real estate matters

>> Adoptions and name changes

>> Immigration and naturalization advice

>> Powers of attorney and notary services

> » Divorce, legal separation, annulment, custody, and paternity advice

> » Consumer fraud and abuse services, including identity theft

If you're still in the military and won't be retiring, you should take advantage of having a free lawyer on your side now. If you're retiring, you'll still have access to the attorneys at JAG or JAD, so there's no rush to get the services you need.

Dipping out on college courses

As a military servicemember, you're entitled to use the College Level Exam Program (CLEP). This program lets you test out on college courses so you don't have to use your GI Bill or pay out of pocket for them later. For example, if you're already pretty handy with numbers, you may want to use the program to take a proficiency test in college algebra. If you pass, you share the results with the college or university you plan to attend; as long as they're one of the nearly 3,000 schools that participate in the program, they'll give you college credits as if you took the course. More than 30 CLEP exams are available in a wide range of subjects, including composition and literature, science and mathematics, business, history and social sciences, and world languages. If you play your cards right, you'll have a healthy head start on college coursework by the time you start school.

TIP

You can still participate in the CLEP program after you're out of the military. The catch is that you have to pay for your exams and administration fees. As of this writing, it's almost $100 for the exam itself — and that doesn't include proctoring fees you must pay to the test administrator (even if you're taking a test remotely), which can vary.

Leaving on a Space-A plane

While you're in the military, you have access to space-available, or Space-A, travel. You can pay a few bucks and get a ticket to your destination if there's already a bird heading that way. That means you can hop on a flight to your next home to get things settled, then come back to gather your stuff and your people. The catch is that Space-A travel depends on availability (it's right there in the name). You have to be willing to risk a delayed return, so it may be best to plan your trip when you're on terminal leave. Check out Chapter 25 for more information on this benefit.

If you're retiring from the military, your spouse is authorized to take one round trip on a military aircraft without you for job- and house-hunting. You can get information on this benefit from your finance office and the personnel at the closest military flight terminal.

RESTOCKING THE MILITARY'S SHELVES

Before I joined the Army, my brother gave me some words of wisdom: "There's only one thief in the military. Everybody else is just trying to get their stuff back." (But he definitely didn't say stuff.) When the military lets you borrow its gear, you have to return it or pay for it if it's gone missing — and Uncle Sam doesn't care either way. For most people, it's smarter to go find missing items at a military surplus store than it is to pay the military for them; surplus stores are usually cheaper.

Maximizing your tax returns

If you're leaving the military around tax time, nab your MilTax benefit before it's gone. MilTax is available through Military OneSource, and it gives you free access to self-paced tax software that walks you through the filing process. It even lets you e-file when you're done, and its results are guaranteed. You can call MilTax consultants with questions whenever you feel like it.

Not into the software? You can use Volunteer Income Tax Assistance (VITA). These tax professionals offer free, in-person tax services (usually around military bases). You can connect with these experts through Military OneSource, and you don't have to pay a dime.

Thinking about What You'll Do on the Other Side

When you leave the military, your next steps are up to you — and you have the option of going straight to work or nailing down an education that will help you earn more down the road. Read more about job assistance programs in Chapters 10 and 11, or flip to Chapter 13 to use your earned GI Bill benefit and all the perks that come with it.

Dusting off your resume

Terminal or separation leave is a great time to get reacquainted with resume-writing. You're looking at paid time off to find yourself gainful employment after you leave military service, so make the most of it. Set up an account with USAJobs at www.usajobs.gov, the federal government's hiring portal, and go over the materials you picked up during your transition assistance program to prepare an unforgettable resume.

You can also pick up Form DD-2586, *Verification of Military Experiences and Training (VMET)* and attend special classes and seminars offered by your branch's transition program. Often, military installations hold special classes related to dressing for interviews, setting goals, managing career changes, evaluating job offers, and negotiating salaries.

Trading in combat boots for school shoes

Grab your Joint Services Transcript (JST for Army, Navy, Marine Corps, and Coast Guard) or Community College of the Air Force Transcript (from each of their websites, respectively) to find out how many college credits the American Council on Education recommends for your military experience. You can download a basic, summary, or complete transcript; you need the complete transcript to send to your school.

When you submit this form to your school, you can earn free college credits. Most veterans get between 10 and 15 college credit hours in things like military science, physical education, and first aid. You can earn credits for Military Occupational Specialty Training, Advanced Individual Training, military job performance, and courses you completed while you were in the service.

You can also earn free college credits by taking advantage of CLEP, which I cover in the section, "Dipping out on college courses," earlier in this chapter.

Selling Back Your Military Leave

If you're being honorably discharged or you're an officer separating under honorable conditions, you have the option to sell the military up to 60 days of your unused leave; that means you get cash for the leave you didn't take. However, doing so almost never makes sense. The military will only pay you your base pay; you don't get money for your entitlements, such as basic allowance for housing or sustenance. Unless you need the extra cash *now*, let the military continue paying you for terminal or separation leave. That's because you earn 2.5 days of leave every month that you're on the military's payroll. That means if you take 60 days of terminal or separation leave, you earn five more paid leave days, which is extra money in your pocket.

GET ON BOARD WITH inTransition

Open to active-duty service members, National Guard members, reservists, veterans, and retirees, the military's inTransition program helps you get access to mental healthcare when you're relocating, returning from deployment, transitioning from the military, or just about any other time. The program is staffed by coaches who understand military culture because they're part of it. Every coach is a licensed, masters-level psychological health clinician with at least three years of experience, and they can connect you with a provider, motivate you to stay in treatment, and put you in touch with local community resources and support groups. They also help you find crisis intervention services in your new location and teach you ways to continue making good life choices. One of the best things about inTransition is that *all* military servicemembers and veterans are eligible to use it; there's no expiration date to enroll, and your discharge status or "time served" doesn't matter. It's completely free, and you can check out the program at http://health.mil/intransition.

Packing with Your Final Move Benefit

The military will cover your final move when you leave the service. During your relocation appointment, the relocation expert you talk to will explain the benefits you're entitled to, such as household goods storage, travel allowances (such as Monetary Allowance in Lieu of Transportation [MALT], which pays for your mileage and some travel costs), and per-diem pay for meals and lodging while you're in transit.

If you separate with fewer than eight years of continuous active-duty service, the military will pay to send your household goods to your home of record or the place you entered military service. If you want to move farther, you're responsible for paying the difference in transportation costs. However, if you served more than eight years or you retire from the military, you can have the military ship your stuff anywhere in the continental United States. Regardless of your length of service, if you're heading out of the country, you have to pay the difference between your total cost and what the military would've paid to move you within the contiguous 48 states.

REMEMBER

Like all other military moves, you're subject to a weight allowance. Your weight allowance is based on your rank at the time of discharge, the number of dependents you have, and where you're going. If your household goods go over your allowable weight, you have to pay the difference. Your relocation coordinator will explain all your allowances and limitations during your relocation appointment.

You can ship just about anything, though some of it is at your own expense. For example, you can ship a motorcycle in household goods or transport it as a privately owned vehicle on the military's dime, but you have to pay out of pocket for pet travel and personal watercraft.

What to Expect from Your Last Paycheck

The military pays like clockwork on the 1st and 15th, but your final paycheck may be a bit different than what you're used to. If you don't owe the military any money, you should get your final pay between 30 and 45 days after separation. However, if you owe a debt, you wait a lot longer for that last direct deposit. The following sections address your final payout from the military and special circumstances that may affect how much you get.

Paying off military debts

If you try to leave the military with a debt, you're going to have to get in the ring with the Defense Finance and Accounting Service (DFAS). (Spoiler: DFAS is going to win, and it's going to be a flawless victory.) My best advice to you is to ensure you pay what you owe before you leave the service. Things can get pretty ugly if you don't.

DFAS collects debts that are left over when you leave. The first thing DFAS does is audit your account — and if the agency finds debts of any amount, you won't see your final paycheck for up to 120 days (or maybe more). It doesn't matter whether DFAS believes you owe $3.40 for a missing grenade pouch or $340 for an MIA Kevlar helmet. That means you could wait several months for your last paycheck to come through, so budget accordingly. DFAS will deduct what you owe from your final paycheck. If you owe more than your check will cover, you have the option of paying your debt in full, working out a payment plan, or protesting the debt. If you protest, DFAS will take another look.

WARNING

If you fail to make a payment on what DFAS considers a valid debt within 30 days, the agency considers your account delinquent. They're not messing around, either; if you don't send in a payment within 62 days of your initial debt notification letter (unless you disputed the debt right away), they'll kick you right in the credit report. DFAS sends delinquency notifications to four credit bureaus: Equifax, Experian, Trans Union, and Innovis.

DFAS also has other options, such as

>> Taking up to 100 percent of your tax refund

>> Nabbing up to 25 percent of your monthly disposable income if you receive Office of Personnel Management (OPM) annuity payments

>> Siphoning off up to 15 percent of your monthly disposable income from Social Security Administration payments

>> Pulling up to 15 percent of your monthly disposable income from non-DOD federal salary

>> Taking up to two-thirds of your military retirement pay

If you're *still* not paying, DFAS will send your debt to a collection agency. After that, you no longer owe DFAS; you owe the debt collector.

Transitioning into retirement pay

More than likely your retirement pay will fall under one of three programs:

>> **CSB/REDUX:** This is for people who joined the military between August 1, 1986, and December 31, 2017.

>> **High 36:** This is for people who joined the military between September 8, 1980, and December 31, 2017.

>> **Blended Retirement System (BRS):** This is for people who joined the military after January 1, 2018. The reason I include BRS here is for people who are medically retired before serving a full 20 years and qualify for this type of pay.

If you're not sure which program is yours, talk to your finance office. The experts there will tell you how much money you'll get and when you can expect to receive it. Even after talking to the pros, retirement pay can be confusing, so I explain each program in greater detail in Chapter 8.

Delving into disability pay

If you ask ten different people about military disability pay, you'll get ten different answers. The fact is that disability ratings and pay are confusing — even for people who work in the VA — and you may fall into a number of different classifications, so every case is different. For that reason, I cover disability ratings and pay in extensive detail in Chapter 9.

CAN YOU GET UNEMPLOYMENT?

Every state, plus Puerto Rico, the U.S. Virgin Islands, and Washington, D.C., has a special program designed for veterans called Unemployment Compensation for Ex-Servicemembers (UCX). The UCX program lets you apply for unemployment benefits right after you leave the military, and all you need is your Social Security number, your DD-214 or other discharge document, and a resume; most UCX programs require you to show that you're actively looking for a job. Though benefits vary from state to state — some pay a lot more than others do — you contributed to this program with taxes withdrawn from your military paychecks. You're entitled to use it while you look for civilian employment. You can get an application from your state's unemployment office (online or in person). You're not allowed to apply while you're on terminal or separation leave, but you're good to go on the day that your orders release you from active duty. Chapter 8 discusses UCX in greater detail.

If you meet all the following criteria, you can apply for a disability rating now using the Benefits Delivery at Discharge program (BDD):

>> You're on full-time active duty.

>> You know your separation date, and it's in the next 90 to 180 days.

>> You're available to go to VA exams for 45 days from the date you submit your claim.

>> You can provide a copy of your service treatment records for your current period of service when you file your claim (find out how to get your records in the section, "Minding Your Medical Records," earlier in this chapter).

When you use the BDD program, you can transition seamlessly from your regular military pay to your disability pay. You'll begin receiving payments when your orders release you from active duty.

If you have fewer than 90 days left on active duty, you can still file a claim; you just can't use the BDD program. You have to file a fully developed or standard claim. In that case, you should receive your first installment of disability pay within 15 days after receiving a notice that the VA has determined your rating to be 10 percent or more.

Dissecting severance pay

The DOD may offer you severance pay if you're being involuntarily separated from the military in an honorable or general (under honorable conditions) discharge. You may also qualify for severance pay for a disability or if you choose to voluntarily separate before retirement under certain circumstances. The following sections explain these special (and somewhat rare) circumstances.

Disability Severance Pay

Some people who are found "unfit for duty" don't qualify for monthly disability payments because their disability rating is under 30 percent. These people receive disability severance pay from the DOD (not the VA). This is a one-time, lump-sum payment that's equal to two months of basic pay for each year of service. The minimum time in service is 3 years (even if you weren't in the military for that long), and the maximum is 19 years. For example, if you were in the military for 3 years and your current base pay is $2,371.80, you receive $(\$2,371.80 \times 2) \times 3$, which is a lump-sum payment of $14,230.80.

You should receive your severance pay within 30 to 45 days of receiving approval. I cover severance pay in more detail in Chapter 8.

TECHNICAL STUFF

The government doesn't consider you medically retired from the military if you receive disability severance pay. However, you may later be eligible to apply for monthly disability payments from the VA — but only if the VA determines that your disability is service-connected.

Full and half ISP

If you're involuntarily separated from the military, you may qualify for full or half involuntary separation pay (ISP). The requirements are as follows:

>> **Full ISP:** You must be fully qualified for retention but be denied reenlistment because of promotion or high year of tenure policies or because of a reduction in force. You may also qualify if you're a commissioned or warrant officer being separated from the military in accordance with Chapter 36 of Title 10 U.S. Code, or Section 580, 1165, or 6383 of Title 10, U.S.C.

>> **Half ISP:** You qualify if you meet time-in-service requirements, your separation is honorable or general (under honorable conditions), and you're being separated instead of board action for specific reasons, such as weight control failure, parenting plan issues, alcohol or drug abuse rehabilitation failure, or a small number of other circumstances. I cover these circumstances in greater detail, as well as how to calculate your ISP, in Chapter 8.

Obtaining a Veteran ID Card

You can get a few types of veteran identification cards after you leave military service, and they come in handy when you want to access your benefits (such as hopping over to the nearest commissary or exchange or taking advantage of discounts offered by civilian stores and restaurants). You can get an ID card in the following situations:

>> **You retire from the military.** In this case, you get a DOD ID card that displays your benefit information, and it gets you access to military installations and all the amenities they contain. You can also use it to identify as a veteran for civilian benefits. This card comes from the Defense Enrollment Eligibility Reporting System (DEERS). You can apply for it when you update your status to "Retired."

>> **You're enrolled in VA healthcare.** In this case, you get a Veteran Health Identification Card (VHIC). You use this card to check into your appointments at your local VA medical center as well as for retail and business discounts. You receive this card directly from the VA after you enroll in VA healthcare.

>> **You served on active duty, in the National Guard, or in the Reserves, and you received an honorable or general (under honorable conditions) discharge.** You can use this card to identify yourself as a veteran for discounts and other perks, but not for access to military installations or VA healthcare. This card comes from the VA, and you can apply for it online.

You can also add an identifying mark to your state-issued driver's license or ID card. All 50 states, D.C., and Puerto Rico offer veteran designations on these identification cards. To get the designation, simply provide a copy of your discharge documents to the issuing authority (and remember that some states may require other documentation). You can use the designation to access benefits and discounts that civilian businesses and establishments offer to veterans.

Chapter **2**

Tying Your Discharge Status into Benefits

As a military veteran, you most likely qualify for at least some benefits — in fact, only a handful of vets don't qualify for anything at all. However, your benefit eligibility is tied directly to your discharge status, and your discharge status determines whether you get all, some, or none of the benefits that Uncle Sam has to offer. Unfortunately, even if you qualify for all the benefits, the government isn't going to chase you down and say, "Hey, you! Come get all this stuff you earned!"

Instead, they're going to set aside funding, make the benefits available, and wait for you to (possibly) discover them. Then, you have to show that you qualify by applying, wait for the government to approve you, and finally get what you earned. This chapter gives you a peek at how your discharge status ties into your benefits and, in case you're researching for a friend or loved one, the types of service that qualify a person as a veteran for benefits.

Identifying Where Benefits Come from

Qualifying veterans are entitled to benefits that come from a variety of government agencies, and those that offer the most are the Department of Veterans Affairs (VA) and the Department of Defense (DOD). You may also qualify for benefits from the Small Business Administration (SBA), the Department of Labor (DOL), the Consumer Financial Protection Bureau (CFPB), and the Departments of Education (ED), Energy (DOE), Housing and Urban Development (HUD), and the Office of Personnel Management (OPM). Your state or U.S. territory has a number of veterans benefits programs, and so do a lot of civilian businesses, nonprofit organizations and charities, and other organizations. I discuss the more prominent benefits in the following sections.

VA benefits

The vast majority of government-issued veterans benefits come from the Department of Veterans Affairs, which you know as the VA. Today's VA offers many more benefits than it ever has. It has an annual budget totaling around $300 billion (though it changes from fiscal year to fiscal year), operates around 1,300 healthcare facilities, and serves millions of vets with benefits ranging from healthcare and home loans to education, apprenticeships, and entrepreneurship training.

Department of Defense benefits

The DOD is the primary source for many of the financial benefits available to veterans and some family members, including retirement pay, separation pay, unemployment compensation for ex-servicemembers (UCX), some types of disability pay, and death gratuity. It also links up with other agencies, such as the DOL and the SBA to offer employment benefits and training. The DOD is also in charge of shopping and travel benefits, oversees military healthcare, and manages a handful of other perks available to many veterans.

A LOOK BACK: HOW MILITARY BENEFITS CAME TO BE

Military benefits started in 1636, when the Pilgrims passed a law that required Plymouth Colony to support soldiers disabled during the war with the Pequot Indians. Then, in 1776, the Continental Congress decided to encourage people to enlist in the Revolutionary War by offering pensions to disabled soldiers; by the 1800s, the United States began to extend pensions to widows and their dependents. A number of veteran-focused government agencies came and went until 1930, when President Herbert Hoover turned the Veterans Bureau into a federal administration.

State and territory benefits

Every state and U.S. territory offers its own veterans benefits, and some are more generous than others. Many states and territories have veterans homes, emergency financial assistance programs, discounts on things you need (like driver's licenses, license plates, and even hunting and fishing licenses), as well as tuition assistance specifically for veterans and their dependents. Head to Chapter 26 to read more about the types of benefits that states offer (and to figure out how you can tap into them).

Benefits from civilians

Thousands of civilian businesses, agencies, and organizations offer special benefits to veterans. Some businesses that hire veterans are eligible for tax breaks (plus they get great employees), and businesses that offer discounts and other freebies tend to get more business from veterans, so it's a win-win.

Qualifying as a Veteran: Types of Service

Not everyone who signs the dotted line and raises their right hand qualifies as a veteran. You must meet certain service requirements to qualify for benefits, and to make matters more confusing, the service requirements are different for different benefits. For example, if you're injured on Day 10 of Basic Combat Training and your injuries are such that you can't continue service, you may qualify for VA healthcare — but you most likely won't qualify for a VA loan to purchase a home.

For some benefits, you must have an honorable discharge; in others, you can have a general discharge or another discharge status; for others, you must meet special circumstances (such as being injured or becoming ill while serving or having served in combat). That's why every benefit has a separate application process. Fortunately, you can apply for all your government benefits online, and there's usually a "Qualifications" or "Requirements" list you must read before you get to the application itself. I describe the current eligibility requirements when I outline each benefit in this book.

Deciphering Different Discharge Types

Your discharge status has everything to do with the benefits you qualify to receive. The following sections discuss the two main military discharge types.

REMEMBER

If your discharge characterization disqualifies you from receiving benefits, you may be able to ask the VA to give you a Character of Discharge Review, which I cover in the later section, "Revisiting Your Discharge Characterization with the VA." Alternatively, you may be able to apply for a discharge upgrade through your branch of service. You can explore that in the later section, "Upgrading Your Discharge."

Administrative discharge

An *administrative* discharge is granted by a discharge authority (a high-ranking commander). Most people who get out of the military do so under an administrative discharge, even if they've been in trouble or were given the old combat boot to the rear.

Here are the three types of administrative discharges:

>> **Honorable discharge:** By far the most common military discharge type, an *honorable discharge* shows that you did government-grade work during your time in the service. As long as you (for the most part) met the standard and didn't get into serious trouble, you earn an honorable discharge. Even some people who have a few scrapes with the Uniform Code of Military Justice

(UCMJ) get honorable discharges, such as when their exceptionally meritorious service makes an honorable discharge the most appropriate type (like those who earn medals for valor or bravery, or other accolades).

>> **General (under honorable conditions) discharge:** *General discharges* are administrative, and they're less common than honorable discharges are. If the overall character of your service was good but you had some issues from time to time, a general (under honorable conditions) discharge may be appropriate. Often, when the military lets people go for failure to progress in training, failure to uphold military standards (including weight and fitness), or medical reasons, it uses a general discharge to do so.

>> **Other than honorable discharge:** *Other than honorable (OTH) discharges* are the worst type of administrative discharges, and the military uses them when a person exhibits a pattern of misconduct or a very serious infraction of the UCMJ (but not serious enough to warrant a court-martial). For example, if you have a series of nonjudicial punishments (such as Article 15s or NJPs), abuse your authority, fraternize, or commit an act of serious misconduct, or if you're convicted in a court-martial but your punishment doesn't include a punitive discharge, you may receive an OTH discharge. If you receive an OTH discharge, the VA must review it through a *Character of Discharge Review* to figure out whether you're entitled to benefits. I cover that in the later section, "Knowing what to expect during a review."

NOT AROUND LONG ENOUGH TO PROVE THEMSELVES

Entry-level separations release a person from military service, but there is no characterization of service (such as honorable, general, or other than honorable) because a person who receives one hasn't been in long enough to prove themselves. These separations are for people who have been in the military for less than 180 days, and they're typically given to people who just aren't a good fit for the military. But know this: A person can still get a different type of discharge within their first 180 days of service. For example, if a person gets in a fist fight with their drill instructor on Day 10 of basic training, they'll be discharged — but it's far more likely to be the punitive type than an entry-level separation.

Punitive discharge

A *punitive* discharge can only be issued by a military court-martial (it's a form of punishment). Here are the three types of punitive discharges:

>> **Bad conduct discharge:** A *bad conduct discharge* comes from a special or general court. However, only enlisted members of the service can get this type of discharge. Usually, people leave the military with a bad conduct discharge for committing crimes, such as being absent without leave, driving under the influence of alcohol or drugs, possessing or using drugs, or other offenses that may or may not come with civilian criminal charges.

>> **Dishonorable discharge:** By far the worst type of punitive discharge, the military hands these out to people whose conduct is reprehensible — the exact opposite of the conduct the military expects from servicemembers. Some examples that qualify people for dishonorable discharges include serious criminal convictions, such as homicide, sexual assault, or sedition. A person can only get a dishonorable discharge (sometimes called a *bad paper discharge*) as a consequence of a court-martial.

>> **Dismissal:** Commissioned officers can be dismissed from military service. The reasons behind an officer's dismissal (or *officer discharge*) are similar to those that would lead to a bad conduct or dishonorable discharge for enlisted servicemembers. (Officers don't receive bad conduct or dishonorable discharges.) This is also a punitive discharge, because only a court-martial can dismiss an officer.

Eyeing the Benefits You've Earned Based on Your Service and Discharge Status

The VA, DOD, and other government agencies that offer benefits use your discharge characterization to determine whether you're eligible for most benefits. (Some benefits, like the veterans crisis line, are available to you regardless of your discharge characterization.) Table 2-1 covers some of the biggest veterans benefits as well as who qualifies for them. If you're looking for disability benefits, head to Chapter 9.

Finding your discharge characterization on your DD-214 or NGB-22

When the military sets you free, you receive a DD-214 (active-duty and federal service) or NGB-22 (National Guard). If you left the military in the not-so-recent past, you may have another type of discharge document. If you had to amend your discharge in some way, you may have additional documentation. However, most people have a DD-214 or NGB-22. Figure 2-1 shows where your discharge characterization appears on a DD-214, *Certificate of Release or Discharge From Active Duty*; it's in Block 24.

TABLE 2-1

Basic Eligibility for Common Veterans Benefits

Benefit	Duty Requirement	Discharge Type
VA healthcare	24 months if you enlisted after September 7, 1980 or entered active duty after October 16, 1981, unless you meet certain criteria (see Chapter 5 for more information)	Honorable, general under honorable conditions, or an acceptable VA Character of Discharge review
Military retirement pay (nonmedical)	20 years	Honorable
Education benefits	Varies based on your state's version of the GI Bill	Honorable
VA home loan	90 or 180 days of active duty (see Chapter 15 for specifics)	Honorable, general under honorable conditions, or an acceptable VA Character of Discharge review
Veterans job preference	Any	Honorable or general
Burial benefits and death benefits for survivors	Any	Anything other than dishonorable

SPECIAL ADDITIONAL INFORMATION *(For use by authorized agencies only)*		
23. TYPE OF SEPARATION RELEASE FROM ACTIVE DUTY	**24. CHARACTER OF SERVICE** *(Include upgrades)* HONORABLE	
25. SEPARATION AUTHORITY AR 635-200, CHAP 4	**26. SEPARATION CODE** MBK	**27. REENTRY CODE** 1
28. NARRATIVE REASON FOR SEPARATION COMPLETION OF REQUIRED ACTIVE SERVICE		
29. DATES OF TIME LOST DURING THIS PERIOD *(YYYYMMDD)* NONE	**30. MEMBER REQUESTS COPY 4** *(Initials)*	
DD FORM 214, AUG 2009	PREVIOUS EDITION IS OBSOLETE. GENERATED BY TRANSPROC	**MEMBER - 4**

I certify this to be a true copy of the original

Office of the U.S. Defense Secretary

FIGURE 2-1: The bottom block of a DD-214.

TIP

If you don't have your discharge documents, you can request that the government send them to you through the milConnect website (`https://milconnect.dmdc.osd.mil/`) or by mailing or faxing (seriously) a request using Standard Form SF-180 to the National Personnel Records Center (NPRC). If you find yourself in St. Louis with some extra time on your hands, you can visit the NPRC to pick up your records. You'll also work through the NPRC if you're requesting someone else's military records to help them get benefits, including burial in a veterans cemetery. But if the person was discharged more than 62 years before the date you apply, you need to go through the National Archives (`www.archives.gov/research/military`).

Talking to specific agencies for waivers

Never assume that you don't qualify for benefits based only on your discharge characterization. When your discharge characterization disqualifies you from getting certain benefits, you may be able to ask the agency that holds the benefit to give you a waiver. Each agency has its own process (and some benefits have more leeway than others), so it's up to you to contact that agency to find out what you can do. The agency may simply tell you to apply for a discharge upgrade, which I cover in the later section, "Upgrading Your Discharge."

Knowing when to share your discharge status

You don't have a choice but to share your discharge characterization when you apply for government benefits; however, when you apply for other types of benefits — such as those that come from civilian agencies — you may not need to disclose your status at all. People can check your service history using a Freedom of Information Act (FOIA) request; even if they can't find your characterization of service, they'll be able to find your final rank, dates of service, and even your final duty status.

People can discover information about your military service in other ways. Figure 2-2 shows what information a person can turn up with only your name, birth date, and the knowledge of one day that you were on active duty in the military by using the Servicemembers Civil Relief Act to make a request. (You can even pull up your own by visiting `https://scra-w.dmdc.osd.mil/`.)

Further, a savvy searcher can find any court-martial trials you've been through to find out more about your military history. All they need is your name to find transcripts, charges, and the outcome of your case; even your sentencing information is a matter of public record, and it's incredibly easy to find. Figure 2-3 shows a sample Statement of Trial Results from JAG's online database (though I redacted the person's name, the government doesn't bother doing that).

On Active Duty On Active Duty Status Date			
Active Duty Start Date	Active Duty End Date	Status	Service Component
Aug-24-2006	May-14-2010	Yes	Army Active Duty
This response reflects the individuals' active duty status based on the Active Duty Status Date			

Left Active Duty Within 367 Days of Active Duty Status Date			
Active Duty Start Date	Active Duty End Date	Status	Service Component
NA	NA	No	NA
This response reflects where the individual left active duty status within 367 days preceding the Active Duty Status Date			

The Member or His/Her Unit Was Notified of a Future Call-Up to Active Duty on Active Duty Status Date			
Order Notification Start Date	Order Notification End Date	Status	Service Component
NA	NA	No	NA
This response reflects whether the individual or his/her unit has received early notification to report for active duty			

Upon searching the data banks of the Department of Defense Manpower Data Center, based on the information that you provided, the above is the status of the individual on the active duty status date as to all branches of the Uniformed Services (Army, Navy, Marine Corps, Air Force, NOAA, Public Health, and Coast Guard). This status includes information on a Servicemember or his/her unit receiving notification of future orders to report for Active Duty.

FIGURE 2-2:
A Servicemembers Civil Relief Act Request.

Office of the U.S. Secretary of Defense

STATEMENT OF TRIAL RESULTS

ADMINISTRATIVE

1. NAME OF ACCUSED (last first MI)	2. BRANCH	3. PAYGRADE	4. SOCIAL SECURITY NUMBER	5. DOD ID NUMBER
	ARMY	E-6		
6. CONVENING COMMAND	7. COURT-MARTIAL FORUM	8. COMPOSITION		9. DATE SENTENCE ADJUDGED
MCOE	GCM	Military Judge Alone		06/09/2021

FINDINGS (ATTACH FINDINGS WORKSHEET)

See attached findings worksheet

TOTAL SENTENCE ADJUDGED (ATTACH SENTENCING WORKSHEET)

10. SENTENCED BY	11. PUNITIVE SEPARATION	12. CONFINEMENT	13. FORFEITURES	14. FINES	15. FINE PENALTY
Military Judge Alone	None	150 Days	None	None	None
16. REDUCTION	17. REPRIMAND	18. HARD LABOR	19. RESTRICTION		20. DEATH
To the grade of E-4	None	None	None		N/A

CONFINEMENT CREDIT

21. DAYS OF PRETRIAL CONFINEMENT CREDIT	22. DAYS OF JUDICIALLY ORDERED CREDIT	23. TOTAL DAYS OF CREDIT
0	0	0

PLEA AGREEMENT

24. LIMITATIONS ON PUNISHMENT CONTAINED IN THE PLEA AGREEMENT
N/A

SUSPENSION RECOMMENDATION

25. DOES THE MILITARY JUDGE RECOMMEND A SUSPENSION OF ANY PORTION OF THE SENTENCE?		No
26. PORTION TO WHICH IT APPLIES	27. RECOMMENDED DURATION	
N/A	N/A	
28. FACTS SUPPORTING THE SUSPENSION RECOMMENDATION		
N/A		

NOTIFICATIONS

29. Is DNA processing required in accordance with 10 U.S.C. § 1565?	Yes
30. Is sex offender registration required in accordance with 34 U.S.C. § 209 or DoDI 1325.07?	No
31. Has the accused been convicted of a crime punishable by imprisonment for a term exceeding one year (18 U.S.C. § 922(g)(1))?	Yes
32. Has the accused been convicted of a misdemeanor crime of domestic violence (18 U.S.C. § 922(g)(9))?	Yes

FIGURE 2-3:
Statement of Trial Results from an Army Court-Martial.

Office of the U.S. Secretary of Defense

DO YOU HAVE TO TELL EMPLOYERS ABOUT A DD?

You're not legally required to tell employers that you were dishonorably discharged from the military (or even that you were in the military at all), but no law is preventing them from asking, either. Employers aren't supposed to ask you about the *nature* of your discharge, but whether you tell or not, some of them may find out anyway (particularly if you hand over a copy of your DD-214 or NGB-22).

Some of your military service file is a matter of public record; if you were ever court-martialed, the transcripts are available to anyone who wants to read them. You need to know that court-martial cases can also appear in the National Criminal Information Center's database, which is what fingerprint-based background checks pull up. Employers that conduct fingerprint-based background checks include those in healthcare settings, some daycare (including adult daycare) facilities, security companies, contractors that work with the government and offer jobs that require security clearances, and federal, state, and local governments.

Saying goodbye to benefits with OTH and dishonorable discharges

Anyone who doesn't have a straight–up honorable discharge from the military has restricted access to veterans benefits. The worse your discharge characterization is, the smaller your pool of benefits gets — and if you have a dishonorable discharge, it's barely even a puddle. That may mean you need to ask Uncle Sam to upgrade your discharge, which I cover later in this chapter (in the section called "Upgrading Your Discharge" — you can't miss it).

Revisiting Your Discharge Characterization with the VA

When you apply for veterans benefits through the VA, the agency looks at your character of discharge (COD) to determine whether you meet basic eligibility requirements under Title 38 of the United States Code. If your discharge was honorable or under honorable conditions, you automatically qualify as an eligible veteran (though you may still have to meet other requirements, such as time in service or disability). But if your discharge characterization *disqualifies* you for benefits, you may be able to ask the VA for a Character of Discharge Review. This review doesn't officially change your discharge status, but it can result in eligibility for some VA benefits. A Character of Discharge Review *only* affects your eligibility for benefits that come from the VA — not from any other government agency.

TECHNICAL STUFF

If you had more than one period of active military service — and one period ended under honorable conditions but the other was characterized as anything other than honorable or general — you may be eligible for VA benefits based on your period of service characterized as honorable. For example, if you served three years and were honorably discharged, but later reenlisted and served another few years before receiving a bad conduct discharge, you could be eligible for benefits because of your performance the first time around.

The following sections address circumstances that may bar you from receiving VA benefits and how you can ask the VA to review your discharge.

Statutory bars to VA benefits

Some issues permanently bar some people from using veterans VA benefits. You can't get a Character of Discharge Review if any of the following situations apply to you (unless you were determined to be insane at the time you committed the offense that led to your discharge):

>> Sentence of a general court-martial

>> Desertion

>> Being AWOL for a continuous period of 180 days or more without providing evidence of compelling circumstances

>> Being an officer who resigned for the good of the service

>> Being a conscientious objector who refused to perform your duties, wear your uniform, or otherwise comply with lawful orders

>> Requesting release from service as an alien during a period of hostilities

You may apply for a Character of Discharge Review if none of these apply to you.

Regulatory bars to VA benefits

The VA will automatically consider your character of discharge to be "under dishonorable conditions," even if it wasn't a bad conduct or dishonorable discharge, if you were released from the military under the following circumstances:

>> Mutiny

>> Espionage

>> Accepting an undesirable discharge to escape trial by general court-martial

>> Any offense involving moral turpitude (to include conviction of a felony in civilian court)

>> Willful and persistent misconduct

>> Sex-related offenses

Knowing what to expect during a review

During a Character of Discharge Review, the VA will attempt to determine whether your discharge was "under conditions other than dishonorable." To do so, the VA requires you to submit evidence that it should consider; it also submits a request to your branch for verification of your COD and the facts and circumstances surrounding your discharge. You may request a hearing to present your evidence, and if the VA grants you one, it'll be held at a VA regional office.

The VA digs into this type of information to review your COD:

>> Mitigating circumstances that can explain why the military characterized your discharge the way it did

>> Supporting evidence from third parties who are familiar with the circumstances surrounding your discharge

>> Your length of service

>> Your performance and accomplishments during your time in uniform

>> The nature of your infraction(s)

>> The character of your service in the time before the incident(s) that led to your discharge

The key takeaway here is that in some cases, people are discharged without the military considering *why* they exhibit certain behaviors. For example, someone suffering from acute posttraumatic stress may find themselves in the kind of trouble that gets them kicked out of the military. These VA reviews seek to address these types of problems, and in some cases, the administration grants benefit eligibility to some people.

REMEMBER

If you have service-connected disabilities, you may still be eligible for treatment at VA medical facilities — even if you don't qualify for any other benefits.

Upgrading Your Discharge

You're not necessarily up the creek without a paddle if you have a discharge that the military doesn't consider honorable or that the VA won't review. In fact, you can petition the government to upgrade your discharge so you qualify for more benefits. The only authority to upgrade your discharge lies with your branch's Discharge Review Board (DRB). The Army, Navy, Air Force, and Coast Guard each has its own DRB. (Marines apply for discharge upgrades through the Navy.)

WARNING

No DRB has authority to rule on medical discharges or those issued by general courts-martials. If you were medically discharged or sentenced to discharge after a court-martial proceeding, you can't use a DRB to change your status.

I'm not going to sugarcoat it. Getting a discharge upgrade can be tough. The process takes time, ample documentation, and a lot of patience. The following sections cover what you need to know to apply for an upgrade and whether you want to upgrade your character of service.

Applying for an upgrade

For most people, the simplest way to apply for a discharge upgrade is to work with a veterans service organization (VSO). These include organizations such as Veterans of Foreign Wars, Disabled American Veterans, American Legion, and American Veterans. If you want this type of help, contact your nearest VA office and ask for help finding a VSO that has VA-accredited representatives. VSOs and VSO reps can't charge you a fee for representing you in your claims for benefits or upgrades. Most VSOs don't even require you to be a member to get the help you need.

Some people choose instead to work with an attorney for a discharge upgrade. If you're thinking about hiring a lawyer, bear in mind that they're going to charge you (most likely by way of an up-front retainer fee *and* an hourly rate after you've used up all the hours your retainer fee paid for).

TIP

Don't hire an attorney who does a little bit of everything. Hire one who focuses primarily on working with former military members. That's because attorneys who handle criminal cases, divorce, personal injury, and a wide range of other issues can't possibly know every little thing about discharge upgrades and benefit claims — but lawyers who focus on working with veterans make it their business to know all the ins and outs of the system.

TIP

Because a VA Character of Discharge Review and a discharge upgrade application take a long time to process (like months . . . or longer), you should file for both at the same time. Doing so covers all your bases, so if one is approved and the other is denied, you're still on your way to getting benefits — and filing both at the same time means you don't have to wait out both processes separately.

Eyeing inequity and impropriety

The DRB will only approve an upgrade if you can prove your discharge was inequitable or improper. Here's what those terms mean in plain English:

>> **Inequitable** means that the reason for your discharge (or the characterization of your discharge) isn't consistent with the military's policies or your service. For example, you may say that your discharge was inequitable because it was based on a minor, isolated incident at the end of five incident-free years.

>> **Improper** means that there was an error in the reason for your discharge or its characterization. For example, if you were discharged for being overweight, but your branch didn't follow the appropriate protocol to get you back on track (such as enrolling you in a weight-control program), you may say that your discharge was improper.

You may have a strong case for a discharge upgrade if you can prove that your discharge was connected to any of the following circumstances:

>> A mental health condition, including posttraumatic stress

>> Traumatic brain injury

>> Sexual assault or sexual harassment (which the VA refers to as military sexual trauma — MST) that occurred while you were in the military

>> Sexual orientation (such as those that occurred while the Don't Ask, Don't Tell policy was in place)

REMEMBER

Here's the catch: You must apply for an upgrade within 15 years of your discharge. This rule has zero exceptions; if you file 15 years and one day after your discharge, you *are* up the creek without a paddle (and you'll have to hope that the VA is willing to favorably review your discharge).

MOVING FORWARD WITH DISCHARGE REVIEWS

A series of DOD memoranda have recently changed the way the military looks at discharge upgrades. The Hagel Memo (2014) and Carson Memo (2016) say that DRBs have to give special consideration to every petition that involves posttraumatic stress; the Kurta Memo (2017) expanded protections to petitions that involve mental illness and sexual trauma. Finally, the Wilkie Memo (2018) requires DRBs to favor giving people a second chance, consider rehabilitation and current character, and look at whether an offense becomes less serious over time (such as marijuana use, which is now legal in many states). In February 2022, a federal judge ordered the Navy DRB to reopen thousands of cases it denied between 2012 and 2022 to look for evidence that points to posttraumatic stress, traumatic brain injury, or military sexual trauma.

Finding the forms for a discharge upgrade

The VA has a handy tool on its website for helping you apply for a discharge upgrade based on the reason you believe you deserve it. Typically, you need to fill out a DD Form 293, *Application for the Review of Discharge from the Armed Forces of the United States.* You may need to fill out and file other forms, based on the reason behind your request. Though DRBs are run by each military branch, you can download all the forms you need directly from the VA's website.

TIP

If you're not so hot on the computer, it's okay; you can request the forms to type or fill out by hand. If you work with a VSO, you don't have to worry about your own computer skills. Your VSO rep will handle the forms for you.

Making your case

Submitting a form and crossing your fingers isn't quite enough to earn you a discharge upgrade — the government wants to see some receipts. That means you have to compile an entire packet to turn in.

TIP

You must include everything you want the DRB to consider. At minimum, you need your DD Form 293 and a statement that explains why you deserve a discharge upgrade (not why you *want* one — DRB members aren't concerned with the fact that you want benefits). You should also include your military records, including your awards, medical and mental health treatment records, and information on your deployments. Finally, consider including the following, which can help sway the DRB in your favor:

>> Statements from other people you served with

>> Character references from people who know you (such as your employer, a clergy member, or a family friend)

>> Your post-service educational records and employment history to show that you're a productive member of society

>> A copy of your credit report to show that you're responsible

>> Any information you have about your good conduct after leaving the service, such as a clear criminal record, proof of volunteer hours worked, or awards you have earned

TIP

I can't stress this enough: Work with a VSO on your discharge upgrade. Working with a VSO doesn't cost you anything (VSOs aren't legally allowed to charge you for help), and it helps ensure your petition is free from errors that could cause delays or rejections. Though there's never any guarantee on a DRB's decision, having a VSO in your corner can make the difference between a denial and an upgrade.

Tracking what happens next

Expect the review process to take several months. A DRB may simply do a records review, or it may call you in for a hearing. You may request the type of review you want when you file your original petition.

In a records review, the board will only look at your military records and the documentation you provide; that's your only opportunity to explain yourself. In some cases, only a records review is necessary. If you were discharged because of your sexual orientation, you don't need to explain anything in a hearing.

However, a hearing may be important in your case. All DRBs hold hearings in and around Washington, D.C., but some travel to other areas. If you're granted a hearing, you or your representative will get a chance to speak to the board; the board members can also ask you questions. You can introduce documents that are important to your case, too. Hearings last about an hour (though they can last longer), and you (or your representative) will go before five active-duty military officers or other senior members.

WARNING

You can request an in-person hearing if the DRB rejects your application after a records review. However, you can't request a records review if the DRB rejects your application after a hearing.

Discharge review boards don't make on-the-spot decisions. The five board members will discuss your case after you're gone, and each will get a vote; the majority rules. After your DRB makes its decision (usually a month or two after a records review or hearing), you receive a written notice that says whether your request is granted or denied. If the DRB grants you a discharge upgrade, it will notify the military and issue you a new discharge certificate — you don't have to do anything. If the DRB denies your upgrade and you have new evidence or documentation that supports your case, such as a change in military regulations or policies, you may file a whole new petition.

Appealing the Decision

If the DRB comes back with an unfavorable decision, you may still have some options. The following sections outline how to climb the ladder of appeals, depending on when you were discharged.

Hitting up the Board of Correction of Military or Naval Records

The DRB isn't perfect, and sometimes it makes decisions that people don't agree with. You can appeal the DRB's decision with the Board of Correction of Military or Naval Records (BCMR), using DD Form 149.

You can also use the BCMR to ask for a discharge upgrade if you were discharged more than 15 years ago, you were discharged through a general court-martial, or you want to correct errors in your military records. In the vast majority of cases, I suggest you work with a VSO; VSO reps know exactly what the BCMR requires in each situation.

TIP

If you're using the BCMR to appeal a DRB decision, you can help your cause by providing new evidence that supports your claim.

Exhausting your almost-final option

If you were separated on or after December 20, 2019, you can take one final shot at an appeal by using the Discharge Appeal Review Board (DARB). The DARB offers one last review of your application for an upgrade, but all it can do is review the existing documentation in your file. The board doesn't even hold hearings. (If you were discharged prior to that, your final option is to file a lawsuit against the DOD, which I cover in the following section.)

Going nuclear — the final option

Though very few people actually exercise the nuclear option in discharge upgrade appeals (and even fewer succeed), it exists: You can file a lawsuit against the government in the U.S. Court of Federal Claims (CFC). However, a statute of limitations on suing exists, and there are far too many potential complications to list in just one book. Besides, you must first exhaust all your other options. If you're at the end of the line and the only recourse you have left is suing the government, it's time to lawyer up.

Chapter **3**

Navigating VA Claims and Appeals

Approximately 17.5 million veterans are living in the United States right now, and according to the U.S. Census Bureau, only *half* have claimed some sort of service-related benefit from the government. Uncle Sam isn't going to knock on your door and let you know he has benefits waiting for you. Instead, he leaves it up to you to ferret out all the opportunities you may be eligible for, waits for you to apply for them, and lets you know whether you're a go or a no-go at each station.

The good news: Applying for benefits from the Department of Veterans Affairs (VA) is easier now than ever before. Almost every VA benefit available has automated processes and online applications. The other news: The VA has (and will have, for the foreseeable future) a deep backlog of claims to sort through. Some benefits take longer to receive than others do, and setting up the right credentials to apply online can be a bit of a pain.

Sometimes the VA turns people down for benefits because their applications are incomplete or incorrect; sometimes the applicant doesn't qualify with the information the government has. If the VA turns you down, don't throw in the towel right away. An appeal process is in place to give you another chance.

This chapter gives you the guidance you need to get your application right the first time, plus what you can do to successfully navigate an appeal if it becomes necessary.

Getting Your Hands on Your Records to Prove Eligibility

Your eligibility for the vast majority of VA benefits depends on your discharge from active military service or a reserve component and a few specific qualifications related to your time in the military. The VA wants to see proof of your service and character of discharge, which you provide by submitting an official copy of your DD Form 214 (or DD-215) or your NGB-22 or NGB-22A. You may also need medical, dental, or mental health records (from the military and, if applicable, civilian providers). I explain each of these records in the following sections.

Diving into DD Forms 214 and 215

Don't say the military never gave you anything — when you leave active service, you get a free stack of paper that contains your DD Form 214, *Certificate of Release or Discharge*. Your DD-214 certifies that you were in the military and gives a quick rundown of the job you performed, the awards you earned, and the schools you attended. Your discharge characterization is also on your DD-214, which enables the VA to determine your benefit eligibility at the most basic level.

The two main types of DD-214 are undeleted and deleted. Most people receive both types when they outprocess from the military. The *undeleted* type is what you need to apply for most VA benefits because it shows your discharge characterization and other information that may be helpful in determining your eligibility when you make a claim.

The DD-215 is a corrected copy of your DD-214. You need this form if your DD-214 is missing awards, schools, or other important information (such as deployment time or additional job codes). You can use the milConnect website (`https://milconnect.dmdc.osd.mil`) to apply, or you can fill out and file Form SF-180 to send to the National Personnel Records Center (NPRC) with proof for the corrections.

Digging up NGB Forms 22 and 22A

The Army National Guard and Air National Guard use NGB Form 22 as a discharge document (technically, it's the *Report of Separation and Military Service*), and NGB Form 22A is the corrected form of an NGB-22. It contains much of the same information a DD-214 does, including the scoop on your job, awards and decorations, reason for discharge, and discharge characterization. You can submit your NGB-22 just like you'd submit a DD-214 when the VA needs to see that you qualify for benefits. Keep in mind that the time you spent in basic training and advanced individual training or technical school is considered active-duty time, and you may also have one or more DD-214s for your qualifying periods of service.

TIP

If awards, schools, or other information is missing from your DD-214 or NGB-22, apply for a correction as soon as you can. You need to provide documentation that backs up your claim, such as copies of official military orders or certifications. I explain how to get the government to make corrections to your military records in the section, "Correcting Errors on Military Records," later in this chapter.

Considering the DD-256

You may have a DD Form 256, *Certificate of Honorable Discharge,* if you served in the National Guard or Reserves. This certificate proves you were in the military and completed a term of duty honorably, and you may use it to demonstrate your discharge characterization.

Accessing your medical records

The military started a medical file on you the day you signed the dotted line. From your first medical exam to your last, every time you received any type of care from a military medical facility, your provider added to your record. Whether it's just a few sheets thick or you're at risk of throwing out your back by lugging it around, your medical file may be the key to getting the VA benefits you need.

REMEMBER

When you apply for medical care or health insurance, disability payments, or some other benefits from the VA, you may need a complete copy of your medical records. Most people score a copy before leaving military service (I cover that in Chapter 1), but if you've misplaced yours or it doesn't seem to be complete, you can request a copy of your entire file through the milConnect website or through the NPRC. You may also be able to request a copy from the VA regional office that has jurisdiction over your claim. Note that the VA will request your records as part of your claim — but it never hurts to have your own copies in case something goes wrong.

Tracking down copies of your discharge documents and other records

Not having your discharge documents isn't the end of the world, but you do need to get your hands on replacement copies. The NPRC maintains copies of all active-duty and reserve military records, and you can request them by visiting the milConnect website or filling out Form SF-180, which you can get at `www.archives.gov/veterans`. Follow the instructions on the form to mail or fax (yes, fax) it to the NPRC in St. Louis.

If you need a copy of your NGB-22 or NGB-22A, contact the National Guard Adjutant General's Office for your state. You can get the most current contact information on the National Guard's website at `www.ngbpmc.ng.mil/Service-Records/`.

Many people file their discharge documents with the county recorder or city hall where they live. Doing so ensures that they're on file somewhere other than at the NPRC, and they may be easier to get your hands on if you need them in the future. If you're worried about the public finding your records, ask the agency what its policy is for releasing information; primarily, you need to know whether it issues copies to anyone who asks and whether the copies it issues are redacted or unredacted.

Correcting Errors on Military Records

The people who put together military records are only human, and sometimes they make mistakes. Unfortunately, errors could make you ineligible for some benefits — but don't worry. They're most likely easy (but time-consuming) to fix, which I discuss in the following sections.

Finding sufficient grounds for changes

If your records have errors you didn't catch before you left the service, it's your responsibility to point them out to Uncle Sam after the fact. Every branch of the military has its own Board for Correction of Military Records (BCMR), but before you reach out to yours, you first have to contact the NPRC to see if it can tidy up your records. If NPRC can't do it, reach out to your branch's HR department; branches can correct more than the NPRC can.

The BCMR has the legal authority to change any military record when necessary. It can fix errors and remove injustices (including unjust discharge characterizations, which I cover in Chapter 2). It's your job to convince the board that the information in your record is wrong or that it's unjust:

>> **In error** means your record has incorrect information. For example, your DD-214 may say that you served 6 months in a combat zone when you really served 16; that's an error.

>> **Injustice** means something is unfair in your record, such as a negative performance review based on your sexual orientation. Because the military has changed its policy on acceptance of sexual orientation, this type of review is unjustly included in your file.

REMEMBER

You have a three-year statute of limitations on filing for a correction, and the clock starts ticking when you discover the error or injustice (though the BCMR can excuse that statute of limitations if it's in the interest of justice to make the corrections anyway). How does the BCMR know when you discovered the error if it's something other than your discharge status? Your guess is as good as mine. But what I do know is this: You have to justify the correction or the board won't make it. The BCMR needs to see proof that something's actually wrong on your discharge document in order to agree to make a change, whether it's something small (like transposed letters in your name) or something big, like an unfair discharge characterization (which I cover in more detail in Chapter 2). That means you need to gather documentation that proves your case before you even bother downloading the application form.

TIP

It may be in your best interest to work with a veterans service organization (VSO) to make changes to your military records. A number of Congressionally chartered VSOs, including Veterans of Foreign Wars, Disabled American Veterans, American Legion, and American Veterans, can help you — and they all offer help for free. However, some VSOs get thousands of requests every year, so their services may be limited. Check with your state veterans office to find out whether it can recommend a good source for help. Alternatively, you may want to work with a lawyer (though that's going to cost you).

REMEMBER

Everything you submit to the BCMR becomes part of your official (and permanent) military record. Working with a pro may help ensure you have the best chance of getting your records corrected.

Backing up claims with evidence

The burden of proof lies with you when you want your military records changed. You may need to submit any of the following:

>> Official military records, such as combat awards, good conduct awards, and positive performance evaluations

>> Proof of your length of service or service performed in a combat zone

>> Documentation that shows military policies have changed since you were discharged

>> Birth certificates, Social Security cards, marriage certificates, or divorce decrees that prove corrections are necessary

>> Treatment records for physical or mental health that occurred within or outside the military (such as seeing a civilian provider while serving on active-duty status)

>> Character references

>> Volunteer awards or proof of volunteer service

>> Vet Center or VA counseling records

>> Proof of your VA disability rating

>> Letters from doctors and other practitioners that state posttraumatic stress or military sexual trauma was likely a factor that led to your discharge

The documentation you send in needs to match the nature of the change you want to see. You don't need mental health treatment records if the military called you *Johnson* instead of *Johnston*, and you don't need your birth certificate if you want a discharge upgrade. You get the picture.

Understanding the advisory opinion

After you file a petition to change your military records, here's what happens:

1. **The BCMR will send it to the Judge Advocate General (JAG) or Judge Advocate Division (JAD) for your branch.**

   That office will write an advisory opinion, which is a professional point of view that makes a recommendation on your petition and send it to the BCMR.

2. **The BCMR will send you a copy of the advisory opinion.**

   You have 30 days to review it and write a response (though you may be able to get an extension if necessary).

3. The BCMR will review the advisory opinion, your response, and all the documentation you sent in at the beginning of the process.

4. The board will make its decision; it may grant all or part of your request, or it may deny it.

If the board denies your petition, you can't appeal. However, if you have new evidence that could impact the BCMR's decision, you can ask it to reconsider your case. Your only other alternative is suing the DOD in federal court.

Starting at Square One When Applying for Benefits

If your military records are squared away, you're ready to file your claim with the VA. A *claim* is any request for benefits, whether you need a certificate of eligibility (COE) for a VA home loan or you're trying to get disability compensation (which I explain in Chapter 9). Sometimes making a claim is as simple as logging into the VA's website and answering a few questions, and in other cases, it's extremely complicated and eats up a lot of time. One thing remains certain, though: All VA claims start on the VA's website, in a Vet Center on a VA campus, over the phone with a VA representative, or with a VSO. Working with a VSO on your claim is usually in your best interest — doing so can save you time and hassle, and sometimes it can maximize your chances of success.

The VA has several portals for applying for benefits, and you need different accounts for different benefits, which I outline in the following sections.

Premium DS Logon

The Defense Self-Service Logon is an account that gives you credentials to access benefit information, applications, and application statuses across DOD and VA partner websites. The two types of DS Logon are standard and premium. After you create a standard account, you'll get the option to upgrade to premium; do it. The government considers a Premium DS Logon more secure because to get it, you need to verify your identity (which you can do at a VA office or online) and answer additional security questions.

Your Premium DS Logon lets you view your financial and benefits information, personal health information, claim statuses, and records. You need to be affiliated with the DOD or VA — and you must be registered in the Defense Enrollment Eligibility Reporting System (DEERS) — to get a DS Logon account. You can create your account through the eBenefits website at www.ebenefits.va.gov/. A DS Logon is valid for the rest of your life, but you have to change your password fairly frequently (and like most other government credentials, you can't reuse one of your last 50 million passwords when it's time to reset it).

ID.me

ID.me is a digital identification card you can use to log into a number of government websites. Many civilian websites use it, too. You can log into the VA's website and several DOD websites with an ID.me account. I'm not going to gloss over this: Applying for an ID.me account is a bit of a headache, and it requires you to download an authentication app on your phone.

When you create an ID.me account, it prompts you to upload copies of various forms of identification, such as driver's licenses, passports, and utility bills. You also need to upload your military discharge documents. If you live overseas or your driver's license address doesn't match your current address, you have to participate in a short video chat with a live agent. I recently had to do that, and it's not a fun experience. However, after you verify your identity through this service, you have free rein to log into all the government websites you need using your ID.me credentials.

WARNING

It's against the law to photograph or copy your military ID card. Instead, use a redacted copy of your DD-214 (or a comparable discharge document) to prove your military service.

eBenefits

When you have a DS Logon, you can access eBenefits. This self-service account lets you research, access, and manage your VA and military benefits. You can use this account to view your official military personnel file, check the status of a disability compensation claim, transfer a Post-9/11 GI Bill to your dependents, and register for direct deposit of some benefits. You can also use your eBenefits account to do any of the following:

>> Apply for some benefits

>> Order prescription medications

>> Securely message your physician

>> Access medical information

>> Get a COE for a VA home loan

HELPING SOMEONE ELSE APPLY FOR BENEFITS

Sometimes veterans aren't able to apply for their own benefits and need a little help. If you're helping someone you care about get the benefits they're entitled to, you need to know that the VA doesn't recognize a simple power of attorney (POA) in the application process if you're not an attorney or an accredited agent or representative of a VSO. Instead, the veteran must appoint you as a representative on a one-time, one-claim basis. However, you're free to help someone fill out and file forms without actually serving as their representative. In many cases, the best way to help someone else apply for benefits is to put that person in contact with a VSO.

>> Get copies of your DD-214

>> Keep up with your Post-9/11 GI Bill payment history

TIP

Go ahead and sign up for all these credentials in one sitting. Different government websites require different credentials, and if you already have them all, you'll be in good shape when you make or track the status of a claim.

Calling on the VA for help

You don't have to apply for all these credentials on your own. You can call the VA for help signing up for what you need or visit a VA regional office. People there can help you sign up and verify your identity. To find your nearest VA regional office, head to www.benefits.va.gov/benefits/offices.asp.

TIP

Sign up for the VA's regular newsletter through its website. It keeps you on top of policy changes, alerts you to new benefits, and gives you fresh information every week.

Working with a VSO

The best way to file a claim with the VA is to get help from a VSO. Several VSOs can help you from start to finish, including gathering your documentation and filling out application forms. Most VSOs don't even require your membership as a condition of helping you, and they're not lawfully allowed to charge you for the services they provide. Their main interest is helping veterans get the benefits they deserve.

I cover some of the biggest and most well-known Congressionally chartered VSOs in the following sections.

Veterans of Foreign Wars

Veterans of Foreign Wars (www.vfw.org/) is the largest organization of combat veterans. It established the National Veterans Service (NVS) to help all veterans (even those who aren't veterans of foreign wars) file claims with the VA. According to the VA, vets represented by the VFW have recouped nearly $10 billion in earned benefits. The service officers working for VFW can help you with disability compensation, rehabilitation and education programs, and even pension and employment training programs.

Disabled American Veterans

Disabled American Veterans (www.dav.org/) has helped veterans get more than $25 billion in earned benefits, and it assists more than a million vets each year. You can find DAV offices all over the country, and DAV service officers can help you apply for any benefit at any time. You don't need to be a member; everyone who has a claim is welcome to free assistance.

American Legion

The American Legion (www.legion.org/) helps all veterans — no membership required — get the benefits they earned during military service. Accredited service officers can petition for disability pensions and the full range of other benefits, as well as offer guidance on education, employment, and business ownership. All the help the American Legion provides is free.

American Veterans (AMVETS)

All veterans can get free help from an American Veterans (https://amvets.org/) service officer. AMVETS National Service Officers are stationed at VA regional offices and VA medical centers, and they can help you with disability claims, pensions, educational and training benefits, dependent and survivor benefits, and burial and memorial benefits (and then some).

Wounded Warrior Project

The Wounded Warrior Project (WWP) (www.woundedwarriorproject.org/) has a VA-certified Benefits Services team that advocates for benefits related to VA disability, caregiver benefits, and more. The WWP can even help you if you've already filed a claim. The caveat: You must be registered with the WWP, and to register, you must have suffered a physical or mental injury, wound, or illness during military service on or after September 11, 2001. Registration is free, and so are all the services WWP provides to registered members.

Other organizations that may help

You can work with any of a number of organizations to file your VA claim, but it's best to only work with an accredited attorney, claims agent, or VSO representative. VA-accredited representatives can help you understand and apply for the benefits you earned, help you gather the evidence you need to back up your claim, and help you request further reviews or appeals. You can find a list of VA-accredited representatives at www.va.gov/vso/.

VA-accredited VSOs and their representatives must provide free assistance; they're not allowed to charge you. Only VA-accredited attorneys and claims agents are allowed to charge you for their representation in appealing or requesting additional reviews of VA decisions — but only after VA has issued an initial decision on the claim.

Scouring Your Documentation to Determine Eligibility

Your time is valuable, and the last thing you want to do is waste one second of it applying for benefits you don't qualify to receive. Unfortunately, a lot of vets apply for benefits that they don't qualify for, and that's part of what contributes to the VA's backlog of claims — the VA has to spend resources on ensuring a person is ineligible and put together a rejection.

All VA benefits have different eligibility rules. Some benefits only require a person to have showed up for work a few times, whereas others require specific types of service (such as time served in a combat zone). The reason is simple: Congress passes the laws that authorize benefits, and those laws are enacted at various times. For example, the Post-9/11 GI Bill was authorized in June 2008, so it reflects lawmakers' wishes from that time.

Every benefit application comes with a list of eligibility requirements. Usually, the VA's website lists one or more conditions you must meet to apply for a particular benefit. For example, in order to possibly qualify for the Post–9/11 GI Bill, at least one of the following must be true:

>> You served at least 90 days on active duty (either all at once or with breaks in service) on or after September 11, 2001.

>> You received a Purple Heart on or after September 11, 2001, and you were honorably discharged after any amount of service.

>> You served for at least 30 continuous days (all at once, without a break in service) on or after September 11, 2001, and you were honorably discharged with a service-connected disability.

>> You're a dependent child using benefits transferred by a qualifying veteran or service member.

If you don't meet the criteria, you shouldn't apply for the benefit. If you do meet the criteria, you need to gather supporting documentation that proves you qualify. The following sections outline the types of documentation that may help you file a successful claim, plus where to turn for help finding sufficient evidence.

Collecting supporting documents

Make sure you include all relevant documentation to support your claim at the time you apply for a benefit. For the vast majority of claims, you must prove at least that you did the following:

>> You served the appropriate amount of time in the military to be eligible for the benefit you want to claim.

>> You have the appropriate discharge characterization (usually honorable, but sometimes general is acceptable) to qualify for the benefit.

>> You meet any other criteria necessary to qualify for the benefit, such as a disability incurred in the military.

You nearly always need a copy of your discharge document to apply for veterans benefits. That document shows your time in service and the characterization of your discharge, which are the most common basic qualifiers for veterans benefits (Chapter 2 discusses discharge characterizations). Remember, you have to prove to the VA that you're eligible for any benefit you want, so you may also need the following documents to prove eligibility:

>> Medical records

>> Buddy statements (letters from people familiar with your time in the service)

>> Citations from military awards and decorations (such as the Purple Heart)

>> Letters from doctors or mental health professionals that include your diagnosis and connect it to your military service

The VA needs three major components to providing the kind of evidence: It should be specific, verifiable, and authoritative, which I examine here.

Specific evidence

The documentation you provide should directly relate to the benefit you're claiming. It needs to be as specific as possible, including exact times and dates.

EXAMPLE

If you suffered a traumatic brain injury on September 26, 2008, a letter from your doctor should note that. It's better for a letter to say, "The patient is suffering from chronic memory loss tied to a TBI received during an IED detonation on September 26, 2008, and this is a classic long-term symptom of TBI received in combat" than to say, "The patient may have suffered a TBI in the military and now has symptoms of memory loss."

Verifiable evidence

Anyone can pay a sketchy Internet doctor to write a letter saying they have a medical condition, even without so much as an in-person consultation or records review, so the VA wants to verify that the claims you're making about your eligibility are true. You need to be able to support any claims you're making through other sources, such as orders to deploy, a unit roster, a buddy statement, or medical treatment records from the military or in-person medical practitioner.

WARNING

Don't use an online doctor to diagnose you with a condition. They often charge more than legitimate doctors do. If you don't have insurance and can't afford a visit to a local physician, don't sweat it; file your claim with all the evidence you have and the VA will most likely schedule a Compensation and Pension (C&P) exam to determine whether there's a service connection for your condition.

Authoritative evidence

You can ask anyone to write you a *buddy statement* — a letter that backs up your claim of eligibility for a certain benefit. However, those that come from credible sources (such as your former platoon sergeant, commanding officer, chaplain, or a doctor who treated you for an injury) carry more weight than statements from your peers, your parents, or your friends.

Using VA's duty to assist

Thanks to a law passed in 2000, the VA is legally bound to help you get the evidence you need to support your case and to develop your claim. It's also required to tell you exactly what type of evidence you need to submit to support your claim. This is called its *duty to assist,* and it prevents you from having to guess what the VA expects from you. The law also requires the VA to make a "reasonable effort" to get supporting evidence for you, which means it must petition the appropriate federal agencies for documentation until it's certain that the documentation doesn't exist or that it's never going to turn up.

Concerning private, nonfederal records, the law requires the VA to request documentation. If it doesn't get the documentation in two months, it's required to request it again. The VA has to keep requesting the records until it believes that the records will never materialize or that they're otherwise unobtainable.

TIP

If you need records to substantiate a claim, try to get them yourself. You may be able to access them faster than the VA can. And when it comes to private, nonfederal records, you need to know that sometimes medical offices ignore VA requests (and all other nonpatient requests). In other cases, they charge to provide copies of records — and by law, the VA isn't allowed to pay fees for documentation. However, if you're having a tough time getting records, rely on the VA's duty to assist; that's what it's there for.

WARNING

Some services request your medical records for you, but they cost money. Call or visit your provider to get your records (or request your records online), work with a VSO, *and* try to get the VA to obtain your records for you before paying anyone to request your records for you.

Hurry Up and Wait: Submitting a Claim

After you have all the required documentation that proves you're eligible, you can submit your claim (or your VSO representative can submit it for you). The VA approves and denies applications on a case-by-case basis, which means a VA official will review your entire packet, including your application and supporting evidence before deciding. Make sure you get your packet right the first time you submit it so you can avoid delays, or worse, have to appeal an unfavorable decision later (appeals are time consuming and require you to come up with even more evidence).

If you're not working with a VSO, your next-best bet is to visit a VA regional office or Vet Center. The counselors there are obligated (by law) to do everything within their power to organize your application and get your supporting evidence in order. This is the best way to speed up the claims process and give yourself the best chance at approval. Few things slow down the VA more than having to stop processing an application to request more evidence.

Because you're a military veteran, you're familiar with hurrying up and waiting — and after submitting a claim, you'll get even more experience with it. The VA can take several months to issue a decision in your case, even without external factors (like global pandemics and labor shortages). The amount of time it takes the VA to review your claim depends on the type of claim you filed, how long it takes the VA to collect evidence that you haven't provided, and how complex your case is (such as when you have multiple injuries or disabilities to claim). As of this writing, it takes the VA 162.4 days to complete disability-related claims but only a matter of minutes to download a COE for a VA home loan or education benefits.

Inspecting the VA's internal processes

If you submit your VA claim online, you see an on-screen message that confirms the VA's receipt of your application. If you mail your application, you receive a confirmation letter a week or so later. From there:

>> The VA will conduct an initial review to determine whether you most likely have enough evidence to support your claim. If the VA official reviewing your file believes you need to provide more evidence, you'll receive a request for more information in the mail and in your eBenefits inbox.

>> The VA will ask you for additional evidence, as well as seek evidence it's required to find through healthcare providers, government agencies, and other entities.

>> The official assigned to your case will review all the evidence and your application before deciding. If the official still needs more evidence, they'll ask you to provide it or continue making requests with the appropriate agencies.

>> The VA will decide. It will put together a packet that includes a "yes" or "no" answer and, if applicable, the reason behind the VA's decision.

>> The VA will mail your decision packet. You should receive your packet within 7 to 10 business days of the VA making its decision. If you don't receive it in that time, you can contact the VA call center to get more information on your case.

Checking your claim's status

You're entitled to check your VA claim's status any time using the VA's website. You need a My HealtheVet account (refer to Chapter 5), a Premium DS Logon account, or a verified ID.me account (head to the section, "Starting at Square One When Applying for Benefits"). You can use the VA's site to find out where your claim (or appeal) is in the review process and when the VA anticipates making its final decision in your case. You can also look at the evidence you filed online, a list of additional evidence the VA needs from you, and your representative's contact information. You can call the VA at 800-827-1000, dial 711 using TTY, or contact your local VA facility to get information on your case. If you're working with a VSO, your representative can keep you updated.

Analyzing the Decision Review Process

The VA doesn't approve every claim, and the people who look at applications are only human — so sometimes they make mistakes. Fortunately, you can ask for a decision review for any unfavorable decision the VA issues. (The process used to be called *filing an appeal*, and if you filed a Notice of Disagreement before February 19, 2019, it's still called that.)

Most commonly, people request decision reviews related to denial of service-connected disability payments, VA pensions, and inaccurate disability ratings, but you're allowed to appeal any type of unfavorable decision that the VA makes regarding your entitlement to benefits. The following sections explore your options for asking the VA to take another look at your case.

Asking for a decision review

If you're working with a VSO, your rep can get the ball rolling on an appeal. If you're flying solo, you need to submit the appropriate form with the VA:

>> Fill out VA Form 10182 to ask the Board of Veterans Appeals to review your case and possibly issue a new decision. You can only use this form if the VA issued its decision on or after February 19, 2019.

>> Fill out VA Form 20-0995 to request a new review of an issue that you previously applied for. You must submit additional evidence with this form.

>> Fill out VA Form 20-0996 to request a higher-level review of the decision you received from the VA. The senior reviewer assigned to your case will determine whether the decision can be changed based on a difference of opinion or an error of fact or law. You can't submit any new evidence in a higher-level review.

EXAMPLE

An example of an *error of fact* is the VA saying a military doctor never treated you for a broken bone, but your service treatment records say otherwise. An example of an *error of law* is something like the VA assigning you the wrong effective date or assigning you a 10 percent disability rating when your records support a 20 percent rating.)

Additional instructions on asking for a review come with VA decision letters. Make sure you carefully follow the instructions.

Choosing the right type of decision review

If you disagree with a VA decision issued on or after February 19, 2019, you have three options: You may file a supplemental claim, ask for a higher-level review, or ask for a board appeal. Table 3-1 outlines the basic types of decision reviews so you can make an informed decision. And don't worry — if you aren't happy with the results of the first option you choose, you can try another option you're eligible for.

TIP

If you submitted your own claim without working with a VSO, it's not too late to use one. In fact, now is the perfect time to start. Your VSO rep can help you with the entire appeals process, including filing your VA Form 10182 and providing supplemental evidence (if necessary) to support your claim.

Hiring an attorney: Yes or no?

Some people choose to work with an attorney when they want a decision review. If you can afford one (they only charge you if you win your case), I say go for it — just make sure you're working with a lawyer who focuses on (and has experience in) these types of cases rather than one who handles all kinds of cases. The reason is simple: Lawyers who handle everything from immigration law and criminal cases to divorce and estate planning can't possibly have all the knowledge necessary to help you succeed.

Of course, I'm also partial to VSOs, at least for initial claims and simple appeals; they don't charge you for the help they provide (and they provide plenty). You can check out the biggest-name VSOs in the section, "Working with a VSO," earlier in this chapter. (If you have a complex appeal, it may be best to hire an attorney. For example, if you have a knee problem that causes you to limp, and your limp led to a hip condition, you may fare better with a lawyer on your side.)

Filing a case in the U.S. Court of Appeals for Veterans Claims

The U.S. Court of Appeals for Veterans Claims (CAVC) is your final chance to get a favorable appeal.

TABLE 3-1

Types of VA Decision Reviews

	Supplemental Claim	Higher-Level Review	Board Appeal
What happens?	A reviewer decides whether new and relevant evidence may change the unfavorable decision.	A senior claims adjudicator (that's a fancy way to say *senior reviewer*) takes another look at your case with the same evidence you originally submitted.	A Veterans Law Judge at the Board of Veterans' Appeals reviews the decision.
Why choose this option?	Choose a supplemental claim if you need to add or identify new and relevant evidence to support your claim. The VA's duty to assist applies here; it can help you gather new and relevant evidence you identify.	Choose a higher-level review if you don't have any new evidence, but you believe that the VA made an error in its prior decision. You can request a one-time, informal conference with a senior reviewer to identify the errors the VA made in your case.	Choose a board review if you want the Board of Veterans' Appeals judge to look at your case and issue a ruling. You can choose a *direct review* if you don't want to submit evidence, *evidence submission* if you do want to submit evidence, or *hearing* if you want to have a hearing (by teleconference, videoconference, or in person) with a Veterans Law Judge.
How long does it take?	Supplemental claims usually take an average of 125 days to complete.	Higher-level reviews usually take an average of 125 days to complete.	Board reviews usually take an average of 365 days to complete, though it typically takes longer for an evidence submission or hearing.
What form do you need?	VA Form 20-0995	VA Form 20-0996 (or you can request a higher-level review online without the form, but only for disability compensation claims).	VA Form 10182
What if you disagree?	You may request another supplemental claim, a higher-level review, or a board appeal.	You may request a supplemental claim or a board appeal. You may not request another higher-level review.	You may request a supplemental claim or appeal to the U.S. Court of Appeals for Veterans Claims.

If you represent yourself in court, you may have a fool for a client. You should absolutely work with an attorney if you intend to take this route, because otherwise, you're at a distinct disadvantage. (How many times have you represented yourself in court proceedings, how familiar are you with court protocol, and how much do you know about the process?)

Attorneys' work at the CAVC is covered by the Equal Access to Justice Act, so if you win, the government may have to pay your lawyer's fees. The court has a list of approved public practitioners, which you can find at https://uscourts.cavc. gov, or you can visit www.vetsprobono.org/ to see if an attorney is willing to represent you for free.

2

Medical Care, Life Insurance, and Compensation Programs

Figure out what types of medical benefits you're eligible for, even if you didn't retire from the military, and find out how to use them.

Get familiar with VA healthcare, including how it works, what it covers, and how to get it.

Discover TRICARE plans that may work for you based on your medical needs, location, and financial situation.

Take a close look at VA life insurance and decide whether it's an expense you need.

Delve into your military retired pay or severance pay so you know what to expect.

Find out how the VA doles out disability ratings and how you can apply for disability compensation.

Chapter **4**

Helping Yourself to Health Benefits

M any veterans have a tough time getting continuing medical care and health coverage from the government after leaving the service. That's because the VA is only able to provide healthcare to a certain number of people, and those people have fallen into the right spot on a priority list. But VA healthcare aside, you're entitled to some medical benefits after you leave the service. Many are for a limited time, whereas you can use others forever.

This chapter explains the health benefits you may be entitled to because you served in the military, as well as mental health resources, what you can do when you or someone you care about is in a crisis, and how to apply for benefits that don't relate to your service.

Using Free TRICARE for 180 Days

While you were in the military, you had TRICARE — even if you didn't realize it. That's what funded your visits to sick call, the boot you got when you sprained your ankle on that battalion run, and the 47 bottles of 800-milligram ibuprofen you were likely prescribed over the course of your military career. It covered your dependents, too; your spouse is probably quite familiar with using the TRICARE website to find a provider, schedule sports physicals, or snag a referral for specialty care.

REMEMBER

The good news: For six months (or 180 days) after you leave the military, you may still qualify for transitional healthcare through TRICARE in one of two ways: the Transitional Assistance Management Program (TAMP) or Continued Health Care Benefit Program (CHCBP), which I discuss in more detail here.

TAMP

The Transitional Assistance Management Program (TAMP) is available to sponsors and eligible family members if the sponsor is

>> Involuntarily separating from active duty under honorable conditions

>> Separating from active duty after involuntary retention

>> Separating from active duty after a voluntary agreement to stay on active duty to support a contingency operation

>> Receiving a sole survivorship discharge

>> Separating from regular active-duty status and agrees to join the Selected Reserve of a reserve component the day after release from active duty

>> Separating from a period of more than 30 consecutive days of active duty under certain conditions as a National Guard or Reserve member

If you qualify for TAMP, you (and your dependents) get all the same benefits you had under your TRICARE plan while you were on active duty.

CHCBP

You may be able to pay for healthcare coverage through the Continued Health Care Benefit Program (CHCBP) insurance plan. CHCBP provides you with temporary health coverage (lasting from 18 to 36 months) when you lose TRICARE eligibility. It serves as a bridge between TRICARE and a civilian health insurance plan, and it provides the same coverage as TRICARE Select does, including prescriptions (see Chapter 6). It's similar to a civilian COBRA program, which gives workers the right to continue paying for health benefits for a limited time. However, you and your dependents are only eligible for CHCBP if you separate under honorable or general conditions.

Seeking Support for Your Mental Health

The Departments of Defense (DOD) and Veterans Affairs (VA) know that there's a mental health crisis among veterans, and though these agencies (and others) do what they can to address the issue, their efforts sometimes fall short. But that doesn't mean you're out of luck when you need mental healthcare. Some programs are designed specifically for veterans, and you can use them — for free — to help you now and later in life. The programs I outline here are largely funded by Congress, though a number of private organizations are also dedicated to helping veterans with their mental health needs.

Accessing free mental healthcare for a year through Military OneSource

Military OneSource (https://www.militaryonesource.mil/) offers free, non-medical counseling for honorably or generally discharged veterans and retirees of the Army, Air Force, Navy, and Marine Corps for up to 365 days after discharge. Though these providers can't prescribe medications, they do provide a listening ear — and they can help you find resources to better address your needs if necessary.

You can use this service to deal with issues such as relationship conflicts, stress management, grief management, and even adjustment to civilian life. However, you can't use it if you're already seeing another therapist, dealing with active suicidal or homicidal thoughts, requiring sexual assault help, or working through a substance abuse issue. It's also not for help with diagnosed mental health conditions, such as posttraumatic stress disorder (PTSD) or child abuse and domestic violence issues. The help Military OneSource provides is completely confidential except in three situations: when there's abuse, a threat of harm, or illegal activity.

TIP

If you're a recently separated member of the U.S. Coast Guard, you can use the CG SUPRT (www.cgsuprt.com/) website for services similar to those that Military OneSource offers. Because the DOD funds Military OneSource, you may only use it if you've been activated as part of the Department of the Navy under Title 10 authority.

Centering yourself with free VA counseling

The VA's Vet Centers offer free counseling that covers a lot of issues. Whether you left the military yesterday or a few decades ago doesn't matter; receiving these services doesn't have a time limit. You can get individual counseling, participate in group counseling, and even get assessed for alcohol or substance abuse issues.

Vet Centers provide military sexual trauma counseling, VA medical benefit referrals, and family counseling for issues related to a veteran's readjustment.

Whether or not you've actively participated in combat, if you've served as active duty in any combat theater or area of hostility (including Desert Storm/Desert Shield, Bosnia, Kosovo, or as part of the Global War on Terrorism, Operation Enduring Freedom, Operation Iraqi Freedom, Operation Freedom's Sentinel, or Operation New Dawn, among others), you qualify for free readjustment counseling. You also qualify if you never served in a combat theater or area of hostility if you

>> Experienced any military sexual trauma

>> Provided mortuary services or direct emergent medical care to treat casualties of war while serving on active duty

>> Performed on a UAV crew that provided direct support to operations in a combat theater or area of hostility

>> Accessed any care at a Vet Center before January 2, 2013, as a Vietnam-era veteran

>> Served on active duty in response to a national emergency or major disaster declared by the president (or the governor or chief executive of a state in response to a disaster or civil disorder)

>> Are a current or former member of the Coast Guard who participated in any drug interdiction operation

>> Are a current member of a reserve component assigned to a military command in a drilling status, if you have a behavioral health condition or psychological trauma related to military service that adversely affects your quality of life or your adjustment to civilian life

Connecting with the Veterans Crisis Line

The Veterans Crisis Line provides free support to veterans and their loved ones all the time — it never closes, and you qualify. Period. That's it. Your discharge characterization doesn't matter, and neither does your period of service, branch, or anything else. All that the providers on the other end of the line (or chat app) care about is getting you the help you need. You'll connect with a real person who's qualified to provide the support you need, whether you're in a crisis (such as thinking about killing yourself or engaging in self-destructive behavior like drug abuse), or you need someone to talk to because you're about to boil over.

The service is completely free and confidential, and though they'll ask you a few questions to start (such as whether you're thinking about hurting yourself or others), you can decide how much information to share and how long you talk.

If you're in a crisis, the responder will help you get through it and then connect you with any additional services you need. Not in an active crisis but coming close? The person you talk to will help you make a plan to stay safe and then connect you with the resources you need. And if you provide your contact information, a suicide prevention coordinator from the nearest VA medical center will contact you by the next business day; all the services they provide are also completely free.

You can use the Veterans Crisis Line in any way that you're comfortable with:

>> **Talk.** Call 800-273-8255 and press 1 because you're a veteran.

   You can also dial 988 from your phone (then press 1). All telecom providers in the United States are required to keep 988 services available to subscribers. But don't worry if you've memorized the 800 number; you can always dial that, too.

   If you use TTY, dial 711, and then the number (or use your preferred relay service).

>> **Text or chat online.** If you're not comfortable talking — or if you can't bring yourself to do it — that's okay, too. You can text 838255 or start an online chat at www.veteranscrisisline.net/get-help-now/chat/.

Veterans and people who care about them are allowed to call the Veterans Crisis Line. It's open to family members, friends, and caregivers. If you or someone you love is in a crisis, reach out — completely judgement-free, immediate, and easy-to-access help is available.

Seeking counseling for military sexual trauma

One in four women veterans and one in a hundred male veterans in the VA health-care system report experiencing military sexual trauma (MST). By percentage, women are at greater risk of MST, but that's partly because there are more male vets; nearly 40 percent of veterans who disclose an MST experience to the VA are men.

The VA provides free counseling and treatment (both mental and physical) for issues related to MST; no documentation is required. You may be eligible for MST care even if you're not eligible for other types of VA care. It's available to those with honorable discharges, other-than-honorable, and uncharacterized (entry-level) discharges, too.

Every VA healthcare facility has a dedicated MST Coordinator who can help you get the care you need, and you can receive MST-related outpatient counseling at your nearest Vet Center. The VA even provides inpatient and residential care for people suffering the effects of MST (even to people who don't qualify for VA healthcare). You can even ask to meet with a clinician of a particular gender and receive care in a gender-separated program.

TECHNICAL STUFF

The VA characterizes MST as sexual assault or sexual harassment experienced during military service. Whether you experienced one event or many doesn't matter, and it's okay if you didn't report the incident(s) at the time. If you were sexually traumatized in the military and are dealing with the aftermath, the VA can help you, regardless of your gender, the amount of time that's passed since the incident, or whether you have evidence of the trauma.

Using PTSD counseling resources

If you have posttraumatic stress, it's never too late to get help — and the VA sees it that way, too. It has numerous PTSD treatment programs available to people who qualify (and don't qualify) for VA healthcare services. I cover VA healthcare in Chapter 5, but if you don't have access to that, you may still use a Vet Center to get free, private counseling (as well as alcohol and drug assessments and other types of support) if you've served in a combat zone. Additionally, if you're homeless or in danger of becoming homeless, you may qualify for free PTSD counseling through the VA.

TIP

Having a PTSD diagnosis may count as a service-connected disability, and you may be eligible to file a claim with the VA for it. If the VA rates you as partially or totally disabled due to posttraumatic stress, you're eligible for disability payments and free physical and mental healthcare. Often, the first (and hardest) step is reaching out for help, but connecting with a Vet Center on a VA campus can ensure that you get the care and treatment you deserve.

Calling the Substance Abuse Hotline

If you're struggling with substance abuse issues or if you're looking for resources to help someone who is, the Substance Abuse and Mental Health Services Administration (SAMHSA) helpline offers free and confidential information on getting support. Call 800-662-4357 (TTY: 800-487-4889), or send a text to 435748 for help any time. The hotline provides referrals to local treatment facilities, community-based organizations, and support groups.

Participating in Red Cross support groups

The VA, in partnership with the American Red Cross, hosts several in-person and online support groups related to mental health and other issues veterans face. Visit www.va.gov/outreach-and-events/events/ to see upcoming events. These events are open to veterans, caregivers, dependents, and others connected to vets.

TIP

Visit the VA's website and sign up for its weekly newsletter. New treatment options, opportunities for veterans, and lists of upcoming events will appear in your inbox each week.

Getting Help with Emergency Situations

Sometimes life just sucks, and you find yourself in a tough spot. First, these are the phone numbers you need to know for help:

>> **Veterans Crisis Line:** 800-273-8255, press 1. This number operates 24 hours a day, 7 days a week, and connects you directly to a VA call center where a qualified responder can talk you through a crisis and connect you with the help you need. You may also dial 988 and press 1; it's the same line with a simpler number.

>> **Domestic Violence National Hotline:** 800-799-7233 or 800-787-3224. Staffed all day, every day; trained counselors can provide you with crisis help and other information.

>> **National Child Abuse Hotline:** 800-422-4453. Professional counselors answer the phone 24-7 and can help you through an emergency and connect you with helpful resources.

With those resources in mind, you can also get emergency help through the VA if you're having a mental health crisis, regardless of your discharge status, your military branch, or how long ago you left the service through the following hospital walk-ins, Vet Centers, and free clinics — even if you're not enrolled in VA healthcare:

>> **VA hospital walk-ins:** If you're experiencing a crisis, such as thinking about harming yourself or others, you can walk into a VA hospital at any time. Every VA medical center has a trained crisis team and can give you immediate help.

>> **Vet Centers on VA campuses:** Vet Centers are located on VA campuses all over the country, and they offer help during emergencies. All the help you receive is free and confidential, and you can walk in during normal business

hours. (If it's outside business hours, you'll need to go to the nearest VA medical center to get immediate help.)

>> **Free clinics:** Community VAs sometimes hold free clinics for specific purposes, such as health screenings, vaccines, and other treatments. If there's a free clinic in your area, you're welcome to attend.

In these instances, the VA doesn't care about your discharge characterization or whether you're enrolled in VA healthcare (or even have any type of insurance).

Applying for Supplementary Benefits

Even if you don't qualify for VA medical care, TRICARE, or other programs based on your veteran status, you may still qualify for a variety of government programs. (I know, this book is about veterans benefits — but I'd be remiss if I didn't tell you about the other types of help you can get when you need it.) As far as your health goes, you may be eligible to participate in four programs, which I discuss in the following sections. I also touch on the Health Insurance Marketplace, where you can purchase a private insurance plan.

Medicaid

Medicaid is a healthcare insurance plan paid for by the U.S. government and individual state governments, and it covers nearly 80 million Americans. It's administered at the state level, but states are required to follow federal requirements. You may be eligible for Medicaid based on your income level; it's also available to many pregnant women, children, and people who receive Supplemental Security Income (SSI). Others are eligible, too, but some states extend coverage to more people than others do.

This government-funded health insurance plan covers routine medical care, emergency care, prescription medications, and a wide range of other services. However, you must make less than a certain amount of money to qualify — and you must usually meet other criteria, too, such as age or parenting status. Some states also offer a *medically needy program*; that's a program for people who make too much money to qualify for Medicaid, but not enough money to pay for their own healthcare services.

Indian Health Service

If you're an enrolled member of a federally recognized tribe, you qualify for healthcare under the Indian Health Service (IHS). The IHS doesn't provide health insurance; it provides care (in that way, it's similar to the VA). To receive these benefits, you can apply in person at the patient registration office of the nearest IHS facility; you must bring proof of enrollment in your tribe. If you don't live near an IHS facility, you may still be eligible for coverage for services you receive at other facilities under the Urban Indian Health Program (UIHP).

Children's Health Insurance Program

Available to kids only, the Children's Health Insurance Program (CHIP) provides low-cost health coverage to children in families that make too much to qualify for Medicaid but still need help paying for medical expenses. Every state has its own rules about who qualifies for CHIP, which covers doctor visits, prescriptions, dental and vision care, hospital care, immunizations, and more. You can call 800-318-2596 or fill out an application through the Health Insurance Marketplace at any time; you don't need to wait for an open enrollment period to apply for health insurance for your kids.

Medicare

Medicare is health insurance for people age 65 or older, and you gain eligibility three months before your 65th birthday. Some people with disabilities are eligible for Medicare earlier. This joint federal and state program provides healthcare coverage for people who have limited income and resources. Medicare is divided into four parts:

>> Part A is hospital insurance that helps cover inpatient stays, skilled nursing facility care, hospice, and home healthcare.

>> Part B helps cover regular doctor appointments and standard care.

>> Part C is a bundled plan that includes Medicare Parts A, B, and D.

>> Part D helps cover prescription drug costs.

The Health Insurance Marketplace

If you need health insurance and your employer doesn't provide it (or you don't yet qualify for it), the Health Insurance Marketplace is the place to go. Visit www.healthcare.gov during an open enrollment period; enrollment for the following year begins November 1 each year.

If you've just lost your TRICARE benefits or another type of insurance, you don't need to wait for open enrollment period. You qualify for a *special enrollment period* that enables you to sign up at any time. (Additionally, you may use the Health Insurance Marketplace to apply for Medicaid or the Children's Health Insurance Program at any time.) The Health Insurance Marketplace is essentially an insurance-shopping site. Big-name insurance providers, alongside some smaller companies, offer a wide range of health insurance plans you can choose from.

Chapter **5**

Exploring VA Healthcare

No matter what you've heard about the level of care it provides, the Veterans Health Administration (VHA) is the biggest integrated healthcare system in the entire country. It provides medical care at nearly 1,300 facilities (with nearly 200 hospitals), and it serves more than 9 million veterans from every era. The VHA's medical centers provide all kinds of services, including surgery, mental health, orthopedics, radiology, physical therapy, and pharmacy. Many VHA medical centers even offer specialty services, such as *geriatrics* (services for older adults), *neurology* (services for brains), *oncology* (services for cancer), and hearing and vision care. Some even offer extremely advanced services, such as organ transplants and reparative plastic surgery. Every VHA has trained patient advocates on staff — they're people who can help resolve your concerns about your healthcare experience on the spot.

Sounds great, right? There's a catch: VA healthcare isn't available to everyone. However, it's not because people don't qualify; nearly every veteran *does* qualify (it's typically open to those who received honorable or general discharges, and others in limited circumstances). The real reason most veterans don't use VA healthcare is that there's only so much of the VA to go around, so it offers health-care to qualifying veterans based on priority groups — those who need healthcare the most — usually because those veterans have service-connected disabilities or low incomes. Like most other VA benefits, you may want to work with a veterans service organization (VSO) to make a claim for healthcare; doing so can boost your chances of getting approved. This chapter focuses on understanding who qualifies through priority groups, exploring the basic benefits VA healthcare offers, and applying for this earned benefit.

Qualifying for VA Healthcare

Eligibility for VA healthcare is based on a lot of factors, and the VA looks at all of them to determine whether a person qualifies for services. For the most part, if you served in the active military and received an honorable or general (under honorable conditions) discharge, then you qualify. If you're a former reservist or National Guard member who was called to active duty by a federal order (sorry — training doesn't count!), provided you completed your full active-duty obligation, you also qualify. You may also qualify based on your income or certain aspects of your military service, such as whether you were injured or became ill while serving, or whether you have a medical condition that your service made worse.

TIP

If you're still in the military and think that you have a condition that the VA will rate as a disability, use the Benefits Delivery at Discharge (BDD) program. You can file a pre-discharge claim if you have between 180 and 90 days left on your contract, which means that the VA can give you a rating before you leave military service. Then, you may begin receiving your disability benefits shortly after you reenter the civilian world. If you have fewer than 90 days left, you can still file a claim before you leave; it simply needs to be a fully developed or standard claim.

The following sections cover the requirements you (and your family) need to meet to qualify for VA healthcare, plus what to do if you have any discharge other than honorable.

Eyeing minimum service requirements

Minimum service requirements to qualify for VA healthcare depend on when you were in the military. You must have served 24 months of continuous active duty (or the full period for which you were called to active duty if you were a reservist or National Guard member) if you enlisted after September 7, 1980, or if you entered active duty after October 16, 1981. But even if you didn't fulfill the minimum service requirement, you may still qualify if you meet one of the following:

>> You were discharged because you were injured and became disabled while you were on active duty.

>> You were discharged because of a disability that your active-duty service aggravated (made worse).

>> You were discharged for a hardship or another reason before completely fulfilling your service obligation.

>> You served before September 7, 1980.

Focusing on enhanced eligibility status

The VA puts people into priority groups, which I dive into in the section, "Understanding VA Priority Groups," later in this chapter. People in higher priority groups are more likely to get free VA healthcare benefits than those who are in lower priority groups. You may qualify for what the VA calls *enhanced eligibility status* if you can show that one of the following situations apply to you:

>> You receive payments from the VA because of a service-connected disability.

>> You were discharged because you were injured or became ill in the line of duty, and that injury or illness caused you a disability.

>> You were discharged because you had a disability that your military service made worse.

>> You're a combat veteran who was discharged within the past five years.

>> You receive a VA pension.

>> You're a former prisoner of war.

>> You received a Purple Heart or a Medal of Honor.

>> You receive or qualify for Medicaid benefits.

>> You served in Vietnam between January 9, 1962 and May 7, 1975.

>> You served in Southwest Asia (in the Persian Gulf War) between August 2, 1990 and November 11, 1998.

>> You served 30 days or more at Camp Lejeune between August 1, 1953 and December 31, 1987.

TECHNICAL STUFF

Wondering why people who served a month at Camp Lejeune get enhanced priority? Between the early 1950s and into the late 1980s, the Camp Lejeune drinking water had toxic chemicals in it. In addition to qualifying for regular VA healthcare, veterans who served there during that time may be eligible for disability compensation.

Examining eligibility based on combat

If you served on active duty during Operation Enduring Freedom, Operation Iraqi Freedom, or Operation New Dawn, you qualify for *enhanced eligibility* — but only if you apply for VA healthcare within five years of your discharge. In that case, you may qualify for five years of free VA healthcare for any illness or injury that may be related to your military service. If all of these apply to you, you can use your enhanced eligibility on your application:

>> You served in a combat theater after November 11, 1998.

>> You were discharged or released from active-duty service on or after January 29, 2003.

>> You did *not* receive a dishonorable discharge.

REMEMBER

Using your combat theater experience means the VA enrolls you in healthcare right away, and you'll receive free care and medication for any condition that could be connected to your service. When your enhanced eligibility period ends (5 years after your discharge date), you keep your VA healthcare coverage — though you may be reassigned to the highest priority group you qualify for at that time. Even if you don't think you need healthcare now, you should apply. Otherwise, you're in the same boat as everyone else; the VA will only base your eligibility on things like your VA disability rating or your income.

TECHNICAL STUFF

You may be able to receive VA medical care for a condition that's possibly connected to your service, but the VA may still deny you disability payments for it. That's because the VA determines eligibility for disability benefits on very specific criteria, which I cover in Chapter 9.

TIP

If you left the service 180 days ago (or fewer), you may be eligible for one-time dental care for any conditions you have. The catch is you have to apply within 6 months of your discharge.

Understanding income-based eligibility

Some people qualify for VA healthcare because of their annual income and net worth. The less you earn, the more likely you are to qualify. These limits are categorized and operate on a tiered basis. The categories are based on your income while qualifying with or without other benefits, such as Housebound Allowance, Aid and Attendance, and a VA pension. (I cover the first two of these benefits in Chapter 9 and the last in Chapter 8.) These income limits change every year, and they're based on your location; they're always published on the VA's website so you can see the most recent figures.

Considering your spouse and dependents

Spouses of permanently and totally disabled veterans, surviving spouses, dependent children of disabled vets (including dependents who have spina bifida), and family caregivers may be eligible for the VA to pay for their healthcare costs — but only in limited circumstances. Coverage is available through the following programs (I delve deeper into these programs in Chapter 21):

» **The Civilian Health and Medical Program of the Department of Veterans Affairs (CHAMPVA):** This coverage is available to spouses or widow(er)s, as well as dependent children of qualifying veterans and servicemembers who have permanent, total service-connected disabilities; deceased veterans or servicemembers who had a permanent, total service-connected disability at the time of their death; died from a service-connected disability; or died while on active duty. It's also available to some primary caregivers who aren't already entitled to other healthcare or services.

» **The Program of Comprehensive Assistance for Family Caregivers (PCAFC):** This program is exclusively for family caregivers of eligible veterans, such as those who were seriously injured in the line of duty during certain time periods, as well as meeting other requirements.

» **The Camp Lejeune Family Member Program:** Family members who lived at U.S. Marine Corps Base Camp Lejeune or Marine Corps Air Station (MCAS) with an active-duty servicemember between August 1953 and December 1987 may be eligible for some healthcare benefits through this program.

» **The Spina Bifida Health Care Benefits Program:** Biological children of veterans who served during the Korean War or Vietnam War who have spina bifida may qualify for healthcare benefits, as well as other disability benefits.

» **The Children of Women Vietnam Veterans Health Care Benefits Program:** This program is for the biological kids of a woman Vietnam War veteran who have been diagnosed with certain birth defects.

Qualifying despite an OTH, bad conduct, or dishonorable discharge

Even if you have an other-than-honorable (OTH), bad conduct, or dishonorable discharge, you may still qualify for VA healthcare. Mental health services related to posttraumatic stress, military sexual trauma, and some other conditions *may* be covered by the VA immediately; in those cases, your discharge status doesn't matter at all. In other cases, you need to ask for a VA Character of Discharge Review or apply for a discharge upgrade, which I explain in Chapter 2.

VETERAN HEALTH REGISTRIES AND FREE EVALUATIONS

The VA runs a total of six Environmental Health Registries (but stay tuned, because as more health conditions come out of the woodwork, the agency may add more). I cover each of them in more detail in Chapter 20, but the main idea is that if you may have been exposed to certain environmental hazards during your time in the military, you get a free medical assessment that can help determine if you have (or will have) long-term health problems due to exposure. You don't have to be enrolled in VA healthcare to put your name on one of the VA's registries.

The registries include the following:

- Airborne Hazards and Open Burn Pit Registry
- Gulf War Registry
- Depleted Uranium Follow-Up Program
- Toxic Embedded Fragment Surveillance Center
- Agent Orange Registry
- Ionizing Radiation Registry

The VA collects the data from the free exams it provides veterans who register, and if it discovers that you're suffering adverse effects that are tied into your service, you could be eligible for additional VA benefits (such as healthcare and disability payments). If you think you qualify for any of these registries, put down the book and sign up right away. Getting your name on the registry can help you get disability benefits now (by assessing your current health) or later, when the VA recognizes certain health conditions as being caused by environmental exposures.

Understanding VA Priority Groups

The VA shuffles veterans into priority groups when determining who's on deck for healthcare services. The lower your priority group's number is, the closer you are to getting VA healthcare. These groups also determine how much (if any) money you'll have to pay for your healthcare. This system lets the VA prioritize veterans who need VA healthcare more than others do.

Priority groups are based on five main factors:

>> Military service history

>> Disability rating, if applicable (I cover disability ratings in more detail in Chapter 9, which also explores how disability pay works)

>> Income level

>> Whether the veteran qualifies for Medicaid

>> Any other benefits the veteran receives (such as a VA pension)

If you qualify for more than one priority group, the VA assigns you to the one that will get you care the fastest and result in the lowest cost to you.

Here I discuss the eight total priority groups. Each has different criteria (and the eighth priority group has six subcategories). You may move between groups after you're enrolled, such as if your income changes or your service-connected disability gets worse and you receive a higher disability rating.

Priority Group 1

Vets who have a service-connected disability that the VA has rated as 50 percent or more, or who have one or more service-connected disabilities that make them unable to work (according to the VA) fall into Priority Group 1. People who receive the Medal of Honor also are in this group. Generally, the vets who fall into this category are fast-tracked on the way to receiving VA healthcare.

Priority Group 2

Priority Group 2 is reserved for veterans who have service-connected disabilities with a VA rating of 30 to 40 percent.

Priority Group 3

Former prisoners of war, Purple Heart recipients, and veterans who were discharged for a disability that was caused by (or got worse from) active-duty military service are part of Priority Group 3. Additionally, those with service-connected disabilities between 10 and 20 percent disabling and those who have received a special eligibility classification fall into this group.

Priority Group 4

If a veteran receives VA Aid and Attendance or Housebound benefits or if they're catastrophically disabled (even if the disability isn't service connected), they're part of Priority Group 4. Veterans are considered *catastrophically disabled* if they have a severely disabling and permanent injury, disease, or disorder that interferes with their ability to perform day-to-day tasks. The disability has to be so severe that the veteran needs personal or mechanical assistance to leave their bed or their home, or they must require constant supervision to avoid harming themselves or others. Often, veterans who meet these criteria also qualify for higher priority groups (in part because they have a high disability rating from the VA), so this group is there to catch people who don't have ratings, as well.

Priority Group 5

The VA puts veterans into Priority Group 5 when they don't have a service-connected disability, or when they have a noncompensable service-connected disability that the VA has determined is 0 percent disabling *and* has an annual income level that falls below the VA's adjusted income limits. (*Noncompensable* means that the VA can't give you disability payments for your condition.) Vets who receive VA pension benefits or who are eligible for Medicaid also fall into this priority group.

Priority Group 6

You can get into Priority Group 6 in several ways:

>> Anyone who has a compensable service-connected disability that the VA has rated as 0 percent disabling (meaning the person has a disability, but the VA believes the disability doesn't prevent the person from working or carrying out day-to-day functions) falls into this group.

>> Anyone exposed to specific environmental hazards that the VA recognizes for causing certain medical conditions, such as being exposed to ionizing radiation during atmospheric testing or during the occupation of Hiroshima and Nagasaki as well as people who participated in Project 112/SHAD.

>> Anyone who served in Vietnam from January 9, 1962 to May 7, 1975; served in the Persian Gulf between August 2, 1990, and November 11, 1998; or who served at Camp Lejeune for at least 30 days between August 1, 1953 and December 31, 1987. I cover these conditions in Chapter 20.

Additionally, veterans who were discharged fewer than five years ago and served in a theater of combat operations after November 11, 1998, fall into this priority group.

Priority Group 7

If a veteran has a gross household income below the geographically adjusted income limits for where they live, and if they agree to pay copays for care, they fall into Priority Group 7. *Gross income* means wages, business income, and other payments that come into your household before taxes or other deductions come out. The term *geographically adjusted income limits* refers to the maximum amount of money you can bring in to qualify for benefits. These limits are based on your ZIP Code and the number of people in your family who you can count as dependents on your tax returns.

Priority Group 8

Veterans who make more than the VA's geographically adjusted income limits *and* VA income limits and who agree to pay copays fall into Priority Group 8. However, some people in this priority group aren't eligible for VA healthcare at all. This group is divided into eight subgroups, which can be a little confusing (and seem a bit nit-picky, though they're outlined in real legislation, so the VA has no choice but to follow them):

>> **Subgroup A:** Veterans with noncompensable, service-connected conditions that the VA has rated as 0 percent disabling who enrolled in the VA healthcare program before January 16, 2003, and who have remained enrolled since that date.

>> **Subgroup B:** Veterans who have noncompensable, service-connected conditions that the VA has rated as 0 percent disabling who enrolled in the VA healthcare program on or after June 15, 2009, and who have an income that exceeds the VA's income limits or geographically adjusted income limits by 10 percent or less.

>> **Subgroup C:** Veterans who don't have a service-connected condition who enrolled in the VA healthcare program as of January 16, 2003, and who also have an income that exceeds the VA's income limits or geographically adjusted income limits by 10 percent or less.

>> **Subgroup D:** Veterans without a service-connected condition who enrolled in the VA healthcare program on or after June 15, 2009, and who have an income that exceeds the VA's income limits or geographically adjusted income limits by 10 percent or less.

>> **Subgroup E:** Veterans with a noncompensable service-connected condition that the VA has rated at 0 percent disabling and who don't meet the criteria for Subgroup A or B. *These veterans are only eligible for care for their service-connected conditions.*

>> **Subgroup G:** Veterans who don't have a service-connected condition and who don't meet criteria for Subgroup C or D fall into this one. (You read that right; there's no Subgroup F. It's almost as if the people who created these groups know what kinds of wordplay this category would be subject to.)

Opening the Medical Benefits Package

The VA's basic medical benefits package includes preventive care, primary and specialty care, inpatient and outpatient services, and diagnostic services. The idea, according to the VA, is to provide care that promotes, preserves, or restores your health. If you get the full enchilada of VA medical benefits, you're entitled to a huge range of services — just like you would be with a top-tier civilian health insurance plan. The big difference is that VA healthcare is a lot easier on your wallet. Some people pay *copays* (money out of their own pockets) for things like urgent care, doctor visits to primary care providers and specialists, tests like MRIs or CT scans, inpatient stays at hospitals, and prescriptions. Those who do pay copays rely on their priority group to tell them how much each copay costs (or if they have to pay one at all), and the prices are subject to change.

All enrolled veterans receive coverage for most services, but only some qualify for additional benefits, such as dental care. The exact benefits the VA covers depend on your VA primary care provider's recommendation and the medical standards for treating your specific health conditions. The following sections explore what is and isn't covered — and what it'll cost you.

Knowing what the benefits cover

The VA's basic medical benefits package includes a wide range of services and treatments you can get from VA medical facilities, emergency rooms, and in some cases, other medical facilities (such as when you live very far from a VA medical center). Table 5-1 outlines the basics.

TABLE 5-1 **VA Medical Benefits Package Coverage**

Type of Care	Specific Services
Preventive care services	Health exams
	Health education
	Immunizations
	Counseling on genetic diseases
Inpatient hospital services	Surgeries
	Dialysis
	Acute care
	Specialized care (such as organ transplants and intensive care)
Urgent and emergency services	Urgent and emergency care at some VA health facilities
	Urgent care for issues that may or may not be life-threatening at other, non-VA medical facilities
Other services	Mental health treatments
	Substance abuse treatment
	Military sexual trauma treatment
	Assisted living and home health care
	Prescription coverage
Ancillary services	Blood tests, X-rays, and ultrasounds
	Therapy and rehabilitation services
	Prosthetics
	Hearing loss care
	Cancer care

Recognizing what isn't covered

The VA's basic medical benefits package doesn't cover everything (though it's always subject to change). The VA won't pay for or perform the following:

>> Abortions or abortion counseling

>> Cosmetic surgery, unless the VA determines that the surgery is medically necessary

>> Gender affirmation surgery

>> Health club and spa memberships

>> Medications or medical devices that aren't approved by the U.S. Food and Drug Administration — unless you're taking part in an approved clinical trial or you're seriously ill and your VA healthcare provider prescribes it for you because no other comparable treatment options are available

>> Inpatient hospital stays or outpatient care if you're a patient or inmate in a non-VA government agency institution, but only if that agency is required by law to provide you with care or services

Delving deeper into VA copays

Some veterans never have to pay copays (including those who are 50 percent or more disabled, are unable to work, or have received a Medal of Honor), but many others do. These fees are based on a number of factors, including your income level, military service history, priority group, and disability rating. Usually, the VA determines whether you have to come up with the money for copays when you enroll; you're required to fill out a financial assessment at that time. Recent combat veterans and those who were exposed to hazardous materials during service (such as Agent Orange, ionizing radiation, and some environmental contaminants, which I explain in Chapter 20) don't have to fill out financial assessments — they're on enhanced eligibility status, so it's not required. See the earlier section, "Focusing on enhanced eligibility status," for more information on this group.

REMEMBER

If you apply for free prescriptions or beneficiary travel pay (but not free VA healthcare), you need to update your income information with the VA every year to continue to qualify. If you're eligible for free VA healthcare based on your income, you don't have to update your income information — but the VA will still get it from the IRS and Social Security Administration. The VA will contact you if the information it receives changes your eligibility or copay requirements. If the VA finds out that you make too much to qualify, it'll send you a notification letter; you can dispute the information by responding to the letter or send in proof of expenses that may help lower your income for qualification purposes.

Caring for Your Eyes, Ears, and Mind

The VA covers basic preventive treatment for vision, hearing, and mental health — which I examine here — though you may need special permission for it to cover things like the cost of eyeglasses. In many cases, if your primary care provider feels that a treatment is medically necessary, it falls under the VA umbrella of coverage.

Peeking at VA vision care

The VA covers routine eye exams, which include preventive screenings for glaucoma and other eye issues. You can schedule an appointment with an eye doctor through your primary care provider or by contacting the nearest VA medical center or clinic. Generally, the VA doesn't pay for eyeglasses — but it may if you have a compensable service-connected disability, are a former prisoner of war or Purple Heart recipient, or you're permanently housebound and receive an increased pension because of it. Additionally, the VA may cover eyeglasses if you have vision problems caused by an illness (or the treatment of an illness) for which you receive VA care, such as diabetes, stroke, vascular disease, or reactions to prescribed medications. You can find out whether you qualify for free eyeglasses by contacting the prosthetic representative at your nearest VA clinic or medical center.

And if you're a blind or low-vision veteran, you may be eligible for more advanced vision care or rehabilitation services. Here are the advanced vision care services:

>> Electronic reading machines and mobility devices, plus training in how to use them

>> Sensory training that helps develop your use of hearing or sense of touch

>> Mobility and orientation training that teaches you how to make mental maps

>> Counseling and group therapy

Your family may also qualify for care that helps them support you.

TECHNICAL STUFF

The VA doesn't provide guide dogs for low-vision or blind veterans, but it *does* work with outside agencies that do provide them. And though it won't provide the service dog itself, it will pay for veterinary care and equipment (such as harnesses, backpacks, and service vests) that you need.

Listening in on VA hearing care

Audiology comes part-and-parcel with the basic VA medical benefits package. In fact, as soon as you're approved for VA healthcare benefits, the agency's own rules say that you "shall receive a hearing evaluation by a state-licensed audiologist to determine the need for hearing aids." If you suffer from hearing loss, you may qualify for free hearing aids from the VA. You may even be eligible to receive free hearing aid batteries and accessories from the VA, which you can order by mail, over the phone, or online using an eBenefits account.

The VA provides other hearing services, too, such as treatment options for tinnitus (ringing ears), cochlear implants, and special examinations.

TIP

Although the VA has gone back and forth over covering tinnitus, if you have a disability rating for it, you qualify for special hearing aids and other services. (Tinnitus is one of the most common service-related disabilities, according to the VA.) If you have tinnitus, hearing loss, or other audiology-related issues, you may be eligible for disability compensation from the VA — and that means you should apply for a disability rating right away. Flip to Chapter 9 for more information on getting a rating.

Using VA mental healthcare services

The VA provides a wide range of mental healthcare services ranging from treatment for posttraumatic stress and military sexual trauma to the effects of traumatic brain injury, depression, anxiety, suicide prevention, bipolar disorder, schizophrenia, alcohol and substance abuse issues, and even tobacco cessation. You can be seen in person, participate in online counseling or therapy, or make phone appointments with your mental health caregiver. The VA also provides the following services to eligible veterans when necessary:

>> Short-term, inpatient care

>> Outpatient care

>> Rehabilitation treatment programs

>> Residential treatment programs (live-in facilities)

>> Emergency mental healthcare services for veterans in crisis

>> Supported work settings to help veterans with mental health needs join the workforce and live in their communities

Some of the most common treatments the VA prescribes are talk therapies (including cognitive behavioral therapy, acceptance and commitment therapy, and interpersonal therapy), and medications. All vets who receive specialty mental healthcare have their own mental health treatment coordinator (MHTC). The MHTC is a specially trained VA worker who helps ensure that veterans have lasting relationships with their mental health providers and oversees care transitions to make sure they go smoothly.

In cases where residential treatment (featuring a supportive environment 24 hours a day, 7 days a week) is in a veteran's best interest, the VA has several domiciliary programs to choose from, including:

>> **Domiciliary Care for Homeless Veterans (DCHV)** provides structured, supportive care and services for homeless vets.

>> **General Domiciliary (General Dom) and Psychosocial Residential Rehabilitation Treatment Programs (PRRTP)** are both geared toward treating medical and psychiatric issues, substance abuse, posttraumatic stress, and other issues.

>> **Domiciliary PTSD (Dom PTSD) or Posttraumatic Stress Disorder Residential Rehabilitation Treatment Program (PTSD-RRTP)** provides residential care for those who have posttraumatic stress or military sexual trauma.

A *domiciliary* is a safe facility where veterans can live for a short time. While living in the home-like environment of a domiciliary, vets get mental health treatments or substance abuse treatments as well as services that can help them get a job, go back to school, work on their social skills, and even address physical health problems.

Mental health support doesn't end there, though. Caregivers and family members of VA healthcare-enrolled or eligible veterans can talk to caregiver support coordinators at VA facilities to learn about the programs in place to help them, such as mental health counseling, respite care, and monthly financial stipends. (I delve into many of the benefits available to family members and caregivers in Chapter 21.)

Checking Out VA Substance Abuse Treatment Programs

If you're dealing with substance abuse issues, you're not alone — according to the National Institute of Health, more than one in ten veterans struggles with alcohol or drug use problems. Fortunately, you can get support and care for substance abuse issues from the VA; it's all part of its basic medical coverage package. (The VA provides treatment for health conditions that relate to substance abuse problems, too, such as posttraumatic stress, military sexual trauma, and depression.)

Here are the treatments the VA offers for substance abuse disorders:

>> Medications to decrease cravings for alcohol

>> Medications that ease withdrawal symptoms

>> Therapeutic substitutes for illegal drugs (like methadone and buprenorphine)

>> Talk therapy (sometimes called *psychotherapy*)

>> Opioid treatment programs that help address issues with heroin and other opiates (including prescription medications)

>> Residential treatment programs, if necessary

TECHNICAL STUFF

The Domiciliary SA (Dom SA) and Substance Abuse Residential Rehabilitation Treatment Program (SARRTP) are the VA's pair of programs designed to provide residential treatment for veterans with substance abuse disorders.

Finding Community Care

When you can't get treatment at a VA medical center because it takes too long to drive there, the one nearest you doesn't provide the services or level of care you need, or appointment wait times at your facility are too long, you may be eligible for community care. *Community care* is access to free healthcare (paid for by the VA) through providers in your local community. If you want to access community care rather than care through a VA medical facility, you need authorization from the VA. If the VA gives you the green light, keep in mind that you may need to get your medical records from your non-VA provider and give them to the VA.

REMEMBER

You still have to pay copays for treatments and medications you'd have to pay if you were being seen by a VA medical provider. However, community providers can't bill you for the copay or collect it directly from you; you pay them to the VA instead, and the VA handles it from there.

The VA also works with the Indian Health Service (IHS) and Tribal Health Programs (THP). If you're an eligible American Indian or Alaska Native veteran, you can seek treatment at an IHS or THP facility and the VA will pay for your care. You don't need preauthorization to go to an IHS facility if you're eligible, and you don't have to pay a VA copayment. However, in Alaska, you do need preauthorization, and you may also have to pay VA copays. (Refer to Chapter 4 where I discuss IHS in greater detail.)

REMEMBER

When it comes to emergency care, you don't have to head to a VA hospital unless it's the closest to you. You can seek treatment for a medical emergency (defined by the VA as "an injury, illness, or symptom so severe that a delay in seeking immediate medical attention would be reasonably expected to be hazardous to life or health") at the nearest medical facility and the VA will pay for it. See the later section, "Seeking Urgent or Emergency Care in Non-VA Facilities," for more information.

If you were previously enrolled in community care under the Veterans Choice Program (VCP), you need to speak to your VA care team or a VA staff member. The VCP program is no longer in use, but you may still be eligible for community care through the current program.

Operating with Overseas Care: The FMP

Eligible veterans who live or travel abroad have access to the VA's Foreign Medical Program (FMP). The FMP is a bit different from standard VA healthcare, but it pays for regular outpatient care, emergency services and hospitalization, medication, skilled nursing care, physical therapy, and durable medical equipment and prosthetics for service-connected conditions. If you're simply traveling abroad, you don't need to notify the FMP program, but if you're moving to a foreign country, you should let the VA know as soon as you get a permanent address. And if you head back to the United States, you'll need to get in touch with the nearest VA healthcare facility before seeking medical treatment.

The FMP doesn't cover experimental drugs or treatments or any of the following (which it may include if you live in the United States or one of its territories):

>> Adult day care or companion services

>> Assisted living, nursing homes, or custodial care

>> Durable medical equipment with "deluxe" or "luxury" features

>> Gender affirmation services, including drugs

>> Family planning services or sterilization

>> Non-acute institutional care (like long-term inpatient psychiatric care)

>> Non-FDA-approved medications

>> Nonmedical home care

>> Physical therapy that isn't under a licensed physician's supervision

Even if you're covered for VA dental care when you're stateside, you may only be authorized to receive dental treatment for VA-adjudicated, service-connected disabilities (or associated conditions). The VA may, in some cases, authorize payment for dental services for veterans who seek dental treatment within 90 days of discharge or whose discharge documents don't indicate a completed dental exam and treatment.

Picking Up Your Prescriptions

The VA will pay the tab for your prescriptions if you're enrolled in its healthcare program. (There isn't a stand-alone prescription program; it only comes as part of the VA healthcare package.) However, in some cases, you have to pay copays for your medications.

The catch: The VA pharmacy can only fill prescriptions written by a VA healthcare provider or VA-authorized provider. If you have a prescription from an outside physician, your VA care provider will review it to determine whether it's appropriate for your condition. If it is, they'll rewrite it so the VA pharmacy can dispense it. The following sections explain prescriptions and copays for people entitled to VA healthcare.

Refilling prescriptions

You can refill some prescriptions through the My HealtheVet website, by calling your local VA medical center, or through a special refill app provided by the VA. You may also request to refill your prescriptions by mail.

Handling non-VA prescriptions

The VA pharmacy can't fill prescriptions that come from a non-VA provider. However, your provider may choose to rewrite a prescription that comes from outside the VA so you can pick it up at the VA pharmacy.

Understanding medication copays

Veterans in Priority Group 1 and those that have certain exemptions (such as those receiving prescriptions for service-connected conditions, former prisoners of war, veterans with low incomes, and those being treated for certain other conditions) don't pay a dime for any VA medications. However, for those vets who do have to pay, copays are based on the type of drug and the length of the supply you need (whether it's a one- to 30-day supply, a 31- to 60-day supply, or a 61- to 90-day supply).

For example, Tier 1 drugs are preferred generic medications and have the lowest copays. Tier 2 drugs are nonpreferred generics and some over-the-counter drugs, and they feature middle-of-the-road copays. Finally, Tier 3 drugs are brand-name drugs and have the highest price tags attached. Don't stress too much, though: Everyone has a medication copay cap, which means the VA won't charge you after your prescription copays reach a certain amount. The cap is subject to change, so if you're not sure what it is this year, contact your VA medical center to ask.

FREE HEALTHCARE FOR RESEARCH SUBJECTS

Between 1942 and 1975, somewhere in the neighborhood of 60,000 servicemembers (now veterans) volunteered for medical research for the United States' biological and chemical programs. If you were a volunteer for this research, which encompassed everything from testing LSD's battlefield applications and vaccine side effects to mustard gas and unknown substances (unknown because the military never disclosed them), you may be entitled to free medical care from the U.S. Army (and/or the VA).

To submit a packet to the Army, you need copies of military-issued documents to prove your participation in chemical or biological substance testing, a diagnosis for all medical conditions that could be a result of your participation in the testing, and a VA determination of service connection (if applicable). You can contact the U.S. Army Medical Command hotline at 800-984-8523 or visit https://armymedicine.health.mil/CBTP to get more information or to get help applying for coverage.

You have to pay copays on all over-the-counter medications you receive from the VA pharmacy, such as cough syrup and vitamins. But it *doesn't* charge you a copay for medical supplies such as syringes and alcohol wipes or for medications you receive during inpatient treatment.

Seeking Urgent or Emergency Care in Non-VA Facilities

You can seek urgent-care or emergency treatment in a non-VA facility if you're covered under VA healthcare. In fact, a number of urgent-care clinics are associated with the VA; they're considered *approved community providers*. As long as you're enrolled in the VA healthcare system and have received care from the VA within the past 24 months (and you choose an approved community provider), you're good to go.

Priority Groups 1 through 5 don't have a copay for the first three visits in any calendar year; Priority Group 6 sometimes has a copay, depending on the condition being treated, and Priority Groups 7 and 8 always have a copay. But if you're only heading to the urgent-care facility for a flu shot, there's no copay at all, regardless of your priority group.

When it comes to emergency care, don't bother asking the ambulance driver to reroute their map guidance to the nearest VA facility. You can get emergency treatment anywhere and the VA will pay for it. Remember, though, the VA defines an emergency as something that poses a threat to your life or health. In order for the VA to pay for your emergency treatment in a non–VA facility, the nearest VA facility "must not be feasibly available" and the medical situation you're in must be a genuine emergency.

You're required to report your emergency treatment to the VA's Centralized Emergency Care Reporting Center online or by calling the VA directly within 72 hours of your treatment (if possible). However, failure to let the VA know within that time frame doesn't mean the agency won't pay for your claim; it just means the payment may take longer because the VA has to use a different authority to process the payment.

WARNING

The VA can pay for emergency care outside the United States only if the emergency is related to a service-connected condition, which I cover in the section, "Operating with Overseas Care: The FMP," earlier in this chapter.

Getting to and from Your Appointments

If you have difficulty getting to and from your appointments, you may qualify for the Veterans Transportation Program (VTP). The VTP gives you three options to get from Point A to Point B at little to no cost; I discuss them here.

Clocking in for travel reimbursement

If you live too far from a VA medical facility to reasonably pay for your travel, or if traveling costs you more than it would cost others (such as when you need to take a taxi), the VA may cover it. Likewise, the VA may pay for transportation if you need a special type of vehicle to get you there (such as an ambulance or wheelchair van). Keep the following in mind:

>> General health care travel is reimbursable if you have a VA disability rating of 30 percent or higher, if you're traveling for treatment of a service-connected condition (even if your rating is under 30 percent), you get a VA pension, if you're heading to a scheduled VA claim exam, you're picking up a service dog, or if you can't afford your travel (as determined by VA guidelines). You may also be eligible for reimbursement if you're traveling to be treated at a special rehab center.

>> Special mode transportation is reimbursable if you're eligible for general healthcare travel reimbursement, your VA healthcare provider says you need an ambulance or specially equipped van for travel, and the VA has approved your travel in advance (unless it's an emergency).

Taking special transportation

The Veterans Transportation Service (VTS) helps vets who are elderly, immobilized, or visually impaired get to and from medical appointments. Vets who are eligible for healthcare benefits and have an authorized appointment are eligible for transportation through VTS, provided that their local medical facility has partnerships with local organizations. Sometimes the VA works with veterans service organizations (VSOs) as well as community transportation providers, governmental transportation agencies, and nonprofit organizations to secure rides for veterans under its care.

Traveling far and wide for VA care

People who live in counties that have fewer than seven people per square mile are often eligible for rides from organizations that receive Highly Rural Transportation Grants (HRTGs). Veterans don't have to pay to participate in the program, which provides funding to VSOs and state veterans service agencies to provide rides in eligible areas. You can find out whether your county makes you eligible by visiting the VA's HRTG page at www.va.gov/healthbenefits/vtp/

Exploring Extended Care

Extended care — sometimes called *geriatric care* — is care for older vets, and the VA provides a pretty decent amount of it. There are home and community-based services, residential programs (such as nursing homes, adult family homes, and assisted living facilities), and special programs for Alzheimer's and dementia. It also covers some exercise programs, advance care planning, and rehab and prosthetics services, which I discuss here.

Home- and community-based services

Older veterans can talk to their healthcare providers about using the following home-based and community-based services:

>> **Adult day healthcare** is designed specifically for veterans to go to during the day to spend time with friends, get peer support, and participate in recreational activities. These programs are often provided at VA medical centers, state veterans' homes, and through community organizations, and they're ideal for isolated vets or those with caregivers who are experiencing burden.

>> **Home-based primary care services** are provided in the comfort of your own home. All care is supervised by a VA physician, and it's designed around vets who have complex healthcare needs, vets who have difficulty making or keeping appointments at medical facilities, and vets who are homebound.

>> **Homemaker and home health aide care** allows a trained professional to visit a veteran's home to help with daily activities. These helpers can often enable a veteran to live independently for longer.

>> **Skilled home health care** is a short-term solution for veterans moving from a hospital or nursing home back to their own home. The services in this program include skilled nursing; physical, occupational, or speech therapy; wound care; and IV antibiotics.

>> **Palliative care** focuses on relieving suffering and controlling symptoms so that a veteran may continue their day-to-day life. This type of care can enhance quality of life, and it can be combined with treatments designed to control or cure an illness.

>> **Remote monitoring** enables a primary care provider or nurse to monitor a veteran using home monitoring equipment.

>> **Hospice care** is for veterans who have a terminal condition with fewer than 6 months to live. This type of care is only appropriate for veterans who no longer want to seek treatment (other than palliative care), and it can be provided at home, in an outpatient clinic, or an inpatient facility.

Residential services

Sometimes veterans need to live in a residential treatment setting or nursing home. The VA *doesn't* cover the cost of residence in a private nursing home or assisted living facility, though it may cover some of the healthcare expenses for veterans who live in them. The following services are available:

>> **Medical foster homes** feature trained caregivers to provide services to a few individuals at a time. These private homes are used as alternatives to nursing homes. Usually, the VA doesn't pay for this service, though it can pay for home-based primary care you receive.

>> **Traumatic Brain Injury – Residential Rehabilitation (TBI-RR) centers** are programs that the VA pays for if eligible vets have TBI or other brain injuries. The VA covers the services provided in the facilities, though the vet is responsible for paying for room and board.

>> **Community living centers** are designed for temporary or permanent stays for veterans. Like private nursing homes, these centers provide rooms,

planned activities, and help with daily living (as well as skilled nursing and medical care). Pets are allowed, and so are visitors. However, there are only about a hundred of these facilities in the country, and eligible veterans still must pay a copay based on their VA service-connected disability status and financial situation.

>> **Community nursing homes** are for veterans who need skilled nursing care around the clock. The VA doesn't provide these homes, but it contracts with community-based nursing homes to pay for services (only if you have a demonstrated medical need and a space is open for you).

>> **State veterans homes** are managed by states, though the VA certifies them. Certified state veterans homes may receive money from the VA to help pay for a veteran's stay. Each state has its own eligibility requirements for these homes. (I cover these and other state veterans benefits in Chapter 26.)

Mental health, brain health, and memory loss care

The VA provides a number of geriatric and elder-care treatments for mental health, brain health, and memory loss. Much of it is covered under standard VA healthcare, though some programs — such as community living centers — require a veteran to pay what the VA doesn't cover. One important thing to note is that the VA handles dementia care, including care for Alzheimer's disease, as part of a regular course of treatment. People who are under a doctor's care for dementia may also be eligible for home-based primary care, home health aides, adult day healthcare, and palliative care, as well as other services, which I cover in the preceding sections.

Health and fitness services

The VA runs a number of health and fitness programs for older veterans, including specific exercise classes designed for seasoned adults. These programs are available at VA facilities all over the country, and they include personalized exercise prescriptions and fun classes (like tai chi, dancing, and balance). If you don't live near one of the locations that offers these programs, you can reach out to the VA to find out whether they may cover your participation in another program.

The VA also handles physical therapy, recreation therapy, and rehabilitation services to treat a wide range of conditions. These types of therapy may include strength and conditioning exercises, balance training and fall prevention, injury prevention, and weight management programs. Recreation therapy (and its companion programs, art therapy, dance and movement therapy, drama therapy, and music therapy) is available through many VA healthcare facilities, as well. Though these are all listed under extended care, which is generally for older veterans, they're available to all eligible vets.

Juggling Health Insurance and VA Coverage

You can use your VA healthcare benefits alongside other types of health coverage, such as private insurance, Medicare, Medicaid, or TRICARE. When you apply for VA health benefits, you have to provide information on your current insurance plan; that's because the VA is legally required to bill your insurer for treatments it provides that aren't related to a service-connected condition.

TIP

Even if your insurance provider doesn't cover all the nonservice-connected care you receive, you don't have to come up with the money to pay for it yourself. However, you may have to pay copays based on your priority group. And if your insurance company does pay for nonservice-connected care, the VA may be able to offset all or part of your copayment.

WARNING

You probably shouldn't give up your private health insurance when you accept VA healthcare benefits. That's because the VA doesn't usually provide benefits to family members (though your private insurance may). Also, the VA's funding is always subject to change, which means it can't predict whether you can stay on VA healthcare forever (or even next year) if you're in a lower priority group.

The VA encourages veterans to sign up for Medicare as soon as they're eligible because that program provides additional benefits (and because if you sign up after you lose VA healthcare benefits, you may have to pay a penalty). You can use Medicare to pay for non-VA prescriptions, outpatient services, and doctor visits that aren't associated with the VA.

Employing Your Form-Filling Skills to the Application Process

If you believe you're eligible for VA healthcare benefits, fill out an application online, by phone (you can call the VA's hotline at 877-222-8387), by mail, in person, or with the help of a professional representative (such as a lawyer, a VA claims agent, or a VSO). The VA will require documentation to process your application and put you in the appropriate priority group.

To apply for VA healthcare benefits, which usually only takes about a half-hour, you need the following documents:

>> Social Security numbers (yours, your spouse's, and your qualified dependents')

>> Your military discharge documents

>> Insurance cards if you have health insurance

You may also need to provide information on your gross income last year (for you, your spouse, and your dependents), as well as your deductible expenses for last year, which help lower the amount of money that the VA counts as your income. The application asks you whether you receive VA disability compensation or have a rating or a VA pension, your start and end dates of active-duty service, and whether you served in a combat area (as well as a few other things). It also asks for household information, such as your spouse and dependents' names and Social Security numbers, and income information. After you fill out your application, it takes the VA approximately a week to put you in a priority group and decide on your enrollment.

LEGISLATION SHAPES VA CARE

From time to time, legislators take up issues involving VA healthcare. In early 2022, Rep. Mark Takano (D-CA) introduced legislation that would require the VA to automatically enroll eligible veterans in the VA healthcare program. Later the same year, legislation passed the House and Senate regarding VA healthcare for conditions related to exposure to burn pits in Iraq and Afghanistan (see Chapter 20 for more on these conditions). If you want to see changes in the way the VA healthcare system works, contact your senator or representative to encourage them to act.

Chapter **6**

Probing into TRICARE

M illions of people in the United States don't have health insurance right now — and many of them who do are paying an arm and a leg for it. Across the United States, annual premiums for individuals average around $5,200 (employers pitch in around $16,000 to cover each worker). Insurance is expensive, and though some plans are pretty cheap, the fact is that more money equals better coverage. Healthcare costs have also risen exponentially in the past couple of decades with people today spending an average of about $12,500 each on care, goods, and services related to health. With that information, it's no wonder health insurance costs keep rising every year.

But if you retired from the military, you may be in luck. Retirees from active-duty military service or a reserve component (including the National Guard) are typically eligible for TRICARE, which is the same program that covers active-duty service-members and their families. Some survivors and former spouses, as well as all Medal of Honor (MOH) recipients and their families are also eligible for this health insurance program. Though the benefits change a bit (and you have to pay for them), it's a pretty sweet deal for most. TRICARE doesn't cost nearly as much as most civilian healthcare plans do, and it provides comprehensive medical coverage through a variety of plans. You can choose a plan that works for your budget and your needs, and unlike VA healthcare, your plan can cover your dependents, too.

You may use TRICARE with other types of insurance (including VA healthcare and Medicare). If you want it, you must enroll in a plan within 90 days of your official retirement, though some exceptions let you stretch your enrollment date to 12 months. This chapter explains TRICARE plans and what they cover, how much you're likely to pay, how to apply when you retire, and then some.

Qualifying for TRICARE

TRICARE is a health insurance program that covers uniformed servicemembers and their families, retirees, and dependents registered in the Defense Enrollment Eligibility Reporting System (DEERS). It's also available to survivors, some former spouses, and MOH recipients. Medical retirees count, too (and if you're a medical retiree, you probably also have access to VA healthcare and a variety of other benefits, such as disability pay, which I explain in Chapter 9).

REMEMBER

Qualifying for TRICARE is generally pretty simple: You have to

>> Fall into one of the appropriate eligibility categories

>> Agree to pay premiums (costs for coverage) and copays

>> Sign a dotted line or two

That's it. Don't worry about preexisting conditions. TRICARE has no restrictions on them, and they won't increase your insurance costs. The following sections cover all the details on qualifying and getting coverage.

Checking the calendar: Age-based qualifications

When you retire from active-duty service at any age (or when you turn 60, if you're a retired reservist), you and your dependents can seamlessly transition into your post-service TRICARE coverage. However, you're not automatically enrolled — you still have to re-enroll in a retiree health plan within 90 days of your retirement date.

Don't freak out if you miss the 3-month window, though. You're allowed to request a retroactive enrollment, as long as you do it within a year of your retirement. After that, you may only enroll in TRICARE or make changes to your plan when there's an open enrollment season (that happens once a year, in the fall) or when you have a *qualifying life event (QLE)*, which means something big happens that necessitates a change in your healthcare benefits. Here are some acceptable QLEs:

- » Birth or adoption of a child
- » Death in the family
- » Kids growing up
- » Loss or gain of other health insurance
- » Marriage or divorce
- » Placement of a child (by a court) in your home
- » Relocation
- » Retirement

Your age matters, and 65 is the golden number. That's when most people become eligible for Medicare. If you're younger than 65, you're eligible for TRICARE Prime, TRICARE Select, TRICARE Select Overseas, and the U.S. Family Health Plan. However, if you're older than 65 or if you're eligible for Medicare in the younger-than-65 set, you're most likely eligible for TRICARE For Life. I cover each of these plans in the following sections.

Keeping DEERS in the loop

TRICARE keeps tabs on your eligibility (and your dependents' eligibility) through DEERS. As a retiree, you're already enrolled in DEERS. However, you have to register your eligible family members. Only a sponsor is allowed to add or remove family members from DEERS; other beneficiaries can't.

TIP

To register dependents in DEERS, visit your local ID card office. Every military installation has one. If all your dependents are already registered from the time you spent on active duty, you're good to go — no further action is necessary. However, you have to keep DEERS updated with things like changes of address and phone number, additions or subtractions of dependents, and marital status changes. Table 6-1 explains what documents you need to enroll a spouse, child, dependent parent, or someone else in DEERS.

WARNING

If you have a dependent who turns 21 while enrolled, DEERS automatically drops their registration unless you prove that they're attending college or otherwise eligible to remain enrolled.

You (or another beneficiary) can make simple changes (like addresses and phone numbers) through the milConnect website, by phone, or by mail.

TIP

If you and your spouse are both retirees (or if one of you is still serving on active duty), you have to pick which one of you will sponsor your kids or other dependents in DEERS. Dependents may only have one sponsor.

TABLE 6-1   **Required Documents to Enroll Dependents in DEERS**

Relationship	Required Documents
Spouse	Marriage certificate
	Spouse's birth certificate
	Spouse's Social Security card with the right name
	Spouse's photo ID
Child	Birth certificate
	Social Security card
	If you're enrolling a stepchild, your marriage certificate
Child older than 21 who is a full-time student	Birth certificate
	Social Security card
	Letter from a school's registrar's office that states the child is enrolled full time in an accredited college to pursue an associate degree or higher
	If you're enrolling a stepchild, your marriage certificate
Child born out of wedlock for male sponsors only	Birth certificate
	Social Security card
	Court order establishing paternity or a state voluntary acknowledgment of paternity form
Dependent parent	Letter of approval from the Defense Finance and Accounting Service (DFAS)
	Sponsor's birth certificate
	Parent's photo ID
	Parent's Social Security card
Dependent ward	Letter of approval from DFAS
	Court document placing the child in your household for one year or more
	Birth certificate
	Social Security card

Maintaining your family's coverage with TRICARE Young Adult

When your children grow up, TRICARE gives them a little bit of a boost by letting them remain on your plan for a while. TRICARE Young Adult (TYA) is a plan for qualified adult kids that you (or they) can purchase. Your child must meet these qualifications:

- » Unmarried

- » At least age 21 but not yet 26

- » Ineligible for an employer-sponsored health plan based on your (the sponsor's) employment

- » Ineligible for TRICARE coverage on their own

How much TYA costs depends on whether you choose Prime or Select, the sponsor's military status, and where the beneficiary receives care. This plan is often a good choice for dependents who have aged out of TRICARE.

TRICARE for survivors, former spouses, and families of MOH recipients

TRICARE continues to provide coverage for eligible dependents when a sponsor dies. That means your family will remain eligible for TRICARE and can continue to use it as long as they want. Your plan may also extend to your former spouse, in some cases, and the families of MOH recipients are always eligible for TRICARE. I cover each of these scenarios here.

Surviving spouses and children

Surviving spouses of active-duty servicemembers, National Guard and Reserve members, and retirees can keep their TRICARE coverage. They still qualify for the same plans and costs they had while the sponsor was alive, too. Surviving spouses remain eligible unless they remarry, and children keep eligibility until they age out or lose their TRICARE eligibility for other reasons. These surviving family members may also qualify for the TRICARE Retiree Dental Program, which I cover in the section, "Drilling into TRICARE Dental Coverage," later in this chapter.

Former spouses

Your former spouse may be entitled to pay for their own TRICARE coverage based on their marriage to you. However, they're only entitled to keep it if they don't remarry; if that happens, they need to start looking for alternative health coverage. To remain eligible, your former spouse needs to provide your marriage certificate, your divorce decree, and your discharge document. I delve into the special circumstances that make former spouses eligible for TRICARE coverage in the section, "Seeing 20/20/20: TRICARE after Divorce," later in this chapter.

TECHNICAL STUFF

If your former spouse qualifies to keep their TRICARE benefits, DEERS will track their eligibility using their Social Security number, not yours.

Families of Medal of Honor recipients

Families of veterans who received the Medal of Honor (MOH) are eligible for TRICARE coverage, even if the servicemember separated from active duty without retiring. In fact, a separated MOH recipient's family gets the same coverage as a retired servicemember's family does. Everyone in the family may also be eligible for dental coverage through the Federal Employees Dental and Vision Insurance Program (FEDVIP), which I cover in the section, "Drilling into TRICARE Dental Coverage" later in this chapter.

Tiptoeing Around TRICARE Plans

TRICARE, like most other insurance providers, has a wide selection of plans. You may choose the plan that matches your lifestyle, budget, and needs, though some plans are only available to certain people based on their military history and current status.

TRICARE is divided into three regions, so depending on where you live, you'll deal with representatives that only work with the insurance company contracted for that region:

>> **TRICARE West Region:** You deal with Health Net.

>> **TRICARE East Region:** Your point of contact is Humana Military.

>> **TRICARE Overseas Region:** You go through International SOS.

Each of these contractors is bound by an agreement with TRICARE to offer identical plans at identical costs. I explain the basics of each TRICARE plan here so you can make a more informed choice when you enroll.

TRICARE Prime

TRICARE Prime is a managed-care option, which means it's a type of health insurance in which the insurer has contracts with healthcare providers and medical facilities. Those contracts enable providers and facilities to care for members of certain insurance plans at reduced costs. All the providers and facilities involved in this type of plan are in the insurer's *network*. Usually, you don't pay to see a network provider. If you seek treatment from a provider or facility that isn't in the network (called a *nonnetwork provider*), you may have to pay for your own care. However, you may be authorized to see nonnetwork providers under this plan only if you choose to use the program's point-of-service option or your regional insurance contractor preapproves your care.

A point-of-service option allows you to see nonnetwork providers, but you have to pay more out of pocket than you would with another option. You pay using point-of-service fees rather than regular copayments as well as any other fees that non-network providers charge. Typically, with this option, you must pay 50 percent of the cost of outpatient services and hospitalization.

This plan is available to retired servicemembers and their families, retired National Guard and Reserve members and their families (when the veteran is age 60 or older), survivors, MOH recipients, and qualified former spouses. Some beneficiaries must pay annual enrollment fees for TRICARE Prime, which enables them to use a military or network provider as a primary care manager (PCM) and get referrals to specialists if they need additional help.

TRICARE Select

TRICARE Select is a self-managed, preferred provider network plan. It's very similar to a civilian preferred-provider organization (PPO). In this type of plan, your insurer contracts with medical providers to create a network. You pay less if you work with providers who belong to that network. However, you may work with out-of-network providers if you want to — you don't need authorization from a PCM. In fact, under this health plan, you don't even *have* a PCM.

Under TRICARE Select, you pay copayments for most outpatient services when you work with a TRICARE network provider. If you work with a non-TRICARE-authorized provider or a provider who isn't in the network, you must pay a cost-share. A *cost-share* is a percentage of the total cost of the healthcare service. Retirees, their families, and other beneficiaries may have to pay an enrollment fee that's based on when the sponsor joined the military. You must also pay deductibles for this plan.

U.S. Family Health Plan

The U.S. Family Health Plan is connected to TRICARE Prime, but it's not available to everyone; it's only open to people who live in the following areas, which are divvied up according to designated providers:

>> Maryland, Washington, D.C., and parts of Pennsylvania, Virginia, Delaware, and West Virginia, are served by Johns Hopkins Medicine.

>> Maine, New Hampshire, Vermont, Upstate and Western New York, and the Northern Tier of Pennsylvania, are served by Martin's Point Health Care.

>> Massachusetts (including Cape Cod), Rhode Island, and Northern Connecticut, are served by Brighton Marine Health Center.

>> New York City, Long Island, Southern Connecticut, New Jersey, and Philadelphia, and its suburbs are served by St. Vincent Catholic Medical Centers.

>> Southwest Texas and Southwest Louisiana, are served by CHRISTUS Health.

>> Western Washington state, parts of Eastern Washington state, Northern Idaho, and Western Oregon, are served by Pacific Medical Centers.

The way this plan works is a little different from other plans. You receive all your care from a primary care provider that you choose from a network of private physicians who are affiliated with the nonprofit healthcare system servicing your area. Your primary care provider coordinates your care and refers you to specialists if necessary. You can't get care at military hospitals or clinics or from other TRICARE network providers.

TRICARE For Life

TRICARE For Life (TFL) is considered *Medicare-wraparound coverage*, which means that TRICARE and Medicare work together to reduce your out-of-pocket medical costs. This coverage is only available to people who have Medicare Part A and Part B, as well as TRICARE. You don't have to pay enrollment fees for this plan, but you must pay your Medicare Part B monthly premiums, which are based on your income. (Refer to the section, "Managing Medicare and TFL," later in this chapter for more specifics.)

Within the United States and its territories, TRICARE picks up the tab after Medicare covers its share of your medical costs. Outside the United States, TRICARE is the first payer. You may use this plan to visit any provider who accepts Medicare. Your provider will file your claims with Medicare, and then Medicare will cover its part. The agency then sends the remainder of the claim to TRICARE. Under this plan, you may be able to get care at military hospitals and clinics — but only on a space-available basis.

TRICARE Select Overseas

TRICARE Select Overseas is only for people who live outside the United States. It's available to retired servicemembers and their families, retired members of the National Guard and Reserves, survivors, MOH recipients and their families, and qualified former spouses.

Under this plan, you may schedule an appointment with any overseas medical provider. You may need preauthorization for some types of services, but you generally don't need referrals for specialty care. You may also have to pay an annual outpatient deductible and cost-shares for covered services.

Typically, you have to pay up-front for medical care you receive overseas under this plan. Then, you file your own claim with TRICARE for reimbursement. If you live overseas, this may be the only TRICARE option available to you.

TRICARE Retired Reserve

TRICARE Retired Reserve is a premium-based plan, so you need to pay a premium each month for your health coverage. You must pay the premium every month, even if you don't use any healthcare services. You also need to pay an annual deductible and cost shares for covered services. This plan is available regardless of where you live, as long as you're a Reserve retiree who qualifies for nonregular retirement, younger than 60, and ineligible for the Federal Employees Health Benefits (FEHB) program. Family members of retired Reservists and some survivors under some circumstances are eligible.

Under this plan, you may schedule appointments with any TRICARE-authorized provider. However, some providers (even when TRICARE-authorized) are in the network, and some are out. If you visit a network provider, you typically pay less in cost shares (and the provider will file your claims for you). If you work with a nonnetwork provider, you may have to pay more for services, and you may also have to file your own claims with TRICARE. You may be able to get care at a military hospital or clinic if space is available for you.

Weeding Out TRICARE Programs You Don't Qualify For

Some TRICARE programs aren't available to retirees, former spouses, and people who fall into other categories. Save yourself a little bit of time by skimming over these:

- **» TRICARE Prime Overseas:** This plan is only available to active-duty servicemembers, command-sponsored dependents, and activated Guard and Reserve members.

- **» TRICARE Prime Remote:** This plan is only available to active-duty servicemembers who live more than 50 miles (or an hour's drive time) from a military hospital or clinic (like recruiters). This plan's cousin, TRICARE Prime Remote Overseas, is only available to active-duty servicemembers, activated National Guard and Reserve members, and their command-sponsored dependents living overseas in remote areas.

- **» TRICARE Reserve Select:** This plan is only for members who are currently in the Selected Reserve and their families.

Saying Goodbye to Services TRICARE Stops Covering When You Retire

When you're a member of the active-duty military, TRICARE covers just about everything from the sniffles and broken bones to mental health services and major surgeries for you and your family. However, upon retirement, you have to kiss some of that coverage goodbye. That's true regardless of the TRICARE plan you choose. The most notable benefits you lose coverage for include the following:

>> Hearing aids (though you may be eligible for them through the VA)

>> TRICARE Extended Care Health Option services for your family members

>> Chiropractic care

>> Eye exams (unless you have TRICARE Prime; then, they're still covered)

You also need to know that as a retiree, you may have to pay for your TRICARE coverage. Your costs may vary based on several factors based on the plan you choose.

Finding a Doctor Who Takes TRICARE

In some TRICARE plans, you get a PCM. This person is assigned to you after you enroll in your plan, and they're your main point of contact for all your healthcare needs. However, in other plans, you're required to find your own doctor. Fortunately, TRICARE takes the guesswork out of hunting for a doctor by giving you online access to a complete list of its network and nonnetwork providers. You may also find a provider by calling your regional TRICARE office or by calling providers near you and asking if they accept this type of insurance.

The TRICARE website even has a "Find a Doctor Wizard," which lets you choose whether you want to be seen at a military hospital or clinic, go to a network or nonnetwork provider, or choose from all your options.

Filling Prescriptions with TRICARE

When you enroll in TRICARE, you automatically get pharmacy coverage. You may fill your prescriptions through military pharmacies, the TRICARE Pharmacy Home Delivery program (which may be limited overseas), TRICARE retail network pharmacies, and some nonnetwork pharmacies. If you get up to a 90-day supply of your prescriptions from a military pharmacy, generic or brand name, you don't have a copay; your prescriptions are free. However, you do have a copay if you use the home delivery program or get your prescriptions from a network or nonnetwork pharmacy.

Drilling into TRICARE Dental Coverage

TRICARE offers dental coverage through FEDVIP. You may choose between major carriers that participate in the program to find the plan that's right for you. FEDVIP plans are available to the following individuals:

>> Retired servicemembers and their family members

>> Retired Guard or Reserve members and their families

>> MOH recipients and their families

>> Survivors — a special program exists for surviving family members (but not retirees) called the TRICARE Dental Program (TDP); this program requires you to enroll for at least 12 months, and you must choose between a single-person enrollment and a family enrollment. If you choose a family plan, you must enroll all eligible family members except children under the age of one, family members who don't live in the same location, or family members who need special medical attention in a hospital or treatment center.

The federal government requires every plan to provide comprehensive dental coverage, which means you get access to preventive services and major dental work. Unlike many other dental insurance plans, FEDVIP covers preventive services at 100 percent; it also doesn't require you to wait for major services such as crowns, bridges, implants, or dentures. Additionally, FEDVIP plans don't have a waiting period or age limit for orthodontic coverage. Your cost for dental coverage will vary based on the dental insurance carrier you choose.

Taking a Peek at TRICARE Vision Coverage

Some TRICARE plans cover routine eye exams. For example, TRICARE Prime and TRICARE Young Adult Prime allow you to get routine eye exams every two years. If you have the U.S. Family Health Plan, coverage for eye exams depends on your provider.

If you don't qualify for TRICARE vision coverage, you may be eligible for separate vision coverage through FEDVIP — the same program that handles dental coverage. Unlike TRICARE, FEDVIP provides pretty comprehensive vision coverage, including routine eye exams, eyeglass frames and lenses, contact lenses, and more.

Managing Medicare and TFL

You become eligible for TFL when you become eligible for Medicare. Usually, that's when you hit the age of 65, but some people are eligible earlier than that. This wraparound coverage complements Medicare and picks up the costs that Medicare leaves behind (which you'd ordinarily have to pay for out of your own pocket). In many cases, having TFL eliminates out-of-pocket costs entirely. Table 6-2 outlines the costs you'll likely be responsible for in specific situations.

TABLE 6-2   **Out-of-Pocket Costs for Medicare and TFL**

Service Conditions	Medicare Payment	TRICARE Payment	Your Cost
Covered by TRICARE and Medicare	The amount Medicare authorizes	All that remains	None
Covered only by Medicare	The amount Medicare authorizes	None	Your Medicare deductible and cost share
Covered only by TRICARE	None	The TRICARE-allowable amount	Your TRICARE deductible and cost share
Noncovered services	None	None	Charges the provider bills you for
Prescriptions	None	All (minus your copay)	Your medication copay, if applicable

You don't have to go out of your way to enroll in this program if you're already enrolled in some type of TRICARE coverage. If you have Medicare Part A and Medicare Part B, you're automatically covered by TFL. However, you *do* need to enroll in both Medicare parts, keeping in mind:

> **» Medicare Part A doesn't have premiums.** This program covers hospitalization and care you receive in other types of inpatient settings.

>> **Part B does have a premium.** This program pays for doctor visits and other forms of outpatient care. Your premium cost will vary because it's based on your income; it may change every year.

>> **You don't need to enroll in Medicare Part D.** This program pays for prescription drugs, but with TFL, your prescriptions are covered at no extra cost. You typically pay a copay to TRICARE for each of your prescriptions, though.

TRICARE and Medicare work together to coordinate your benefits, which means you don't normally need to file claims. You may be able to use your TFL coverage to get care at military hospitals or other military treatment facilities, as long as space is available for you. However, more than 90 percent of physicians accept Medicare patients, which means you have plenty of treatment options. You can use TFL with any provider who accepts Medicare.

Exploring Special TRICARE Programs

TRICARE offers several special programs for those who qualify. Most of these programs revolve around certain health conditions, or they're available to certain populations. Here are some of its most popular programs:

>> **Autism care demonstration:** This special program is for children who have been diagnosed with autism spectrum disorder (ASD) and covers applied behavior analysis services such as one-on-one therapy.

>> **Cancer clinical trials:** You may be eligible to participate in clinical trials if your doctor agrees. If you are, TRICARE covers all medical care and testing needed to determine your eligibility and all medical care needed during this study.

>> **Childbirth and breastfeeding support demonstration:** This program covers the costs of certified, nonmedical labor doulas as well as certified lactation consultants and counselors. However, this program is only for TRICARE Prime enrollees.

>> **Combat-related special compensation travel benefit (CRSC):** If you get retired, retired retainer, or equivalent pay and if you have a combat related disability, you may be eligible for CRSC. This benefit is available to people who have TRICARE Select or TFL and need specialty care more than 100 miles from home. You may use this benefit to cover your costs for lodging, fuel, meals, and other costs associated with getting your specialty care.

>> **TRICARE Plus:** This is a primary care program that some military hospitals and clinics offer to people who are eligible for TRICARE but aren't enrolled in Prime, the U.S. Family Health Plan, or a civilian or Medicare Health Maintenance Organization (HMO). It's also open to dependent parents and parents-in-law. TRICARE Plus allows people to get primary care at a military hospital or clinic without paying any money out of pocket.

You can check your eligibility for any of these programs using TRICARE's website or by calling the number for your regional office. TRICARE adds and removes programs periodically, and program requirements may change. Get the most current information by visiting `www.tricare.mil/Plans/SpecialPrograms`.

Enrolling in TRICARE When You Retire

To participate in TRICARE, you must enroll in or purchase a health plan. As a retiree, you don't have to wait for an open enrollment season. You may enroll within 90 days of your retirement or after any qualifying life event, such as a marriage, the birth or adoption of a child, or a divorce. You can enroll online at `www.tricare.mil/enroll`, by phone (just call your regional office), or even by mail.

TRICARE AND THE AFFORDABLE CARE ACT

Most TRICARE plans that are available to you meet the requirements for healthcare coverage in the Affordable Care Act (ACA). That means you'll receive an Internal Revenue Service Form 1095 in the mail; that form lists the coverage you had in the previous tax year. Though it's no longer required to prove your healthcare coverage when you file your federal taxes, you may need to prove it when you file your state taxes if you live in the District of Columbia, California, Massachusetts, New Jersey, Rhode Island, or Vermont. Even if you don't need to prove coverage to anyone, keeping this form on hand in case you need it in the future is wise.

Doing an About-Face When You Lose TRICARE Eligibility

Sometimes people lose TRICARE eligibility. This can happen to a dependent child who reaches the maximum age limit, or when a former spouse, surviving spouse, or widow remarries. It can also happen when the sponsor doesn't properly update beneficiary information in DEERS.

Dependents who age out of benefits may be eligible for the TRICARE Young Adult program, and sponsors can update DEERS to regain coverage — but former spouses, surviving spouses, and widows can never regain coverage if they remarry unless they're eligible for coverage through their new spouse.

TIP

If you or your dependents lose coverage because you didn't update the information in DEERS, don't panic. All you need to do is go to a local ID card office and update your information to restore your coverage. You should be able to find an ID card office on the nearest military installation, which you can access with your retiree ID card.

Seeing 20/20/20: TRICARE after Divorce

After you divorce, your former spouse may be eligible to keep TRICARE coverage in only two ways, which I discuss here.

The 20-20-20 rule

Under the 20-20-20 rule, a former spouse may keep their coverage if all of the following are true:

>> The sponsor has at least 20 years of creditable service toward determining retirement pay.

>> You were married to each other for at least 20 years.

>> All 20 years of marriage overlap the 20 years of creditable service that counted toward the sponsor's retirement.

If the sponsor's original personnel component determines that a former spouse meets these eligibility criteria, they'll receive a new identification card the first time they renew their card after the divorce. The new identification card will include their own name and Social Security number where the sponsor's information ordinarily appears.

The former spouse will automatically lose their coverage if they remarry.

The 20-20-15 rule

Under the 20-20-15 rule, a former spouse qualifies if all are true:

>> The sponsor has at least 20 years of creditable service toward determining retirement pay.

>> You were married to each other for at least 20 years.

>> Fifteen of the years you were married overlap the 20 years of creditable service that counted toward the sponsor's retirement.

Like the 20-20-20 rule, the former spouse will receive a new identification card with their information in the sponsor's spot. They'll remain eligible for coverage according to the divorce's effective date. Have a peek:

>> If you divorced before April 1, 1985, the former spouse's eligibility continues as long as they meet eligibility requirements.

>> If your marriage ended between April 1, 1985 and September 28, 1988, the former spouse isn't currently eligible for care.

>> If you divorced on or after September 29, 1988, the former spouse is eligible for TRICARE for only one year from the date of the divorce.

Regardless of which rule applies to a former spouse, TRICARE eligibility disappears if they remarry, purchase and are covered by an employer-sponsored health plan, or were the former spouse of a North Atlantic Treaty Organization (NATO) or Partners for Peace nation member.

IN THIS CHAPTER

» Finding out whether you're eligible for life insurance

» Zeroing in on the right policy

» Getting benefits for disabled or terminally ill policyholders

» Using free financial planning services

» Making a claim

Chapter **7**

Securing Your Family's Future with VA Life Insurance

When you were in the military, you had the option to purchase Servicemembers Group Life Insurance (SLGI). That insurance provided your family with up to $400,000 in coverage in the event of your death. But when you leave military service, you lose your SGLI benefit, which means if something happens to you, your family is on the hook for funeral expenses and other costs associated with your loss (including lost income).

The average funeral costs between $7,000 and $12,000, and unless you're eligible for VA burial benefits (see Chapter 22), your family will also have to pay for a lot of associated costs. Many people choose to buy life insurance — not only to cover funeral expenses, but also to provide their families with a safety net when they're not alive to contribute income. (If you're receiving a military pension, those payments stop altogether when you die. Your spouse or dependents don't receive them.)

TIP

The good news is you may be eligible for life insurance through the VA. You can apply online through the VA's website at www.va.gov/life-insurance, or you can apply by mail or fax. Some people choose to work with a veteran service organization (VSO) to apply for life insurance and other benefits.

Several types of VA life insurance are available. Each program has its own eligibility requirements, so you may be eligible for some and not others. Different programs carry differing costs, which are generally based on your age and the amount of coverage you want. I examine them here so you can decide whether to purchase and which plan may be right for you.

Deciding Which Policy Is Right for You

The Department of Veterans Affairs offers four main types of veterans life insurance, each for different circumstances. Every VA life insurance plan has its own eligibility requirements, but generally, you must be considered a veteran to be eligible. In some cases, you must have a disability rating from the VA (even 0 percent counts), you must be in good health, or you must receive certain benefits from the VA to qualify. I cover the four main types in more detail, including eligibility, in the following sections. Refer to the nearby sidebar for more on the rare fifth type.

Here are a couple important definitions you need to know:

>> **Term life insurance:** This insurance covers you for a specific period of time (that's where the *term* comes in). For example, if you purchase a 20-year policy, you're covered for that term. If you die during those 20 years, your beneficiaries are covered. However, if you die outside those 20 years, your beneficiaries don't receive any money. You'd need to purchase a new term life insurance policy to ensure they were covered for the next specific period of time. Term life insurance only pays out if you die; it has no cash value while you're alive.

>> **Whole life insurance:** This insurance builds cash value while you're still alive. It pays out when you die, but the policy owner can borrow from the cash value before death. These policies generally earn a fixed rate of interest, but if you borrow against one, your outstanding loan principal and interest reduce the amount of money your beneficiaries receive when you die.

Veterans Group Life Insurance

Veterans Group Life Insurance (VGLI) enables you to keep your life insurance coverage after you leave military service. You can keep your coverage for as long as you keep paying your premiums. This is a term life insurance program.

Eligibility for VGLI

You may be eligible if at least *one* of the following is true about you:

>> You were in the National Guard or Reserves and had part-time SGLI, and you suffered an injury or disability while you were on duty (to include traveling to and from duty) that disqualified you for standard premium insurance rates.

>> You had SGLI when you were in the military, and you're now within 1 year and 120 days of being released from an active-duty period of 31 or more days.

>> You're within 1 year and 120 days of retiring or being released from the Ready Reserve or National Guard.

>> You're within 1 year and 120 days of assignment to the Individual Ready Reserve or to the Inactive National Guard.

>> You're within 1 year and 120 days of being put on the Temporary Disability Retirement List (TDRL).

If you're outside of these time windows, you don't qualify to purchase VGLI and you need to look at alternatives.

TIP

If you apply for VGLI within 240 days of leaving the military, you don't need to prove that you're in good health to get a life insurance policy. But if you sign up after 240 days have passed, you do need to prove that you're healthy.

Benefits with VGLI

VGLI offers you the opportunity to get between $10,000 and $400,000 in term life insurance benefits. The amount you receive depends on how much SGLI coverage you had at the time you left the military ($400,000 is standard coverage in the military unless you actively opt for less). It's possible to convert an active VGLI policy into a commercial whole life insurance policy, and you can do so without providing evidence of good health.

One other benefit that VGLI offers is the Accelerated Benefit Option (ABO), which many term life insurance policies don't have. With the ABO, terminally ill veterans are allowed to access a portion of the death benefit while they're still alive. To qualify for this benefit, a veteran must provide a valid written prognosis from their physician that states that the veteran has fewer than nine months to live. In that case, the veteran may apply to receive a lump-sum payment of up to 50 percent of the face value of the insurance. That means if you have a $400,000 policy, you may be able to get up to $200,000 to use however you want.

VGLI cost and claims

Your life insurance costs with VGLI depend on how old you are when you apply or renew your coverage, as well as how much coverage you want. Monthly premium rates are subject to change, so you can find the latest figures on the VA's life insurance website (www.va.gov/life-insurance). To make a claim, file Form SGLV 8283.

Veterans Affairs Life Insurance

The Veterans Affairs Life Insurance (VALife) policy is whole life insurance, and it offers guaranteed acceptance; you don't need a health exam or even to answer health-related questions.

Eligibility for VALife

You're eligible for VALife if you have any level of VA disability rating, even 0 percent, and you're under 80 when you apply (though some who are 81 or older may still qualify). You may sign up at any time after your grand exit from the military, regardless of your disability rating.

Benefits with VALife

You can get coverage in increments of $10,000 for a total of up to $40,000. You don't have to meet any medical requirements or answer health-related questions to qualify, and it offers cash value that builds over the life of the policy after you've been enrolled for two years.

VALife cost and claims

Your cost for VALife depends on your age at the time you sign up and the amount of coverage you want. The VA locks in your rate, so it never increases; if your rate is $50 a month when you sign up, it remains $50 a month as long as you're enrolled. To file a claim, use Form SGLV 8283. Like its cousins SGLI and VGLI, you may choose to receive a lump-sum payment or monthly installments.

Service-Disabled Veterans Life Insurance

Service-Disabled Veterans Life Insurance (S-DVI) is available to veterans who have service-connected disabilities. If you don't have service-connected disabilities, you can't get this type of life insurance.

Eligibility for S-DVI

You may be eligible for S-DVI if *all* the following apply to you:

>> You were released from active duty on or after April 25, 1951, and received any type of discharge other than dishonorable.

>> You have a VA disability rating; even 0 percent ratings count toward this requirement.

>> You're in good health outside of any service-connected conditions that you have.

>> You apply within two years of receiving a disability rating.

Benefits with S-DVI

With this form of insurance, you may be eligible for up to $10,000 of coverage and up to $30,000 of supplemental coverage. Supplemental coverage can be used for things like burial costs and other expenses related to your death. In the case of S-DVI, you're eligible for this coverage if you become totally disabled and unable to work while you have standard S-DVI coverage. You may also qualify for this supplemental coverage if you qualify for a premiums waiver, which I explain in the section, "Premiums waivers and S-DVI," later in this chapter.

S-DVI cost

The amount of money you need to pay to get S-DVI coverage depends on how old you are, how much insurance you want, and the coverage plan you request. You may purchase this insurance in amounts from $1,000 to $10,000 using multiples of $500, and you pay in monthly installments. To check the most current rates, call the VA or visit its life insurance website at www.va.gov/life-insurance.

Premiums waivers and S-DVI

In some cases, waivers are available for veterans who are totally disabled. However, the waivers are only good for the basic S-DVI coverage; you must pay premiums if you want supplemental S-DVI. You may be eligible for a waiver if you have a mental or physical disability that prevents you from being able to work, you already have S-DVI, you become totally disabled before you reach the age of 65 (but after you begin your life insurance policy), and you're totally disabled for at least six consecutive months.

Veterans Mortgage Life Insurance

Veterans Mortgage Life Insurance (VMLI) is a form of mortgage protection for the families of veterans who suffer from severe service-connected disabilities and who have adapted a home to fit their needs.

Eligibility for VMLI

You may be eligible for VMLI if *all* of the following statements are true:

>> You have a severe disability that the VA has determined was caused or worsened by your military service.

>> You received a Specially Adapted Housing Grant for your home (see Chapter 20 for more info).

>> You have the title of the home and have a mortgage on the home.

>> You're younger than the age of 70.

Benefits with VMLI

VMLI provides you with up to $200,000 in mortgage life insurance. If you die, the VMLI program will pay your entire coverage amount to the lender that holds your mortgage. No money goes to your beneficiaries with this type of insurance, and the amount of money the program pays out will equal the amount you still owe on your mortgage. If you pay off your mortgage, your VMLI coverage ends; it goes down as your mortgage balance decreases. These policies have no loan or cash value.

VMLI cost

Like most other types of life insurance, your premiums are based on your age and how much coverage you want. They're also based on the current balance of your mortgage loan and how many more payments you have before your home is paid off.

SERVICEMEMBERS' GROUP LIFE INSURANCE TRAUMATIC INJURY PROTECTION

Very few people are eligible for this type of life insurance, but it's worth mentioning. This insurance is for people who were insured by SGLI when they experienced a traumatic injury and meet very specific requirements. The reason I bring it up here is that you may be eligible for retroactive TSGLI payments if you were injured between October 7, 2001, and November 30, 2005. It doesn't matter whether you were on- or off-duty when your injury occurred. If you qualify for this program, you may get between $25,000 and $100,000 in short-term financial support that helps offset the costs of your recovery.

Accessing Free Financial Planning

The VA offers free financial counseling services for beneficiaries of TSGLI and VGLI policies. (It's also available to SGLI and Family SGLI beneficiaries.) These services are available at no cost, and they come from professional financial counselors associated with the VA. Some of the most notable services include the following:

>> Budgeting help

>> College tuition planning

>> Debt-reduction help

>> Education in investment strategies

>> Estate planning

>> Long-term care planning

>> Pre- and post-retirement financial planning

>> Savings plan development

These services are only available for two years from the date the claim is paid. Another benefit is the online will-preparation service that comes with every policy. Beneficiaries may quickly and easily prepare a will without needing an attorney; they simply answer a series of questions and automated software creates a legal will that's valid in all states.

Making a Veterans Life Insurance Claim

Each type of VA life insurance requires a different claims form, and they're all available on the VA's website at www.benefits.va.gov/insurance/sglivgli. asp. Different types of beneficiaries must file different documents with a VA life insurance claim, but the most necessary document is a photocopy of the veteran's death certificate.

EXAMPLE

A principal beneficiary only needs the appropriate form and the veteran's death certificate, whereas a contingent beneficiary also needs photocopies of the death certificates of all principal beneficiaries showing dates and causes of death.

You may file a claim online or by mail. Your claim will be processed faster if you file online.

TIP

You're allowed to request monthly payments instead of one lump-sum payment. However, if you do so, you need to provide the VA with additional documentation. You can find out what you need to submit by calling 800-669-8477.

» Crunching the numbers on your monthly pay

» Applying for a VA pension

» Cashing in on severance pay

» Holding on to your TSP money

Chapter **8**

Cashing In on Military Pensions, Severance Pay, and the TSP

Spending 20 or more years in the military is no small feat. From long hours with no overtime pay and frequent permanent change of station moves to back-to-back deployments and whatever the military did to your knees, every retiree has an origin story that spans a sizeable portion of the globe. Fortunately, surviving a couple of decades giving Uncle Sam your blood, sweat, and tears earns you the ultimate reward: monthly retirement checks for the rest of your life. You also get other perks, such as unlimited access to the nearest commissary and all the Space-A travel you can handle — and if you're a medical retiree, you're entitled to many of the same benefits (and possibly some others, which I cover in Chapter 9). Only about 17 percent of servicemembers make it to military retirement, so you're in good, but limited, company.

As with most of the benefits the government offers, there are a couple of minor catches: After you retire, you're still governed by the Uniform Code of Military Justice, and the military can call you back out of retirement for just about any reason. For most people, neither of these things matter (and neither is likely to have any impact on your post-military life).

Some servicemembers who are forced out of their jobs without retiring are entitled to severance pay, but that can be a bit complicated to figure out. Don't worry, though — the Defense Finance and Accounting Service (DFAS) counts every penny. And if you had a little forethought when you joined the military (or at any point during your service), you stashed away some cash in the Thrift Savings Plan. I cover all these things, plus a few more, in this action-packed chapter.

Differentiating between Retirement and Retainer Pay

The military's retirement plans are a bit different from those you encounter in the civilian world (though if you have a few good working years left in you, it's not a bad idea to start exploring other career paths that offer their own retirement benefits so you can collect *two* retirement checks each month). Depending on the branch you served in, as well as how long you stuck it out, the Department of Defense may consider you a retiree or a retained member. It's more confusing on paper than it is in real life, though; either way, you get the same pay to stop showing up at work.

Here's what you need to know about these terms:

>> **Retired member:** If you completed your career in the Army, Air Force, Coast Guard, or Space Force, you can officially retire with 20 years of service under your belt. The government considers you a *retired member* of the armed forces.

>> **Retained member:** If you wrapped things up in the Navy or Marine Corps, you're a *retained member* after 20 years of service and a retired member after 30 years.

That's where things get sketchy (but again, only on paper — and I'm only telling you so you understand what's going on if you have to call DFAS support).

In the Navy and Marine Corps, you're retired if you were enlisted with more than 30 years of service, or if you were a warrant officer or commissioned officer with more than 20 years of service. If you have between 20 and 30 years of service on your record, the government sticks you in the Fleet Reserve or Fleet Marine Corps Reserve. The government can recall you to active-duty service at any time during this stint, which ends when 30 years have passed since you signed your first enlistment contract (unless you had a break in service).

REMEMBER

If you're in one of these two components, you still receive your monthly pension payments; it's just called *retainer pay* rather than *retirement pay*. After you hit 30 years (your active-duty time plus your time in the Fleet Reserve or Fleet Marine Corps Reserve), the government starts calling your monthly stipend "retired pay." Either way, it's the same amount, and it all spends the same.

Reeling you back in through reactivation

Uncle Sam couldn't quit you. In fact, retirees are on the military's short list of people to call in an emergency. That means the government can order you to get back to work, even after you're retired. Though it's really unlikely that'll ever happen, a *recall* means that you haul out your dusty combat boots and start shopping for new, and maybe bigger, uniforms. (You didn't think that the government let you keep your unfettered access to Military Clothing and Sales for nothing, did you?)

Department of Defense Instruction 1352.01 governs the reactivation of regular and Reserve retired members. It says, and I quote, "Regular retired members and members of the retired Reserve may be ordered to active duty as needed to perform such duties as the Secretary concerned considers necessary in the interests of national defense as described in Sections 688 and 12301 of Title 10, U.S.C." Don't stress just yet though; the instruction also says that retirees may be used as a "source of last resort after other sources are determined not to be available or a source for unique skills not otherwise obtainable." That means plenty of people are in line in front of you, including the Individual Ready Reserve (IRR), which is where the military places people who served fewer than eight years before ending their contracts.

REMEMBER

Even if you *do* make it to the front of the recall line, you fall into one of three categories:

>> **Category I** is for vets who didn't retire due to disability, are younger than 60, and who have been retired for fewer than five years.

>> **Category II** is for vets who didn't retire due to disability, are younger than 60, and who have been retired for more than five years.

>> **Category III** is for those retired for disability or who are older than 60.

The DOD instruction specifies that Category I and II retirees who are physically qualified may be identified for work similar to what active-duty servicemembers do, but that Category III retirees should generally be placed in civilian defense jobs unless they have critical skills or volunteer for a particular job.

Being subject to the UCMJ

The Uniform Code of Military Justice (UCMJ) is in most veterans' rearview mirror — after they receive a DD-214, they never have to think about the UCMJ again. But because you're reading this chapter, it probably still applies to you. The government wants to keep you in line if you're still on its payroll, so it reserves the right to haul you back on active duty and try you through a court-martial. A court-martial, even after you're retired, can result in a change to your discharge status and affect your military benefits (including your future pension payments). Though it's rare for the military to bring in a retiree for trial, it happens.

TECHNICAL STUFF

If you retire from a Reserve component and aren't entitled to your pension until you're older, the UCMJ most likely doesn't apply to you.

Investigating the IRR

If you leave the military without completing your entire military service obligation (MSO), you're automatically placed in the Individual Ready Reserve (IRR). You remain in the IRR until your initial service obligation is complete (usually five to eight years, though there are some exceptions), and you may volunteer to stay in it, too. As an IRR member, you may accrue retirement points. However, you don't get access to military healthcare or other active-duty or reserve component benefits (or pay).

REMEMBER

Retirees may elect to remain in the IRR; if you do, you'll be among the first called up to serve when the military needs you. More than 800,000 people are in the IRR right now, and somewhere in the neighborhood of 2,000 get called up each year (though during Operation Enduring Freedom and Operation Iraqi Freedom, the numbers were much higher).

Focusing on Military Retirement Plans

The U.S. government has offered a wide variety of retirement plans since 1776, when the Continental Congress resolved to provide payments of a half-month's salary to officers, noncommissioned officers, and private soldiers who lost limbs or were otherwise disabled to the point where they couldn't earn a living. I'm happy to report that pensions have come a long way since then when infantry captains earned $26 per month and privates earned $6. Thanks to the evolution of government pension plans for retirees, three main types are in effect today, depending on when you joined the military: High-3 or High-36, the Blended Retirement System (BRS), and CSB/REDUX.

High-3

The High-3 (or High-36) retirement system determines your retirement benefit based on the number of years you served times the average of the highest 36 months (three years) of pay you received. That's usually the last three years of your service.

The percentage multiplier is 2.5, which means for every year you remained in the military, you earn an additional 2.5 percent of your base pay. The math works out so that if you serve 20 years, you receive half your highest-averaged base pay as a monthly retirement check (because $2.5 \times 20 = 50$). If you serve 40 years, you receive 100 percent of your highest-averaged base pay.

REMEMBER

Years of service are calculated differently for servicemembers in a reserve component. Your retirement points are divided by 360 to calculate the number of "active-duty years" they count for (they're like dog years, but harder on your back). The 2.5 percent multiplier applies to the number of years you served in active-duty time. You also aren't eligible for reserve retirement pay until you reach the age of 60 unless you were called into active service after January 28, 2008; that reduces your age 60 requirement by 3 months for every cumulative period of 90 days active service you performed in the years after that. The government won't automatically pay you when you reach the right age, either — you must request retirement payments to get the ball rolling.

Blended Retirement System

The Blended Retirement System (BRS) went into effect on January 1, 2018, and it's the only option for people who joined on or after that date. It's a blend of the High-3 system and the Thrift Savings Plan (TSP), which I cover in the later section, "Managing Your Thrift Savings Plan." It's also the most complicated system the government offers.

Under the BRS, the government multiplies your highest 36 months of basic pay by 2 percent (rather than the 2.5 percent allowed in the High-3 program). It also contributes to your TSP account to the tune of 1 percent of your basic pay each month. (That money doesn't come out of your pay; it's a gift from your friendly neighborhood government.)

When you joined the military, you also agreed to contribute 3 percent of your own basic pay to your TSP account (though you can change or stop those contributions at any time). After two years of service, the government matches your contributions to the TSP up to 5 percent; if you put in 5 percent and the government matches it, that means 10 percent of what you earn in basic pay goes into your TSP. You can contribute more, but the government's matching cap is 5 percent.

But wait! There's more! The BRS also includes *continuation pay*. After you serve between 8 and 12 years, you get the chance to commit to another 36 months of service in exchange for immediate cash. The amount of continuation pay you receive depends on your branch of service, and it's always subject to change (just like retention bonuses do), but by law, it's supposed to be between 2.5 times and 13 times your monthly base pay. (In the reserve components, it's between 0.5 and 6 times your monthly base pay.) Continuation pay is taxable, and if you don't complete your obligated service, you may have to pay it back.

Upon retirement (or at the age of 60 if you're in a reserve component), you get the choice: You may receive standard monthly retirement pay checks or take a lump-sum payment of 25 or 50 percent of your gross estimated retired pay (after the deduction of a "discount," which changes every year) and receive smaller payments each month. If you elect to take 25 percent of your gross estimated retired pay, your checks will be 25 percent less than they would have if you didn't grab the cash; likewise, if you take 50 percent, you lose 50 percent. That fat stack of cash is taxable, too, so keep that in mind.

CSB/REDUX

Servicemembers who joined the military after July 31, 1986, but before January 1, 2006, were given a choice between two retirement plans upon reaching 15 years of service: The Career Status Bonus (called CSB/REDUX) or the High-3 Year Average. If you chose the CSB/REDUX plan, you may have received a $30,000 bonus at that time in exchange for a lower rate of retired pay. If you were a nondisabled retiree, you saw a 1 percent reduction for each full year of creditable service (less than 30 years) and one-twelfth of 1 percent for each full month of creditable service less than a full year, as well as a 1 percent reduction in cost-of-living adjustments (COLA).

The reduction stays in effect until you reach the age of 62; at that time, your retired pay is restored to the same amount paid under the High-3 system.

Figuring Out How Much You Get

Planning for retirement is a lot easier when you know how much money you'll have on hand when the time comes. Fortunately, the DFAS's website has a handy calculator that you can use to calculate your monthly retirement payments based on the retirement plan you fall into — or you can use the basic calculations in the following sections to get a ballpark idea.

Calculating active-duty retirement

If you're on the High-3 retirement system, you can get an idea of your monthly retirement payments through a simple math formula:

Basic pay × number of years of active-duty service × 0.025

Imagine that you're a servicemember with 20 years of service earning base pay of $4,000 per month. Here's how the formula applies:

$4,000 × 20 years = $80,000
$80,000 × 0.025 = $2,000

Remember, though, military service comes with annual pay raises. You need an average of your highest-paid 36 months to get an accurate look at how much the government will send you in each retirement check. DFAS keeps all previous pay tables on its website, so you can go back and look at the charts to see how much you made in the past. Then, you can do the math to determine your average base pay over those three years to your monthly retirement pay.

Adding up reserve retirement points and pay

If you served in the Army National Guard, Army Reserve, Navy Reserve, Marine Corps Reserve, Air National Guard, Air Force Reserve, or Coast Guard Reserve, your retirement pay is calculated differently than it is for active-duty troops. You earn one point for each day of active service, so technically, you could earn 365 or 366 points per year (during a leap year). If you weren't activated at all in a year, your points come from other sources:

>> **15 points** for each year of your membership in a reserve component

>> **1 point** for every unit training assembly

>> **1 point** for each day you're in a funeral honors duty status

>> **1 point** for every three credit hours you earn in accredited correspondence courses

Qualifying years

If you earn 50 or more retirement points in a year, it's considered a *good year*, which simply means you hit the minimum number of points to count toward your retirement. A typical drill weekend is worth a total of four retirement points, so you get 48 points just for showing up; you should get around 15 points for Annual

Training (AT), which puts you over the top with 63 points. You also get 15 points for membership in your branch, so that puts you over the top with 78 points. As long as you don't miss any drills or training, you should be more than good to go (though you should keep tabs on your retirement points at least every year, just to make sure that your readiness team is properly recording your attendance and points).

The 60/75/90-point rule

Caps on the number of inactive points limit what you can accrue in a year, and those limits have been in existence for the past few decades. In any reserve year ending after October 30, 2007, you can earn a maximum of 130 points. However:

>> You may only count 90 points for reserve years ending between October 29, 2000 and October 30, 2007.

>> You may only count 75 points for reserve years ending between September 23, 1996 and October 29, 2000.

>> You may only count 60 points for reserve years ending before September 23, 1996.

Converting points to years

Generally, members of reserve components need a minimum of 20 good (qualifying) years to retire and earn retirement pay. If you served on active duty before switching to a reserve component, you already have good years on your record; the number you have depends on how long you were on active duty. You can mix and match your service to qualify for retirement — it all counts.

Here's how you convert points to years:

1. **Divide the number of retirement points you have by 360.**

   That gives you the number of comparable years you served as an active-duty servicemember, which is what the government uses to calculate your retirement pay. For example, if you serve 30 years and earn 78 retirement points each year, you have a total of 2,340 retirement points:

   $$2,340 \div 360 = 6.5 \text{ active-duty years}$$

2. **Multiply your basic pay by the number of years of equivalent active-duty service.**

3. **Multiply that by 2.5 percent (which is 0.025 in mathematical terms).**

If your basic pay is $750, your equation looks like this:

$$\$750 \times 6.5 \times 0.025 = \$121.88$$

I round up; there's an extra half-penny in there.

This calculation tells you that you'll receive $121.88 each month in retirement pay. Naturally, your points will vary, especially if you have active-duty time (which counts for 365 or 366 points per year) or activations. Note that real retired pay is rounded down to the nearest dollar.

Note: If you joined after September 8, 1980, but before December 31, 2017, you're on the High-3 retirement system. If you joined after December 31, 2017, you're on the BRS. If you're on the BRS, you multiply your service by 2 percent after calculating your years. See the earlier section, "Blended Retirement System," for more information on how that works.

Cashing in

You can't begin collecting payments until you reach the age of 60 (except in special circumstances such as being called to active service). You must apply for your retirement pay through your branch before the government will begin paying it out.

Eyeing What Else You Need to Know

Collecting retirement pay is simple; the cash shows up in your bank account. But the actual amount you receive can fluctuate based on taxes and cost-of-living adjustments the federal government passes down in its annual budget. In the following sections, I cover those issues, plus how many times you have to refresh your online account screen to check for your first payment.

Taxes, Social Security, and retirement

Your military retirement pay is taxable. In addition to federal income tax, you may have to pay state income taxes on it, depending on your state's rules. You don't have to pay federal Social Security taxes on it, though. Like any other type of income, you may declare how many tax exemptions you want to claim.

Your military retirement pay won't affect your Social Security benefits. You're entitled to your full Social Security benefit based on your earnings.

Annual pay raises through COLA

Your retirement base pay won't go up, but you get an annual cost-of-living adjustment (COLA) in December of each year. That adjustment equals the inflation rate of the previous year, based on the Consumer Price Index (CPI). However, if you accepted a career status bonus (under the CSB/REDUX retirement plan), your COLA is capped at one percentage point beneath the rate of inflation.

Waiting on your first retirement check

Your first retired pay generally takes DFAS between 30 and 45 days to process. However, that depends on you correctly submitting documentation. And though you're used to being paid on the first and 15th of every month in the military, retired pay only comes in once a month — on the first. Like military pay, though, if the first falls on a weekend or holiday, you get it on the last business day of the prior month.

THIS AIN'T YOUR GRANDPA'S RETIREMENT

The earliest military pensions were only based on disability or death, but today, you can earn a retirement check by showing up at the right place, at the right time, in the right uniform, for 20 years. Over the years, a number of pension plans and government pay-outs overlapped, both in time and funding. For example, between 1788 and 1855, the War Department gave some veterans and their heirs *bounty land warrants*, which were certificates that gave their bearers rights to free public land, in addition to the benefits they received from other government agencies. Dozens of laws have since passed to govern how much money retirees and disabled veterans receive in compensation from the government.

But retirement pay is expensive; the government paid out around $60.5 billion to retirees and survivors during 2019 alone. Sometimes, Congress decides it wants to tighten the purse strings and make budget cuts, and military pensions are an easy target. However, the military maintains that a good retirement plan is essential to its retention efforts — more people stay in when they know there's a bigger reward at the end. That's why you see so many different retirement plans in this book, and why there's always potential for a new retirement plan on the horizon. It's also part of the reason that the military switched to the Blended Retirement System (BRS) for those who joined on or after January 1, 2018; the government only pays 2 percent rather than 2.5 percent of your basic pay, and servicemembers contribute to their own Thrift Savings Plans (TSP — with matching government contributions, to a point).

Spreading the Wealth

Military retired pay stops when the retiree dies; the surviving spouse and other dependents won't receive it. (And for the record, disability compensation stops, too. However, other survivor benefits may be available to those you leave behind, which I cover in Chapter 23.)

Furthermore, you may not be the only person entitled to your military retired pay. Though your pension pay is exempt from garnishment for commercial debts, it's *not* exempt from garnishment for child support or spousal support, and you may have to share your pension with your former spouse if you divorce. I discuss these factors in the following sections.

Setting up payments for your spouse

The Survivor Benefit Plan (SBP) is a form of insurance that pays out upon your death so that your survivors continue receive monthly payments. Unless you opt in to the SBP, your dependents won't see any of your retired pay after you pass. Through the SBP, you pay monthly premiums from your gross retired pay; in turn, the government will pay your spouse or dependents up to 55 percent of your retired pay. (If you retired under the CSB/REDUX plan, that amount is calculated based on what you would have received if you were under the High-3 program.) Eligible children can be SBP beneficiaries, too, and so can *insurable interests,* such as business partners or parents. You may also contribute your SBP payments to a special needs trust, which allows a disabled dependent to receive monthly payments after your death without compromising their ability to receive federal disability payments.

Payments from the SBP continue until the beneficiary dies, and they increase with COLA each year. But because the SBP coverage amount increases with COLA, your premiums do, too. If your beneficiary dies before you do, you can't get a refund for what you've paid into the program.

REMEMBER

There's one big catch, though (in addition to the payments you make from your retirement checks): You *must* choose SBP at the time you retire. If you don't, you aren't eligible to pick it up later to cover the same spouse (or even a different spouse). And if you choose less than full coverage or choose not to enroll in SBP, your spouse must provide consent in writing. If you aren't married at the time you retire, you're allowed to get SBP coverage later, as long as you elect coverage before your first anniversary with your first new spouse.

Divvying up retirement pay after divorce

If you divorce, your spouse may be entitled to some of your pension under the Uniformed Services Former Spouse Protection Act. Under that law, state courts may (and do) treat retired pay as community property. Your former spouse won't qualify for *any* of your pension unless it's awarded to them in your divorce decree; even then, the most a court may award them is 50 percent. That means if your divorce decree says that your former spouse gets half your pension and you receive $800 per month, they receive $400.

TECHNICAL STUFF

You may have heard the popular and persistent myth that you have to be married for ten years before your spouse is entitled to some of your pension, but that's all it is: a myth. However, ten years is important. If you were married to your spouse for at least ten years with ten years of your marriage overlapping your service (as long as that service is creditable toward your retirement pay), the DOD will be authorized to pay your former spouse directly. Otherwise, you have to make the payments on your own.

Payments from your TSP are also divisible in divorce, but only if your former spouse requests them. The same is true with the SBP; it must be addressed in your divorce settlement.

Looking At VA Pensions for Low-Income Veterans and Survivors

Disabled veterans who didn't retire from the military and those who are older than 65 with low income may be eligible for a VA pension. These sections discuss the three main types of VA pension benefits: the VA Pension, Housebound Allowance, and Aid and Attendance Allowance.

REMEMBER

The VA asks for documentation when you apply for any of these benefits. In the case of a VA Pension, you have to supply information on your current income and net worth. If you're applying for the Housebound Allowance or Aid and Attendance, you must provide medical documentation that substantiates your claim.

VA Pensions

The VA Pension is for any veteran who received a discharge other than dishonorable and meets certain income and net worth limits, provided at least one of the following is true:

>> You entered active duty before September 8, 1980, and served at least 90 days on active duty with at least one day during wartime.

>> You started on active duty as an enlisted person after September 7, 1980, and served at least 24 months or the full period for which you were called or ordered to active duty, with at least one day during wartime.

>> You were an officer and started on active duty after October 16, 1981, and hadn't previously served on active duty for at least 24 months.

REMEMBER

Additionally, you must be at least 65 years old or have a permanent and total disability (regardless of your age or whether your disability is service-connected). If you're a patient in a nursing home for long-term care due to a disability, or if you receive Social Security Disability Insurance (SSDI) or Supplemental Security Income (SSI), you may also qualify for a VA service pension.

Eligible wartime periods include the following:

>> World War II

>> The Korean War (June 27, 1950 to January 31, 1955)

>> The Vietnam War era (November 1, 1955 to May 7, 1975 for veterans who served in the Republic of Vietnam, and August 5, 1964 to May 7, 1975 for veterans who served outside the Republic of Vietnam)

>> The Gulf War (August 2, 1990 through today, though a future law or presidential proclamation may set an end date)

Congress sets the income limits for this pension, which are subject to change. However, you need to know that your annual income is the total amount of money you earn in a year from a job or from retirement or annuity payments. That includes your salary or hourly pay, bonuses, commissions you earn, overtime pay, and tips. When the VA is calculating your net worth, it subtracts educational expenses and medical expenses you're not reimbursed for.

Your net worth must also fall below a certain limit, and it includes all the personal property you own except your house, car, and furniture (but minus any debts you owe). Things like investments, boats and recreational vehicles, and money you have stashed in a savings account are all assets that count toward your limit. Your net worth also includes your spouse's net worth for the purposes of receiving this pension benefit.

EXAMPLE

If the net worth limit is $140,000, you have $100,000 in assets and $39,000 in annual income, you're eligible for veterans pension benefits. That's because your net worth is $139,000, which falls under the limit.

VA Housebound Allowance

If you're a veteran who receives a VA pension, you may be eligible for the VA Housebound Allowance. These funds are reserved for people who spend most of their time in their home because of a permanent disability.

VA Aid and Attendance

You may be eligible for VA Aid and Attendance if you receive a VA pension and meet one or more of the following criteria:

>> You need someone to help you perform daily activities, such as bathing, eating, and getting dressed.

>> You have to stay in bed (or at least spend a lot of time in bed) because of illness.

>> You're a nursing home patient because of the loss of physical or mental abilities related to a disability.

>> Your eyesight is limited, even when corrected (you must see 5/200 or less in both eyes, or have concentric contraction of the visual field to 5 degrees or less).

WARNING

You can't get VA Housebound Allowance and Aid and Attendance at the same time. You may only receive one of these two benefits in addition to your VA Pension.

Estimating your payment

The VA bases your payment amount for the VA Pension, Housebound Allowance, and Aid and Attendance on the difference between your countable income and the maximum amount you can receive set by Congress, which is called the Maximum Annual Pension Rate (MAPR).

REMEMBER

Here's a closer look at these two factors:

>> **Countable income:** Your *countable income* is the amount of money that the VA is legally allowed to count as income. Basically it's how much you bring in, including Social Security benefits, retirement payments, investment payments, and income that your dependents receive while living with you. However, some expenses (like medical care that your insurance provider won't pay for) may reduce your countable income.

>> **Maximum Annual Pension Rate (MAPR):** The MAPR is based on the number of dependents you have, whether you're married to another veteran who qualifies for a pension, and whether you qualify for Housebound Allowance or Aid and Attendance benefits. MAPR amounts change every year with COLA, but the VA keeps them updated on its website.

EXAMPLE

Joe Snuffy is a qualified veteran with a nonveteran spouse. He has a countable income of $10,000 per year. His MAPR is $29,000 per year, so the government will deduct the $10,000 of Joe's countable income from that number. His annual benefit from a VA pension is $19,000. He receives $1,583.33 per month (because $19,000 \div 12 = \$1,583.33$).

Supplementing Your Retirement Check with Other Government Income

You may be eligible for other types of benefits based on your military service and contributions you've made during your career, such as unemployment compensation immediately after your retirement and Social Security benefits when you meet certain criteria. Here I delve deeper into the additional benefits you need to know about.

Filing for unemployment after leaving the military

Though most retirees don't qualify for unemployment compensation because they receive income through pension payments, some do. Every state and U.S. territory has a program called Unemployment Compensation for Ex-Military (UCX). Because eligibility for unemployment benefits varies between states, contact your local unemployment office to find out whether you qualify. Regardless of your state's requirements, you only qualify for UCX if you were on active duty, separated under honorable conditions, and in most cases, are actively seeking employment.

You can only file for UCX through your state unemployment office. If you don't qualify for UCX, you may still qualify for regular unemployment compensation. Check with your state's unemployment office to find out whether you're eligible and how to apply.

Collecting Social Security with your military retirement benefits

First things first: Your military pension has no bearing on your ability to collect your full Social Security benefits. But in order to qualify for Social Security benefits, you must earn *credits*. The government gives you these credits for working and paying Social Security taxes. You need a certain number of credits in order to collect your benefits, and you can typically only shore up four credits per year. Nobody in the United States needs more than ten years of work (usually 40 credits) to qualify for Social Security benefits when the time comes to cash in.

Usually, the more money you earned while working, the higher your Social Security benefits are. That's because you paid more in Social Security taxes based on your income. You put more into the pool, so you're entitled to take more out. You can use your Social Security benefits for anything you want; it's a direct deposit into your bank account, just like your pension payments are. The Social Security Administration may even continues paying these benefits to your dependents when you die. (It also offers payments to people who develop disabilities, which I cover in Chapter 20, and if you're a wounded warrior, you likely qualify for expedited processing.)

You're allowed to request your benefits as early as age 62, but if you do so before reaching full retirement age (which is 67), your benefits will be permanently reduced. As long as you don't apply for Social Security benefits before your 67th birthday, you receive your full entitlement.

Saying Hello to Severance Pay

The DOD sometimes offers severance pay to people who are involuntarily separated from the military. You only qualify for severance pay if your separation is classified as honorable or general (under honorable conditions) and you completed at least 6 (but fewer than 20) years of service, and if you don't qualify for retirement. You could be entitled to this involuntary separation pay, or ISP, if

» You're fully qualified to stay in the military but are denied reenlistment because of established promotion or high year of tenure policies (and that goes for officers who decline continuation, as well) or because of a reduction in force.

» You're a warrant or commissioned officer being separated in accordance with Chapter 36 of Title 10, U.S.C. or Section 580, Section 1165, or Section 6383 of Title 10, U.S.C.

To calculate the full ISP amount, multiply your number of years of active service by 12 times the monthly basic pay you received at the time of your discharge or release from active service.

EXAMPLE

Consider this example: If you're an E-5 with 7 years of service, your monthly pay is about $3,200. If you qualify for full ISP, your math looks like this:

$$\$3,200 \times 12 = \$38,400$$
$$\$38,400 \times 7 = \$268,800$$
$$\$268,800 \times 0.1 = \$26,880$$

The military would fork over $26,880 in separation pay if you were in this situation. (Check the most recent pay chart on DFAS's website if you're not sure exactly how much you make every month. DFAS updates its pay tables every year.)

Not everyone qualifies for full ISP. If your involuntary separation is honorable or general (under honorable conditions), you meet the time-in-service requirement, and you're being separated instead of board action for one of the following reasons (or for similar reasons), you may qualify for half ISP:

>> Weight control failure

>> Lack of a parenting plan

>> A disability that existed before you joined the military

>> Failure of alcohol or drug abuse rehabilitation

>> Failure to meet minimum retention standards

>> Ineligibility for security clearance

You only qualify for any form of ISP if you agree to spend up to three years in the IRR following your separation. You must also sign a declaration that acknowledges that if you later become eligible for retired or retainer pay or for disability compensation, the full amount of ISP you received will be deducted from that pay. You absolutely *won't* qualify if you do the following:

>> You separate at your own request (including declining training, requesting a separation, or declining a regular appointment).

>> You haven't completed your initial active service obligation.

>> You're eligible for retired or retainer pay.

>> You're separated as punishment through a court-martial.

>> You're enlisted and are separated for unsatisfactory performance or misconduct.

>> You're an officer and are separated for substandard performance, acts of misconduct, or moral or professional dereliction.

Managing Your Thrift Savings Plan

The TSP has been available to all servicemembers since 2001, so if you served since that time, the option to stash away some of your paychecks has been there regardless of the retirement plan you fall into. Designed to supplement your retirement pay, your TSP may have a few thousand dollars or several hundred thousand; it depends on how much you set aside, how much the government matched, and how long you've been saving.

REMEMBER

When you retire from the military, you have to stop making employee contributions to your TSP account. However, you may be able to transfer money into the account from an IRA (but not a Roth IRA) and eligible employer plans. The money can shelter in place and keep earning for you until you withdraw it whether or not you contribute any more.

You may withdraw money from your TSP whenever you want — it's your money. However, if you take it all, it'll close your account and you can never reopen it again (unless you start a federal job that offers TSP as one of its benefits). There's no limit to the number of withdrawals you can make after you retire, but you can only withdraw once every 30 calendar days or until you run out of money.

You may also elect to receive distributions in a number of ways:

>> You can take regular income from your TSP account monthly, quarterly, or annually.

>> You can request a specific dollar amount or have TSP administrators apply a formula to compute a monthly payment for you based on your life expectancy (based on your age and your account balance) each year.

>> You can also choose a *life annuity*, which is a monthly benefit the TSP pays to you every month for the rest of your life.

>> You can even do a combination of individual withdrawals, regular withdrawals, and annuity payments.

Any way you slice it, the TSP has the potential to keep earning while your money is in it — and it can be a nice supplement to your retirement pay.

- » Making the connection between your service and your disability

- » Getting the VA to rate you

- » Puzzling together retired pay and disability pay

- » Familiarizing yourself with additional disability benefits

- » Figuring out who can take your money in special situations

Chapter **9**

Taking a Close Look at Disability Pay

When the VA decides you're disabled — and that your disability is directly connected to your military service in some way — you're entitled to disability pay. Sure, you've heard the stories about Joe Snuffy, who got some hot brass on his neck at the range and now has a 10 percent rating, or about Seaman Jones whose back injury netted her a 70 percent rating. You may have also heard that VA disability pay is a percentage of your active-duty pay (it's not), that you receive back pay from the date of your injury (nope), or that you won't qualify if you wait too long to apply (also not true).

Regardless of what you've heard, one cold, hard fact is that somewhere between 25 and 30 percent of veterans currently have a disability rating. Post-9/11 vets who deployed to a combat zone have more disability ratings than those from other service eras, clocking in at around 40 percent. Whether that's because the VA and DOD now recognize more conditions as disabling (such as tinnitus and breathing problems caused by burn pits in Iraq and Afghanistan) or because today's servicemembers have deployed more and been subjected to more hazards than those in the past, you may qualify, too.

Though you won't be able to afford a million-dollar mansion or a private island on your disability paychecks, these monthly payments can help you cover your bills and make up for what you can't earn in the civilian workforce. In some cases, disabled vets are eligible for other benefits, too, such as clothing allowances and money for adaptive equipment or adapted housing. This chapter helps you slog through the sometimes-muddied waters of disability pay, how it works, and how much you're entitled to receive.

Understanding Uncle Sam's Definition of Disability

Though you may have a different idea of what a disability is — whether or not you're living with one — the VA defines a person with a *disability* as one who has a physical or mental impairment that substantially limits one or more major life activities, has a record of the impairment, or is regarded as having such an impairment. A *disabled veteran* is someone who applied for and received a disability rating from the VA or DOD. You can be considered a disabled veteran whether you have a 10 percent disability rating or a 100 percent disability rating; I explain ratings in the section, "Breaking Down Your Rating," later in this chapter.

Discovering Your Disability Pay's Origin Story: VA versus DOD

Some people get disability pay from the VA, whereas others receive what's called disability retirement pay from the DOD. It spends the same, so the only important distinction lies in knowing what the jargon means in plain English:

>> *VA disability pay* is money you get from VA because you left the military and have an injury or medical condition that's connected to your military service.

>> *Disability retirement pay* is money you get from the DOD because you were medically retired from service. Your branch determined that you were no longer able to successfully perform your job, so it discharged you and kept you on (reduced) payroll.

In a nutshell, if you get out of the military without being medically retired (and if you have a disability), you can apply for VA disability pay. If you're medically retired from the military, you may be eligible for disability retirement pay from the DOD — but you can't apply for it; you only get this pay if a medical examination board (MEB) or physical examination board (PEB) determines that you're unfit for continued service. The MEB and PEB are the same thing, and both are commonly called *med boards*, but the difference in names comes from the branch of service you're in. I cover DOD disability retirement pay in the section, "Receiving DOD Disability Compensation," later in this chapter.

Connecting the Dots Between Service and Your Disability

The VA is only authorized to make disability payments for conditions that were caused or aggravated by military service. The key is that your disability *must be connected to your service in some way.*

EXAMPLE

If you tripped and fell while taking an Army PT test, broke your wrist, and now have limited mobility in that wrist, you may qualify for VA disability pay. If you have migraines due to a TBI or noise exposure, cervical strain (a literal pain in your neck) from a physical injury you sustained in the military, or the surprisingly common-among-veterans condition of degenerative arthritis, you could be eligible for compensation from the VA as well. Many other conditions, such as post-traumatic stress, anxiety, amnesia, gastrointestinal issues, eating disorders, and mood disorders also qualify you for VA disability payments if they're connected to your military service.

If your condition wasn't caused or aggravated by your military service, or if you became ill or injured because you did something you weren't supposed to do, the VA isn't going to pay you a dime for conditions stemming from that incident. For example, if you were hurt in an alcohol-related crash that you caused, the VA won't give you disability pay for the ongoing conditions you have from that incident (though it will consider other disabilities that are connected to your service).

REMEMBER

You can't get VA disability compensation if you received a dishonorable discharge. However, you may be able to apply for a discharge upgrade or ask the VA to review your discharge; I explain these approaches in Chapter 2.

COMMONLY AWARDED COMPENSATION CLAIMS

Some VA compensation claims are far more common than others are. Your mileage may vary on your rating if you have one of these common conditions. They're the most commonly awarded compensation claims in order from most to least:

- Tinnitus (ringing ears)

- Hearing loss in one or both ears

- Posttraumatic stress

- Scarring

- Limited knee flexion

- Lumbosacral and cervical strain (back and neck pain)

- Sciatic nerve paralysis (nerve damage)

- Limited ankle motion

- Migraine

- Degenerative arthritis

Other common ailments veterans have include sleep apnea, traumatic brain injury, respiratory problems, Type 2 diabetes from Agent Orange exposure, cancer, and a variety of secondary conditions. (*Secondary conditions* are conditions caused by another condition that's related to military service.)

Getting Your Disability Rating

To determine how much money it should pay you, the VA gives you a *disability rating*. The VA bases this rating on how severe or serious your service-connected condition is. The more serious your condition is, the higher your rating is.

TIP

You can have multiple disability ratings, such as one for posttraumatic stress and one for hearing loss. When that happens, the VA combines all your ratings to make a final determination. I explain that process in the section, "Breaking Down Your Rating," later in this chapter. I explain how to relate your disability to your military service and when to apply for benefits in the following sections.

Your VA disability rating is also used to help determine other VA benefits, such as VA healthcare, as well as in veterans hiring preference.

Establishing a service-connected disability

Before you can even ask the VA to give you a disability rating, you need an official diagnosis from a doctor or other healthcare professional. You may also need to undergo a VA exam (called a *compensation and pension exam*, or C&P). Simply saying that you have headaches now because you breathed in too much sand during a deployment isn't going to cut it. The VA is tasked with being a good steward of taxpayer money, so it wants you to bring receipts. You may want to ask your healthcare provider to fill out a VA Disability Benefits Questionnaire (DBQ) to help the VA make its decision. These questionnaires are available for most conditions, and they're all on the VA's website.

If your doctor or the VA discovers that your condition was caused by your own willful misconduct, you can't make a claim. Additionally, if you had a medical condition related to your service but have since been cured, you don't qualify for VA disability payments. That means if you developed cancer, got treatment, and are now cancer-free, you can't make a VA disability claim. (However, if your cancer comes back, you're eligible to file a claim.)

TIP

If you have undiagnosed symptoms that you believe are related to your military service, file a claim. The VA will examine you to determine their cause.

I cover the four main types of service-connected disabilities in the following sections.

Direct service connections

Sometimes proving a direct service connection to your disability is easy. If you're a Purple Heart recipient and your disabilities (including posttraumatic stress) stem from the incident that earned you that medal, the VA can easily connect the dots. But sometimes it's not that simple; you have to provide the VA with evidence that shows your military service caused or worsened your condition. To do that, you must have a current diagnosis from a healthcare provider.

You also need to pinpoint the cause of your condition (or the cause of your worsening condition), and that cause has to be related to your military service. You can do so by isolating a specific event, injury, or illness in your military service records (such as that time you fell off the back of an LMTV when the driver hit a pothole) or by creating what's known as a medical nexus. A *medical nexus* is a link between your continued symptoms and your service. If a medical nexus exists, you can provide the VA with a *medical nexus letter* from a healthcare provider that says that it's "at least as likely as not" that your condition was caused or aggravated by your time in the military with rationale to back up their opinion. (Alternatively, you can ask for a VA exam to connect your symptoms with your service.)

Presumptive service connections

In some cases, the VA presumes that you have a service-connected disability — even if you don't provide any proof that your disability was caused or aggravated by your military service. The VA can approve your claim based on its presumption that you were exposed to certain conditions or circumstances known to cause disabilities like yours.

For example, if you served in the Republic of Vietnam during the Vietnam War, the VA presumes that you were exposed to herbicides such as Agent Orange. Additionally, if you're a Persian Gulf War veteran who served in Southwest Asia between August 2, 1990, and today, the VA presumes that you were exposed to certain environmental toxins. If you develop one or more medical conditions related to those toxins, you don't need to create a direct service connection because the VA already knows that the toxins were *at least as likely as not* to have caused your condition.

When it comes to certain chronic conditions, you may be eligible for a presumptive service connection if the condition became what the VA considers 10 percent disabling within a year of your discharge (even if you weren't diagnosed or didn't file a claim within a year). The chronic conditions eligible for this type of presumptive service connection are outlined in 38 CFR, Section 3.309 and include arthritis, some cancers, hypertension, malaria, stroke, irritable bowel syndrome, and a number of others.

REMEMBER

The following chronic conditions don't have to manifest within a year of your separation from service to qualify you for service-connection:

>> **Amyotrophic lateral sclerosis (ALS, which is commonly known as Lou Gehrig's disease):** At any point after serving in the military, the VA presumes that it was caused by your service. (Veterans are about twice as likely to be diagnosed with ALS than members of the general public, which is likely at least part of the reason the VA presumes ALS is connected to military service.)

>> **Hansen's disease (leprosy) or tuberculosis:** You have three years for both those conditions to become at least 10 percent disabling for a presumptive service connection.

>> **Multiple sclerosis (MS):** If you developed MS within seven years of the date you separated from the military, you're also eligible for a presumptive service connection.

>> **Any disease known to affect prisoners of war:** If you were a POW and developed any disease known to affect POWs, and if your disease manifests to a degree of 10 percent or more at any time after your discharge or release, you don't have to prove a service connection.

Secondary service connections

The VA recognizes that some vets have *secondary service connections* — that is, they have a condition caused or aggravated by military service and that original condition causes or aggravates another condition that's not directly related to their service. An easy way to say that is "Condition A was caused by military service, and Condition A caused or led to Condition B."

EXAMPLE

If you have a service-connected condition such as Type 2 diabetes and your diabetes led to vision loss or blindness (which it's known to do), you have a secondary service connection. With a secondary service connection, you may be entitled to additional disability compensation from the VA.

Service connections based on aggravation

Service connections based on aggravation relate to conditions that were aggravated by your military service. That means you had a condition before you joined the military or developed one while you were in (but not as a result of your service), and your service in the military made it worse. The VA will consider whether your service worsened your condition or the condition naturally became worse on its own.

REMEMBER

If the VA denies your disability claim by saying that your condition existed before you entered the service, it must provide "clear and unmistakable evidence" that your condition predated your service. Then, it must prove that your military service didn't aggravate the condition. The *presumption of soundness* is a legal concept that means someone joining the military enters service in sound condition. That means any conditions that arose during your time in the service may possibly be connected to your service — unless those conditions were noted on your entrance examination records. The burden of proof lies entirely on the VA in cases like this. In other words, you don't have to prove that your condition *didn't* exist before you joined the military; the VA has to prove that it *did*.

Asking for a rating before discharge

You may ask the VA to give you a disability rating before you even leave the military through the Benefits Delivery at Discharge (BDD) program. You can use the BDD program if you meet all of the following:

>> You're currently on active duty.

>> You have a separation date within the next 180 to 90 days.

>> You can be available for VA exams for 45 days from the date you submit your claim.

>> You can provide a copy of your service treatment records for your current period of service at the time you file your claim.

The BDD program can help you speed up the process so you receive your benefits sooner after discharge. However, you may not use it if your case requires what the VA calls "special handling," such as if you need case management for a serious injury or illness, you're terminally ill, or you're pregnant. The BDD program is also off-limits to you if:

>> You're waiting on a discharge while being treated at a military treatment facility or VA hospital.

>> You're waiting for the VA to determine your character of discharge.

>> You need to have a VA exam done in a foreign country (unless you're in Landstuhl, Germany, or at Camp Humphreys, South Korea).

WARNING

You can't use BDD if you have fewer than 90 days left on active duty. However, you can still start filing your claim before you're discharged; you just need to file a fully developed or standard claim, which requires you to provide medical evidence and proof that your disability is service-connected. I cover fully developed and standard claims in the following section.

If you're wounded, injured, or ill and are no longer able to perform your duties, your branch of service will refer you to the Integrated Disability Evaluation System (IDES). Under IDES, the VA will work with the DOD to give you a proposed disability rating before you leave the service. (And as a side note, if you're referred to IDES, you're automatically entitled to Veteran Readiness and Employment. or VR&E, services. I take a deep-dive into the VR&E program in Chapter 20.) If your branch decides to medically retire you, you may qualify for disability payments from the DOD rather than the VA, which I explain in the section, "Receiving DOD Disability Compensation," later in this chapter.

Getting a rating after discharge

If you have fewer than 90 days left on active duty or if you've already been discharged, you can file what's called a *fully developed* or *standard claim* with the VA for disability compensation. You need evidence to support your claim, such as medical records, supporting statements from people who can tell the VA more about your condition (including how and when it happened), and your discharge documents.

Under federal law, the VA has a *duty to assist*. That means the VA has to help you get the evidence you need to support your claim, such as medical records. However, the VA can only do so much — such as obtaining your military treatment records (if they still exist). It can't chase down people who know you to provide supporting statements, nor can it require your current civilian doctor to diagnose you with a condition. The VA's duty to assist only applies when you file your initial claim or when you file a supplemental claim.

If you don't have any medical records or other evidence to support your claim, don't stress too much. (It can be tough to get, or pay for, treatment after you're out of the military, and the VA knows this.) The VA will most likely schedule a claim exam at your nearest VA medical center or with a contractor so it can learn more about your condition and help determine whether you have a disability it can compensate you for.

You can file your claim online through the VA's website, bring a filled-out application form to your nearest VA regional office, or mail your claim to the VA. All the forms you need are available on the VA's website, but if you can't access them there, you can ask for help at any VA campus.

TIP

If you intend to file your claim by mail, you should submit what's known as an "Intent to File" form first. That way, you become eligible for retroactive payments (kind of like back pay) if your claim is approved. You then have a year to complete your claim. You don't need to submit this form if you file your claim online, because your effective date is the day you begin filling out your claim forms online. That means if you're thinking of filing a claim online, you should open it as soon as possible — even if you don't plan to complete it right away.

Breaking Down Your Rating

After the VA determines you have a disability, it can assign you a disability rating. This rating determines how much money you receive in compensation each month. It also affects your eligibility for and access to other benefits (including your veteran hiring preference in federal and state employment). Your disability rating is based on the severity of your service-connected condition, and the VA rounds it to the nearest ten for compensation purposes. That means if you have a 77 percent rating, you receive compensation at the 80 percent level. If you have a 73 percent rating, you receive compensation at the 70 percent level.

TIP

You're allowed to work and collect VA disability benefits at the same time in most cases. However, if you receive IU payments, your work must meet certain conditions that I explain in the section, "Qualifying for Individual Unemployability," later in this chapter.

Making the connection with a single rating

The VA determines how disabled you are based on your medical records and other evidence. If it's not sure how to rate you or if you don't have any evidence to back up your claim, the VA will send you to a medical appointment with one of its doctors; the doctor will evaluate you and submit a report to the VA.

After the VA makes its determination, it assigns you a disability rating that's expressed as a percentage. For the most part, less severe disabilities receive lower ratings than more severe disabilities do. The VA's Schedule for Rating Disabilities (VASRD) dictates the percentages for a huge range of disabilities. The Schedule tells the VA what percentage to assign; for example, tinnitus makes a person 10 percent disabled, and "hearing impairment with attacks of vertigo and cerebellar gait occurring more than once weekly, with or without tinnitus," makes a person 100 percent disabled (at least for purposes of VA benefits). In other categories, ratings are outlined based on severity. For example, a severe duodenal ulcer gets someone a 60 percent rating; a moderately severe one nets them 40 percent, a moderate one is rated at 20 percent, and a mild one is rated at 10 percent.

That's where your medical diagnosis comes in. The person evaluating your claim looks at the condition you suffer from, finds it in the VASRD, and then searches for the diagnostic code that best matches your symptoms. The VASRD tells the reviewer exactly what rating to give you based on your condition and symptoms.

TIP

You can find the VARSD on the VA's website or by searching the Internet for "38 CFR Book C, Schedule for Rating Disabilities" if you're looking for an idea of what the VA may rate you after you make your claim.

TECHNICAL STUFF

Getting a 0 percent disability rating is possible, and though it won't get you any monthly disability payments, it's still important. Having a disability rating may qualify you for VA healthcare, which I explain in Chapter 5, and some other benefits.

Combining ratings for two or more disabilities

If you have two or more service-connected conditions or if you have secondary conditions (additional medical issues caused by your first condition), the VA will give you a combined disability rating. Your *combined disability rating* is your total rating, but the VA doesn't simply add two ratings together; it uses a specific formula to determine your total rating, which can't exceed 100 percent. The VA stores all its calculations in a table governed by 38 CFR 4.25. You can also use the VA's combined disability rating calculator on its website to determine your total rating, but bear in mind that if you have special circumstances, such as two or more disabilities that affect both sides of your body, your total rating may be a bit different when calculated by the VA.

REMEMBER

If you entered the military with a disability that your military service aggravated, the VA calculates the rating your preexisting disability was worth. Then it deducts the original disability rating from your current disability rating. For example, if you joined the military with migraines that the VA considers 10 percent disabling and left the military with migraines the VA considers 30 percent disabling, it pays you the difference by rating your migraines at 20 percent.

Getting a 100 percent disability rating

Receiving a 100 percent disability rating for a single disability from the VA is tough; getting a combined rating of 100 percent (or 95 percent, which the VA rounds up to 100) is easier. A 100 percent rating means that you receive the maximum allowable amount in monthly disability payments.

REMEMBER

A 100 percent rating isn't always permanent. In some cases, the VA can attempt a *rating reduction*, which is an evaluation of your current condition to determine if you've gotten better; if the VA finds that there's been an improvement, it can reduce your disability rating. However, if you've had a 100 percent rating for 20 years or more, the VA will only reduce your rating if it finds evidence of fraud from your initial rating.

If the VA finds that your condition is permanent and total — that is, it'll last the rest of your life with no improvement, and that it's totally disabling — you get a *permanent and total rating* that the VA can't reduce in the future.

Some people are eligible for temporary 100 percent disability ratings. The VA sometimes awards these ratings when a person is hospitalized for more than 21 days, is recovering from surgery or a broken bone, or has an unstabilized condition that's causing severe disabilities. The VA will reevaluate your situation and readjust your disability rating after you recover.

If you have a 100 percent disability rating from the VA, you qualify for additional benefits, such as being in the first priority group for VA healthcare (I cover that in Chapter 5), CHAMPVA (Chapter 23), Survivors' and Dependents' Educational Assistance (Chapter 21), and commissary and exchange benefits (Chapter 24). You may also qualify for special benefits from your state.

TECHNICAL STUFF

If you have service-connected cancer, the VA gives you a 100 percent disability rating. You keep that rating while your cancer is active, and for six months after you successfully complete a treatment program. At the six-month mark, the VA reevaluates your case to determine your level of disability.

Qualifying for Individual Unemployability

You may be eligible for Individual Unemployability (IU) benefits if you can no longer perform substantial gainful employment due to one or more service-connected conditions but don't qualify for 100 percent disability.

REMEMBER

In order for a job to be considered *substantial gainful employment*, it must pay more than the federal poverty level. To even qualify for IU payments, you must have a disability that's already rated at 60 percent or higher. If you have two or more disabilities, at least one must be rated at 40 percent, and your combined rating must be greater than 70 percent.

If you qualify for IU benefits, you receive the same amount of pay as a 100 percent disabled veteran receives. Additionally, you may qualify for VA healthcare and other benefits available to 100 percent disabled vets.

TIP

You're still allowed to work if you receive IU payments, provided that your earnings fall under the federal poverty line or you work in a protected work environment. A *protected work environment* is one that provides you with specific accommodations for your disability. You may make more than the poverty level and still qualify for IU if you work in a protected work environment.

Addressing important points on ratings

Here are a handful of things to keep in mind when the VA is rating you for a disability:

>> If you have service-connected disabilities and disabilities that aren't connected to your time in the military, although it's difficult to tell which condition is causing your symptoms, the VA is required to give you the benefit of the doubt. That means if the VA can't determine the cause of your symptoms, it's required to assume that the cause is your service-connected disability.

>> If your disability becomes worse while you're waiting for the VA to approve your claim, you may ask for staged ratings. *Staged ratings* are different ratings for the same condition. You may ask for staged ratings if you first sought treatment for a mild duodenal ulcer, which is rated at 10 percent, but your condition became severe enough for a 60 percent rating while the VA was processing your claim. This can increase your payments (which you'll receive as back pay) from the time your condition became worse.

>> You may be eligible for special monthly compensation if you have a certain type of severe disability, such as the loss of sight, loss of use of limbs, erectile dysfunction, or loss of use of your hands or feet.

Receiving Monthly VA Disability Pay

After the VA assigns you a rating, your claim is complete (though you may appeal if you're not happy with your rating). If the VA rates you at least 10 percent disabled, you receive your first disability payment within 15 days. It pays through direct deposit or by check. If you don't receive your payment within 15 days of the VA issuing its decision, call the Veterans Help Line at 800-827-1000. The following sections explain special payment circumstances that may apply to you.

Waiting on your back pay

If the VA gives you a 10 percent or higher rating, it most likely owes you back pay. Your *disability compensation effective date* is the date that you're entitled to receive compensation — and because that date passed before the VA approved your claim and gave you a rating, you're entitled to retroactive pay.

In some cases, your disability compensation effective date is the date that you filed your original claim; in others, it's the date you first became ill or injured (whichever is later). For example, if you were injured in the military in 2020, discharged in 2021, and filed a claim in 2022, the VA will provide you with back pay from the date that you filed your claim or sent in an intent to file letter, which I discuss in the section, "Getting a rating after discharge," earlier in this chapter.

REMEMBER

Sometimes the VA conducts an audit to ensure that you don't owe Uncle Sam any money before giving you back pay, which can delay your receipt.

Pocketing Special Monthly Compensation

Special Monthly Compensation (SMC) is a tax-free payment to compensate some veterans who suffered the loss (or loss of use) of specific body parts. For example, if you can't move a joint, you're paralyzed, or have had a body part amputated, you may qualify for SMC. This compensation also covers deafness, loss of a percentage of breast tissue from mastectomy or radiation treatment, or an inability to communicate by speech.

You can get SMC in addition to your VA disability payments, and in some cases (such as erectile dysfunction with a 0 percent disability rating), you may receive it without receiving any disability payments. The amount of money you receive in SMC depends on your condition as well as whether you have any other disabling conditions. You may be eligible for more SMC if you're housebound, bedridden, or require aid and attendance. You may apply for SMC through your VA regional office.

Qualifying for Extra VA Disability Benefits

With a disability rating from the VA, you may qualify for additional disability ben-efits. Though I explain each of the following benefits in Chapter 20, here's a quick rundown of what you may be entitled to:

>> **180-day Family Housing Extension:** If you live in military family housing but are being separated from active duty because of your illness or injury, you may be eligible to shelter in place for an additional six months.

>> **Aid and Attendance:** Aid and Attendance is a higher monthly pension amount that you may be eligible for if you need help to perform activities of daily living.

>> **Automobile allowance and adaptive equipment:** The automobile allow-ance and adaptive equipment is for veterans who have a service-connected disability that prevents them from driving. You may receive a little more than $21,000 to help you buy a specially equipped vehicle.

>> **Clothing allowance:** If your clothing is damaged by a prosthetic or orthopedic device (such as a wheelchair), or if it's damaged by medications you take or use for a skin condition, you may receive a clothing allowance from the VA.

>> **DEA:** Dependents' Educational Assistance (DEA) is for spouses and kids of disabled veterans (as well as some others). Commonly called *Chapter 35,* DEA provides money for school, apprenticeships, and other educational benefits.

>> **Housebound allowance:** If you receive a VA pension and you spend most of your time in your home because you have a permanent disability, you may be eligible for a *housebound allowance* — extra money tacked on to your VA pension amount.

>> **SAH grants:** If you need to buy, build, or change your permanent home because of your disability, you may be eligible for a Specially Adapted Housing (SAH) grant. This benefit is only available to 120 veterans and servicemembers each year, but it's significant; you could receive more than $100,000 to adapt your home. The maximum grant amount changes every year.

>> **SHA grants:** Special Home Adaptation (SHA) grants are available to some veterans with certain service-connected disabilities, and like SAH grants, they're designed to help you buy, build, or change your permanent home. The VA can award you just a bit over $20,000 for an SHA grant, and the maximum award changes each year.

>> **S-DVI and VMLI:** Service-Disabled Veterans Life Insurance (S-DVI) is low-cost life insurance coverage for people with service-connected disabilities. Veterans Mortgage Life Insurance (VMLI) is mortgage protection insurance for

vets with severe service-connected disabilities who have adapted a home (with or without a grant from the VA).

>> **Service dogs:** Some service-disabled veterans qualify for free service and guide dogs. Though the VA doesn't provide the dog, it does connect veterans with accredited agencies and pays for everything, including the dog, veterinary care (including office visits, dental procedures, prescribed medications, and vaccinations), and necessary equipment like harnesses or backpacks.

>> **TRA grants:** If you live with a family member and need to make changes to meet your needs, you could be eligible for a Temporary Residence Adaptation (TRA) grant. These grants vary based on whether you qualify for an SAH or SHA grant; the award is higher if you qualify for SAH and lower if you qualify for SHA.

>> **VR&E:** VR&E is available to service-disabled vets who need job training, education, employment accommodations, job seeking skills, and resume development help.

Combining Retired Pay and VA Disability Compensation

Until 2004, vets couldn't receive full retirement benefits and VA disability compensation; they had to choose which they wanted to receive. If they chose to receive VA disability compensation, that money was deducted from their retired pay. Fortunately, times have changed — and in some circumstances you get to keep all your retirement pay and collect your VA disability payments. However, in many cases, your retirement pay will still be offset by your VA disability payments. The following sections explain.

Disability ratings of 50 percent or greater

You may keep all your retirement pay *and* collect VA disability payments if you have a VA disability rating of 50 percent or more. Thanks to the Concurrent Retirement Disability Pay (CRDP) system, you receive both payments at 100 percent. There is no pay offset.

Disability ratings of 40 percent or lower

If you have a disability rating of 40 percent or lower, your retirement pay is offset by the amount of money you get from the VA. I'm going to ask you to put on some rose-colored glasses here, because in my humble opinion, this system isn't ideal. You earned your retired pay and it's not your fault you were disabled, so you may need a nudge to help you "hunt the good stuff."

Here you go: VA disability compensation is tax-free, so many vets choose to receive it and offset their retired pay. You still receive the same amount of compensation you would have received as a retiree without a disability, but you have a VA disability rating (which makes you eligible for other benefits), and you may have more spending power because you aren't required to pay taxes on the VA portion of your monthly payment.

EXAMPLE

Here are a couple examples (with fictional numbers, of course) to give you a better look at how each scenario works:

>> You retired from the military after 20 years of service and have a 50 percent disability rating. Your retired pay is $2,000 per month, and your disability pay totals $500 per month. You receive a total of $2,500 each month. Over the course of a year, you receive $6,000 in nontaxable income and $24,000 in retired pay that's subject to federal (and sometimes state) taxes.

>> You retired from the military after 20 years of service and have a 40 percent disability rating. Your retired pay is $2,000 per month, and your disability pay totals $400 per month. You choose to receive your VA disability compensation, which lowers your retirement pay to $1,600 per month. The $400 you receive from the VA is tax-free, while the remaining $1,600 is subject to federal (and often state) taxes. You still get $2,000 per month, but that's it; nothing extra for your disability. Over the course of a year, you receive $4,800 in nontaxable income and $19,200 in taxable retired pay.

TIP

If you're a retiree with *any* physical or mental ailments that are connected to your military service, grab your medical records and prepare to make a case to the VA. The seemingly small difference between a 40 percent rating and a 50 percent rating seriously affects the amount of pay you receive from today until the day you die.

Getting Combat-Related Special Compensation

You may be eligible for Combat-Related Special Compensation (CRSC), which enables you to keep your retired pay and collect disability payments. You may only receive this tax-free benefit if your branch determines that your disability is combat-related (you apply for it through your branch — not through the VA). To qualify, you must be retired and entitled to military retirement pay, have a VA disability rating of at least 10 percent, and your DOD retirement payments would be reduced by the amount of your VA disability payments. One of the following must also be true about you:

>> You served 20 or more years of service on active duty, the National Guard, or Reserve (and have reached retirement age for the Guard or Reserves, if applicable).

>> You retired for medical reasons with a disability rating of at least 30 percent.

>> You're covered under the Temporary Early Retirement Act (TERA), which ended in 2002.

>> You're on the Temporary Disability Retired List (TDRL) or Permanent Disability Retired List (PDRL), which I cover in the next section.

If you retired after at least 20 years and have a 10 percent disability rating for a combat-related issue (which may include an injury or condition caused by training for combat), you're eligible to apply for CRSC. You need your service medical records from the date you were injured, and they must show the severity of your combat-related medical condition. You also need all your official service records, such as performance evaluations, personnel action requests, and investigative reports if there were any related to your incident. Finally, you also need your decorations and award recommendations, such as a Purple Heart citation, orders for a Combat Action Badge, other medals, and decorations for valor. You also need to provide your retirement records, DD-214, and any VA decision notices you have.

Your evidence must show that your injury occurred when you were doing any of the following:

>> You were engaged in armed conflict (in combat or during an occupation or raid).

>> You were participating in hazardous duty, such as parachuting, flying, or demolition activities.

>> You engaged in war simulations, such as live-fire or hand-to-hand combat training.

>> You were exposed to instruments of war, such as chemical agents, weapons, or military vehicles.

>> You engaged in an activity for which you received a Purple Heart.

WARNING

There's a six-year statute of limitations on CRSC, which means that you must apply for it within six years of becoming entitled to military retired pay or of receiving any VA rating decision, whichever comes first. If you file your claim after the six-year statute of limitations expires, you're only eligible to receive up to six years' worth of payments that the government owes you.

You may only apply for CRSC through your branch. Use DD Form 2860, which is available on the VA's website, and mail it to the appropriate address for your branch (though the Army also accepts email submissions; you can find the most current email address on the VA's website).

Receiving DOD Disability Compensation

Some people receive disability compensation from the DOD rather than the VA. It all comes down to whether you're medically retired from service, which I cover in the section, "Discovering Your Disability Pay's Origin Story: VA versus DOD," earlier in this chapter. When this type of compensation comes from the DOD, it's called *disability retirement pay*. The DOD only sends a monthly direct deposit to people who are deemed unfit to perform their duties because they were injured in the line of duty. Another type of DOD disability pay comes in the form of severance. I cover both in the following sections.

Qualifying for disability retirement pay

To qualify for disability retirement pay, you must have completed at least 20 years of creditable service *or* have one or more service-connected disabilities that make you unfit for duty — and in the latter case, the disability or disabilities must amount to a combined disability rating of 30 percent or more. If your combined disability rating is less than 30 percent, you may receive a disability severance payment; you can read more in the section, "Getting your cut through disability severance pay," later in this chapter.

You can't apply for DOD disability retirement pay; it's not like VA disability pay. The only way to get this pay is if a doctor examines you and discovers a qualifying disability, then refers you to a medical examination board (MEB) or physical examination board (PEB). (An MEB and a PEB are the same thing; they're just called different names in different branches.) Usually, people simply refer to these boards as med boards; when you hear someone say, "I was med-boarded," they mean that they were found physically unfit for duty and medically retired.

The MEB or PEB will determine whether your disability is severe enough to qualify you for a medical retirement and assign you a disability rating (kind of like the VA does, though the VA does it after the fact). These boards also consider whether your disability is likely to be permanent or temporary, and based on their evaluations, the members will put you on the Permanent Disability Retired List or the Temporary Disability Retired List, which I explain in the following sections.

WARNING

If you had a medical condition or physical defect prior to joining the military, the military may administratively separate you without referring you for DOD disability compensation under certain circumstances.

You may qualify for a medical retirement if you have 20 or more years of active service, regardless of your disability rating (which the medical board assigns to you regardless). If you have fewer than 20 years of active service, you must have a disability rating of 30 percent or higher to qualify for retirement. If your disability rating is lower than 30 percent, you'll be separated. And if your disability existed before you joined the military, the board will recommend you for discharge without benefits. That doesn't mean you have a dishonorable discharge. It simply means you won't get medical retirement pay from the DOD; you may still apply for VA disability pay if this happens in your case.

When the military gives you a medical retirement, you get all the same benefits a regular retiree gets — you can shop at the commissary, use military Space-A flights, and spend time at Armed Forces Resorts.

Looking long-term at the permanent disability list

If the MEB or PEB believes your condition is permanent — that is, it's not going to improve, even with treatment — it can choose to put you on the PDRL. Your disability rating, which the MEB or PEB board assigns you, determines whether your disability qualifies you for a medical retirement or separation from the military. You must have a service-connected disability rating of 30 percent or greater to get retired disability pay, which is calculated in one of two ways (based on the way that's most beneficial for you):

>> Retired pay base × disability percentage (not to exceed 75%)

>> Retired pay base × (2.5% × years in service)

Your retired pay base is the average of your three highest-earning years in the service. It's what you receive under the High-3 retirement system I describe in the High-36 system (see Chapter 8).

Finding a spot on the temporary disability list

If your MEB or PEB puts you on the TDRL, you get retirement benefits for the duration of time you're on it. You also receive medical coverage for you and your dependents until your conditions are stabilized or corrected, or until your healthcare provider and your branch determine that your disability is permanent. You'll be reexamined at least every 18 months while on the TDRL (unless you're put on it for posttraumatic stress; in that case, you need an additional exam at the six-month mark). After every examination, your healthcare provider will forward their findings to the board. And if you skip an exam, your retired pay will be suspended until you decide to show up.

Nobody can stay on the TDRL for more than three years. During those three years, your healthcare provider can find you fit for duty; if that happens, lace up your boots — you're going back to work. However, if your condition stabilizes and is rated at 30 percent or greater, the DOD puts you on the PDRL. If you're stable and rated at below 30 percent but you don't have 20 years of service under your belt, the DOD discharges you from the list with severance pay. (If you have more than 20 years of service, you go straight to the PDRL, regardless of your disability rating.)

Getting your cut through disability severance pay

Disability severance pay is a one-time, lump-sum payment that you may be eligible to receive if you have fewer than 20 years of creditable military service, you're unfit for duty based on a service-connected disability, and your disability is rated at less than 30 percent. Your disability must be permanent or a physician must determine that it may be permanent. The amount of severance pay you receive is based on your basic monthly pay and years of service (as long as you served fewer than 19 years), and it varies based on whether you incurred your disability in a combat zone.

WARNING

It's against the law to get VA compensation for a disability for which you received disability severance pay. However, you may be able to reimburse the severance pay you received and receive disability pay. You may also apply for VA benefits based on other disabilities not related to your medical discharge from the military.

Losing Disability Pay to Outside Sources

Disability pay is yours — except when it's not. In some cases, other people can get their hands on it. The following sections explain when your disability pay may not end up directly in your bank account (and when nobody can touch it but you).

Divvying up disability in divorce

When it comes to family matters, your disability pay isn't entirely off the table. Federal law doesn't count it as *marital property* (that is, property that you and your spouse are both entitled to), which means it can't be divided like your retirement pay can. But it still plays a role; though the court won't divide it between you and your soon-to-be ex, disability pay does count toward your income concerning child support or spousal maintenance (alimony). That's because in a 1987 Supreme Court Case, *Rose v. Rose*, the court found that VA disability payments were "to be used, in part, for the support of veterans' dependents."

Courts use your total income when determining how much child support or spousal support you're required to pay. That means your income from work (if you're working), your military pension, and your disability pay are all rolled together. The court then applies that amount to your state's support formula (most states have child support formulas, but fewer have spousal support formulas). The result is the amount you're required to pay.

REMEMBER

Your VA disability compensation can't be garnished to pay for your alimony and child support obligations *unless* you waived part of your taxable military retired pay to receive nontaxable disability compensation. (Head to the section, "Combining Retired Pay and VA Disability Compensation," earlier in this chapter for more information.)

Getting the scoop on garnishment

Though a court can garnish your VA disability pay to cover what you owe in child support or spousal maintenance, debt collectors have no such luck. Usually, debt collectors aren't allowed to take your VA disability benefits; a U.S. Treasury rule requires your bank to automatically protect that money if it's direct deposited into your account. When a creditor tries to garnish money from your account, your bank has to look at your account history for the past two months to determine how much you received in benefits during that time. If your account has more than two months' worth of benefits in it, your bank can garnish or freeze the extra money — and if that happens, you may need to go to court to have your money released to you.

For the record, creditors can't garnish your Social Security or Supplemental Security Income (SSI), either. If you receive either of those benefits, your bank is required to protect two months' worth of that cash, as well.

WARNING

Though this doesn't apply to most people, if you receive a paper check from the VA and then deposit your checks into your bank, your bank doesn't have to protect two months' worth of your money. Your bank could freeze your entire account and require you to go to court to prove that the money came from the VA as a disability benefit.

Paying back into the system through tax

Unlike a military pension, VA disability pay is nontaxable at the federal, state, and local level. (Very few states tax military pensions, but the federal government does.) The IRS doesn't include disability benefits received from the VA in a person's gross income. You also don't have to pay taxes on:

>> Disability compensation or pension payments for disabilities paid to you (or your family)

>> Grants designed to help you modify your home for living with a wheelchair

>> Automobile grants for veterans who have lost their sight or the use of their limbs

>> Benefits you receive under a dependent-care assistance program

>> Education, training, or subsistence allowance

>> Veterans' insurance proceeds and dividends (including the proceeds of a veteran's endowment policy paid before death)

>> Death gratuity paid to survivors whose veteran died after September 10, 2001

>> Payments made under the Compensated Work Therapy program, which I tell you about in Chapter 10

Check out IRS Publication 525, available on the IRS's website.

3

Employment, Education, and Housing Programs

Explore government programs that can help you find and keep a good job.

Discover how to ferret out good government jobs and how to get an edge with veterans preference.

Check out self-employment opportunities and the government programs that help you build an enterprise from the ground up.

Get the scoop on using your GI Bill and other programs that provide funding for higher education.

Put your money where your house is by exploring your VA home loan benefit.

Collect information about spending your golden years in a military-only retirement home, on a military installation, or in a military-only community.

Chapter **10**

Applying to Employment Programs

U nless you're wealthy, you're going to need a job after leaving military service. According to the U.S. Department of Labor, the unemployment rate for veterans is lower than it is for nonveterans, which may be due to the programs Uncle Sam has in place for people who trade in their combat boots for professional footwear. It probably also has something to do with the fact that employers that hire veterans receive certain incentives, including tax cuts and bragging rights for putting vets to work. Regardless, as a veteran of the U.S. military, you're more likely to find employment than a civilian is. And don't forget: Your military experience translates into valuable characteristics employers are looking for.

That doesn't mean you're going to find your dream job right away (though if you had an eye toward the future, you began looking for employment before you even left the military). However, it does mean that additional opportunities are available, including employment training programs, hiring preference in government agencies (see Chapter 11), and access to jobs.

Many vets aren't aware of all the programs available to give them a head start. If you're one of them, use this chapter to look at all the current government programs — as well as civilian programs and opportunities — designed to put you into the workforce.

Getting into Government Programs that Put You to Work

The VA and other offices of the government, such as the Small Business Administration and the Department of Labor, are always looking for ways to create meaningful programs for veterans. This section outlines several of the most beneficial, explains who qualifies for each, and tells you what to do if you want to participate.

VR&E tracks

Veteran Readiness and Employment, commonly referred to as the VR&E program, provides service-disabled veterans with access to job training, resume development, coaching in job-seeking, and more. The program offers five tracks, though one is only for Reserve and Guard members who became disabled on a deployment and want to return to their former employer with disability accommodations, and another is for veterans who need help with activities of daily living (I cover it in Chapter 20). Here are the other three, which primarily deal with putting you to work:

>> **Rapid Access to Employment** gives you counseling and rehabilitation services that help you find employment using your existing skill set. You get access to tools to help with your job search, professional or vocational counseling, help writing a resume and preparing for interviews, and help figuring out whether you're eligible for veterans preference points.

>> **Employment through Long-Term Services** is for people with a service-connected disability that makes it hard to succeed in employment in their current field. Under this track, you get the education or training necessary to find work in a different field. This program also offers you a complete skills assessment, career guidance, job market evaluation, and opportunities for apprenticeship and on-the-job training. It also provides you with volunteer opportunities and employment assistance.

>> **Self-Employment** is for veterans with employment barriers (that is, things that prevent them from working or finding a job) who want to start their own businesses. If you participate in this program, you get coordination services, help developing your business plan, and receive analysis of your business concept as well as training in small business operations, marketing, and finances. The VA will point you in the right direction to get the resources you need to implement your business plan.

To qualify for the VR&E program, you must have a service-connected disability rating of at least 10 percent from the VA and a discharge other than dishonorable. After you apply, the VA schedules you an evaluation with a Vocational Rehabilitation Counselor (VRC) who will determine whether you're eligible to participate in any of the VR&E tracks.

In some cases, family members who support a service-disabled veteran facing employment challenges also qualify for some VR&E benefits, like career assessments, readjustment counseling, education and career counseling, and Dependent Educational Assistance (DEA), which I cover in Chapter 21.

WARNING

If you were discharged from active duty before January 1, 2013, you're only eligible for 12 years after the date you received notice of your date of separation from active duty or the date you received your first VA service-connected disability rating. However, the VA may extend your eligibility period if you have a serious employment handicap. If you were discharged after that date, there is no time limit on your eligibility for the VR&E program.

Compensated Work Therapy

The Veterans Health Administration runs the Compensated Work Therapy (CWT) program to provide support to veterans living with mental health conditions (including posttraumatic stress) or physical impairment. Your conditions *don't* have to be service connected to be eligible for CWT services. Some of the services that CWT programs provide (but that may not be available in every location) include the following:

>> **Transitional Work (TW):** Participants in this program, which operates out of VA medical centers and some private companies, are matched with work assignments on a time-limited basis. Though these participants aren't considered employees, they receive base pay determined by the prevailing wage.

>> **Supported Employment (SE):** SE is for veterans who have significant barriers to employment due to mental health conditions or physical disabilities that require additional support in the workplace.

>> **Community-Based Employment Services (CBES):** This program is less intensive than SE and provides a wide range of services that lead to direct placement in a job.

>> **Supported Self-Employment (SSE):** SSE gives veterans guidance on business practices, offers networking opportunities and training, and even helps veterans connect with community financial institutions for help in starting a business.

>> **Vocational Assistance:** This program provides short-term help such as assessment, counseling, and related services that help veterans pinpoint their skills, find resources, and meet expectations during job searches, interviews, and employment.

In order to participate in the CWT program, you must be eligible to receive VA healthcare services, have barriers to obtaining or retaining employment, and have the goal of returning to competitive employment.

On-the-job training programs

If you're looking at a job that offers on-the-job training (OJT) and you don't intend to use your GI Bill entitlement to go to college, you may still get some of the financial benefits associated with it. Here's how it works: The VA gives you a monthly housing allowance (MHA) and some cash for supplies while you're participating in on-the-job training, provided that you're working for an organization that's been VA-approved.

REMEMBER

The MHA comes from your GI Bill entitlement and counts against the total amount you're allowed for the lifetime of your GI Bill.

That money shows up in your bank account *in addition to* the wages you're earning through your OJT opportunity so you can advance in your field. Your MHA payments are tiered this way: If you have the Post-9/11 GI Bill, you get 100 percent of your MHA during your first six months of training. However, every six months that figure drops by 20 percent. That means in your second six months, you receive 80 percent of your MHA (and 60 percent in your third six months, 40 percent in your fourth six months, and so on). If you have any other GI Bill, you get 75 percent of the full-time GI Bill rate for your first six months of training, 55 percent of the full-time rate for your second six months, and 35 percent of your full-time GI Bill rate for the rest of your training period. You can collect your cash until the money runs out.

TECHNICAL
STUFF

The OJT benefit from your GI Bill doesn't count for training at a standard job; it only counts in jobs where OJT is common. That means subway operators, commercial pilots, detectives and criminal investigators, railroad conductors and yardmasters, and other, similar jobs that don't require apprenticeships (but that do require extensive training) can get you MHA from your GI Bill.

You're only eligible for payments while conducting OJT if you're a veteran, a spouse or child of a veteran who receives benefits through the Fry Scholarship or the Survivors and Dependents' Educational Assistance Program (I describe both in Chapter 23), or child of a veteran who is receiving transferred benefits from the Post-9/11 GI Bill. Spouses who are using transferred GI Bill benefits can't access these payments for OJT.

Non-Paid Work Experience program

The VA's Non-Paid Work Experience (NPWE) program is for veterans with a distinct career goal in mind and who learn best through hands-on training. It's particularly helpful to those vets struggling to find a job due to lack of experience (experience you can only get by — you guessed it — having a job). Through this program, you're not paid by the local, state, or federal agency that brings you on board; in that way, it's like an internship. However, if you participate in this program, you're entitled to a monthly subsistence allowance from the VA to help with your living expenses.

You can also view these internship programs as your proverbial foot in the door to government employment. The agency you intern for has the option to hire you directly (and noncompetitively, which is a special tool the government can use to hire someone it really wants; see Chapter 11). The proposition is relatively risk free for the government, too; it's only paying you a subsistence allowance, and the agency you work for doesn't have to pay anyone for your labor. If you strike out, the agency can simply bring in another intern — and if you knock it out of the park, the agency has its next employee vetted and ready to go.

Apprenticeship.gov

Just like its name implies, Apprenticeship.gov is an official program that helps veterans (and others) gain experience through apprenticeship with approved companies. If you participate in this program, you get paid to learn — and typically, the pay is pretty competitive. You also gain knowledge through on-the-job practice and job-related classroom training. After your apprenticeship is finished, you earn a portable credential in the industry. That means you can find a job at another company using all the things you learned at the company that gave you the apprenticeship (or you can stay in place, like about 92 percent of apprentices do). Some of the things you learn may even count as college credits, which can be helpful if you intend to go back to school in the future. And get this: The average starting salary of a former apprentice is $77,000 per year.

REMEMBER

Here's where it gets good for veterans: If you're eligible for the Post-9/11 GI Bill, you can take advantage of its housing allowance and stipend for books and supplies while you're learning as an apprentice. You still get paid for your apprenticeship work, too. And if you have a service-connected disability, you may be eligible for a customized apprenticeship program through the VR&E program.

Apprenticeships are available in a huge range of industries, including software development, IT, coding, healthcare, hospitality, electrical, plumbing, and carpentry. You can visit www.apprenticeship.gov/ and use its job search tool to see if any apprenticeships are available in a field that interests you, or you can check out the special programs for veterans here: www.apprenticeship.gov/career-seekers/service-members-and-veterans.

Veterans Employment and Training Service and CareerOneStop

The Veterans Employment and Training Service (VETS) is a U.S. Department of Labor program that gives you access to job listings, entrepreneurship programs, and other services through CareerOneStop (www.careeronestop.org/), which is a huge repository of information about getting back to work, changing careers, and more. CareerOneStop also gives you tools to find jobs similar to your military work. When you enter your military job title on the site, it returns similar civilian fields, typical job requirements, the career's outlook, and even links to jobs that match what you already know how to do.

You can also use it to get information on the following:

>> How-to instructions to help you get certifications in your field

>> Internships through federal and state government agencies (including active job listings for internships)

>> Professional development through networking, professional associations, and local training programs

>> Ways to set career goals, dig up salaries for jobs you may enjoy, and access to local resources based on where you live

Through the VETS program and legislation passed in 2014, the Department of Labor also requires American Job Centers — one-stop shops for employment training, career counseling, training referrals, job listings, and other employment services — to prioritize veterans. You can find more than 2,400 American Job Centers across the country so there's a good chance there's one near you. Refer to the later section, "Scouring State Employment Services," for more information about American Job Centers.

VA for Vets

The VA's Veteran Employment Program Office (VEPO) provides vets with a number of employment readiness programs, including

>> Job opportunities within the VA and other federal agencies

>> Recruitment and career readiness support

>> The Disabled Veterans Affirmative Action Program (DVAAP), which promotes the recruitment and hiring of injured and disabled veterans

VA for Vets is the "Gateway to VA Careers" under VEPO. It offers access to job listings within the VA for veterans and their spouses as well as other opportunities to work for the federal government. Its website, www.vaforvets.va.gov/, also offers training and resources that familiarize you with USAJobs (the federal government's official job website, which I cover in Chapter 11), shows you how to write an irresistible federal resume, and walks you through standard interview procedures so you can make a great impression on prospective employers. It even explains the federal hiring process in great detail so you know what to expect, including how to fill out and file the appropriate forms for government employment, how to claim veterans preference, and more.

My Next Move

My Next Move (www.mynextmove.org/), developed for veterans by the National Center for O*NET Development and sponsored by the U.S. Department of Labor/ Employment and Training Administration, is a web portal that helps veterans find out about their career options. You can explore the salaries for more than 900 different careers, discover required tasks and skills to perform each job, and find open job listings that interest you.

REMEMBER

This web portal is a one-stop shop for employment information when you're just testing the waters, whether you're still in the military or you already have a civilian job but want to make a change. If you're looking for jobs that relate to what you did in the military, you can use the site to find them by entering your military occupational specialty or rating. The site also classifies jobs and career fields according to their outlook, which refers to estimates of future demand across the United States using data from the Bureau of Labor Statistics; that information may help you determine whether a career field is the right long-term choice for you.

CTAP and ICTAP for government jobs

The U.S. government has special programs for "displaced" or "surplus" federal employees that were subject to reduction in force (or force shaping), separated due to a compensable injury, retired due to disability, or discontinued service. These programs offer special hiring preference to those who are eligible.

Career Transition Assistance Plan (CTAP)

The Career Transition Assistance Plan (CTAP) is an intra-agency program you can use to find a new job in the same agency. In order to be eligible for CTAP, you must apply for a new position by your official date of separation.

Interagency Career Transition Assistance Plan (ICTAP)

The Interagency Career Transition Assistance Plan (ICTAP) is an interagency program you can use to find a new job in a different agency. You must be in the local commuting area to apply for an ICTAP job, and the job must be offered to people outside the agency. You must apply for the job within one year of your separation except in certain circumstances, which are listed in the job description.

Eligibility for CTAP and ICTAP

These programs offer special hiring preference if you meet the following criteria:

>> You received a Reduction in Force (RIF) separation notice, a notice of proposed removal for declining a reassignment, or a certificate of expected separation, or if you have another official certification that indicates your position is surplus and that your employment is being terminated.

>> You're adequately qualified for the job.

>> The agency is accepting applications from people who are eligible for one of these programs.

Eligibility begins when you receive a notice that you'll be separated through a RIF. Though being CTAP- or ICTAP-eligible doesn't *guarantee* you a job, it does help you get an edge over other candidates who haven't been displaced from federal employment.

WARNING

If you're CTAP- or ICTAP-eligible and take a temporary job, you may lose your eligibility. That's because the other job means you're not faced with unemployment, which may signal to the government that you no longer need hiring priority. However, every case is different, so you should talk to the HR specialist overseeing the job you want to apply for to check.

Warriors to Workforce

The Warriors to Workforce (W2W) program from the Veterans Affairs Acquisition Academy gives vets an opportunity to start a career in the federal government. Designed to shorten the learning curve and give people a foot in the door, the W2W program trains people to become contract specialists. Program participants are hired directly as GS-5 government employees and earn educational credits while working. You can find out more at www.acquisitionacademy.va.gov/.

Personalized Career Planning and Guidance (VA Chapter 36)

The VA's Personalized Career Planning and Guidance (PCPG) program offers free career and educational guidance, planning, and a wide range of resources to veterans and their dependents. However, the veteran must be eligible for a VA education benefit to qualify (and for any dependents to qualify), and the veteran must have separated from active duty under conditions other than dishonorable within the past year. (It's also open to anyone who qualifies as a veteran or servicemember for educational assistance under a VA educational program as well as to active-duty servicemembers who have six months or fewer left on their military contracts). The PCPG program provides

>> Career counseling to help you decide what job is right for you

>> Educational counseling to help you find the right field of study or choose the ideal training program

>> Adjustment counseling to help you address barriers to your success

>> Resume support

>> Goal planning

Vets First Verification Program

The Office of Small & Disadvantaged Business Utilization (OSDBU) runs the Vets First Verification Program, which gives veteran business owners advantages when bidding on government contracts. You may also get some forms of tax relief, enhanced access to capital, extra support if your business is "poised for high growth and innovation," and support in finding VA procurements, contract awards, and acquisition resources. The VA also gives you specialized resources, education, training to help you learn how to do business with the VA (and other government agencies), and help building partnerships with other businesses and people who can help you succeed.

REMEMBER

Your company is eligible for Vets First if you — or another veteran at your company — are a veteran and meet all these requirements:

>> You own 51 percent or more of the company.

>> You have full control over your company's day-to-day management, decision-making, and strategic policy.

>> You have the necessary experience to manage the business.

>> You (or another veteran) are the highest-paid person in the company, or you can provide a written statement that explains why you making less helps your business.

>> You work full time for the business.

>> You hold the highest officer position in the company.

You may also be eligible to register your business as a service-disabled veteran-owned small business if you meet all the requirements previously listed *and* you have a VA disability rating letter that confirms you're rated somewhere between 0 and 100 percent, or if you have a disability letter from the DOD.

USMAP

The United Services Military Apprenticeship Program (https://usmap.osd.mil/) is similar to Apprenticeship.gov, but it's run by the DOD — and you don't complete your apprenticeship in a civilian company. Instead, you complete it while you work in your military job. The reason it's so beneficial is that through your military service, you can easily log 2,000 apprenticeship hours in a year and earn a journeyman's card before you even leave military service.

REMEMBER

There's a catch, though: USMAP is only open to current enlisted servicemembers who have a minimum of 12 months remaining on active duty (so if you're reading this book early in preparation for your transition, you're on the right track). You get all the benefits of your military pay (including housing allowance and basic allowance for subsistence), and you still report to work in your normal place of duty. You log your work hours and report them through the USMAP portal to earn your certification.

And don't worry if you're already out of the military and ineligible for USMAP. Instead, head to the section, "Apprenticeship.gov," earlier in this chapter to find information on how to jump into an apprenticeship with both feet while earning competitive civilian wages.

SkillBridge

The DOD's SkillBridge program is open only to active-duty servicemembers and National Guard and Reserve members on active-duty orders. It provides regular pay, allowances, and benefits while these servicemembers train for employment with a SkillBridge industry partner. *Industry partners* are companies that have agreed to allow servicemembers to participate in their workforces; the program doesn't cost the company anything because the DOD foots the bill.

The program is open to servicemembers of any rank, enlisted or officer (including warrant officers), as long as the servicemember is within their last 180 days of military service. If you're still on active duty, you can find out more about Skill-Bridge by visiting https://skillbridge.osd.mil/military-members.htm.

Support for dependents' employment

Many dependents of veterans with service-connected disabilities qualify for employment benefits through the VA, other government agencies, and civilian companies. Your state government likely has employment (and other) programs designed for veterans' spouses as well. These benefits may include things like career exploration programs, job training programs, and career counseling. And if the veteran family member is unable to use their veterans preference in employment (see Chapter 11), spouses, widows and widowers, and even parents of veterans may.

One notable program is Transition Employment Assistance for Military Spouses (TEAMS). Despite its name, veterans' spouses can also use it. The DOL sponsors this virtual workshop-packed program that offers guidance on career credentials, resume writing, self-marketing, and federal hiring. Workshops include how to create a LinkedIn profile and use it to find jobs, nail an interview, and negotiate a salary. You can read more at www.dol.gov/agencies/vets/programs/tap/teams-workshops.

EMPLOYERS GET TAX BREAKS FOR HIRING VETS

The federal government incentivizes employers to hire veterans. One program in particular, called the Special Employer Incentive (SEI) program, applies to companies that hire vets working through Veteran Readiness and Employment (VR&E). In this program, the government reimburses the employer up to 50 percent of the veteran's salary; it also pays for tools, equipment, uniforms, other supplies, and any workplace accommodations that need to be made so the veteran can work.

Additionally, some employers get great tax breaks and income tax credits when they employ veterans for at least 27 consecutive weeks. The same is true if a company hires a veteran who has received unemployment compensation for at least four weeks, a veteran who has received food stamp benefits, a wounded warrior, or an otherwise disabled veteran. Credits can be nearly $10,000 under the right circumstances, so it's no wonder many businesses are on the lookout for vets. (It's a win-win situation — you benefit, too, because you get a job with a steady paycheck.)

Special veterans programs from government agencies

Many federal, state, and local government agencies offer vets special preference in hiring, which I cover in Chapter 11. But vets may also qualify for *special hiring authorities*, which are pathways; they're like doors that open to make it easier for vets to enter government service. Here are some of the most common special hiring authorities for veterans:

>> **Veterans Recruitment Authority (VRA):** The VRA enables government agencies to appoint an eligible veteran without making that veteran compete against others for the position.

>> **Thirty Percent or More Disabled Veteran:** This authority permits government agencies to noncompetitively appoint any veteran who has a service-connected disability rated at 30 percent or greater.

>> **Veterans Employment Opportunities Act (VEOA):** The VEOA gives eligible veterans (including CTAP and ICTAP eligibles) a chance to compete for some positions that are ordinarily only available to current competitive service employees and some prior employees.

A number of other special hiring authorities may also apply to you, but they aren't restricted to veterans. For example, Schedule A Appointing Authority enables agencies to give preference to people with certain disabilities; the Pathways Programs (Internship, Recent Graduates, and Presidential Management Fellows) allow agencies to scout for recent high school and college graduates. Individual state governments may offer additional types of special hiring authorities. Usually, you can find out about these opportunities for veterans by visiting your state's employment agency's website.

Comparing Civilian Back-to-Work Programs for Vets

Civilian employers and organizations often have programs to put veterans to work. Sometimes these programs are run in conjunction with government agencies, and other times, they're completely civilian initiatives. Often, the civilian programs that help with employment aren't as concerned with a veteran's discharge status as government-based programs are. They're also more likely to provide employment assistance for veterans' spouses and other dependents. The following sections outline some of the most prominent programs.

Onward to Opportunity

Onward to Opportunity (O2O) is a free veterans career training program that provides professional certifications and employee support services. It offers dozens of in-classroom and web-based courses on topics related to information technology, business management, and customer service that lead to industry certifications. Those certifications can help you enter the workforce or change fields. The program also provides its participants with a direct connection to more than 400 military-friendly employers that are actively seeking new hires.

This program is available to veterans who are separated or retired from the military with an honorable discharge and their spouses. It's also available to active-duty servicemembers who are transitioning within the next six months and members of the National Guard and Reserves.

IVMF ARSENAL

The Institute for Veterans and Military Families (IVMF) at Syracuse University in partnership with J.P. Morgan Chase offers entrepreneurship programs to veterans and their spouses. The IVMF's program, ARSENAL, provides a wide range of services that includes one-day training events, workshops, and conferences that cover getting started in business, maintaining an existing business, and scaling a business to earn more. Special programs are geared toward women veterans, vets who have families they need to care for, and people who need more education before searching for a job. IVMF has a huge repository of resources for existing business owners who are ready for their companies to grow. You can find out more about IVMF entrepreneurship programs at `https://ivmf.syracuse.edu/programs/entrepreneurship/`.

Hire Heroes USA

Hire Heroes USA (`www.hireheroesusa.org/`) provides free job search help to veterans and their spouses; it's funded entirely through public donations and private grants. When you register with the organization, you get access to career coaching that helps you learn effective job search techniques, interviewing techniques, and even networking skills. You also get expert guidance in resume writing, the chance to take part in mock interviews, and even mentoring from professionals in your chosen field. The organization also connects veteran job seekers with companies that are actively hiring. As a veteran, you're automatically eligible to apply for help through this organization.

Hiring Our Heroes

Hiring Our Heroes (www.hiringourheroes.org/) hosts more than 50 hiring events each year, provides virtual and in-person networking opportunities, and holds virtual training programs that can help you find and hold a job (including leadership training). The organization also connects vets with internship programs and skills training in a wide range of fields, including data analytics, solar and renewable energy, Salesforce and applied technology, and IT support. It offers opportunities for you to earn Google Career Certificates in a range of digital fields. Many of the services HOH provides are open to all vets, and some are open to veterans' spouses as well.

Veterans Career Program by PVA

Paralyzed Veterans of America (https://pva.org/) runs the Veterans Career Program; they call it a "high-touch" program because you work directly with employment analysts and vocational rehabilitation counselors to overcome employment barriers and other obstacles that affect your ability to find or keep a job. Unlike many other programs, you receive one-on-one support every step of the way; they'll even help you write your resume (and cover letters), practice interview skills, and create an effective profile on LinkedIn. According to the PVA, more than 80 percent of the people who work with them stay in their positions for more than a year. You don't have to be a paralyzed veteran to get help from the PVA; they offer free employment support and vocational counseling to veterans (and their caregivers).

Veterati

Sponsored by USAA, Veterati (www.veterati.com/) is a mentorship platform that connects veteran job seekers to mentors who can coach and guide them throughout their entire search for employment. Signing up for mentorship is free, and when you do, you can start connecting with mentors immediately. You can connect with any number of mentors, and they can answer your questions about everything from what it's like to work at a Fortune 500 company to how to negotiate a salary after you get a job offer. All the mentors are successful professionals who have specialized expertise.

American Corporate Partners Mentoring program

American Corporate Partners (ACP) (www.acp-usa.org/) is a nationwide nonprofit that helps veterans find their next adventure through mentoring, networking, and career advice. They offer a women's veterans' mentoring program and an online community where you can get advice on job searches, networking, small business development, and leadership. You work one-on-one with a mentor who can review your resume and help you prepare for your next job interview. The help is free, but you do have to apply to participate.

American Legion's Veterans Career Center

The American Legion is a veterans service organization that provides employment assistance through training and resources, including American Legion–supported career fairs and other events. It has relationships with a number of employers that hire veterans, including Lockheed Martin, Northrop Grumman, Synchrony Financial, Oracle, and other big-name companies. You can check out its career-help section here: www.legion.org/.

AMVETS Career Services

AMVETS (https://amvets.org/) runs a service called America's Virtual OneStop. It contains labor market information, employment and wage data, career tips, and a learning center filled with self-paced training videos and tutorials. AMVETS also has career centers with career coaches and job placement services all across the United States.

DAV employment resources

Disabled American Veterans (www.dav.org/) regularly holds job fairs all over the country open only to vets, transitioning military members, and the spouses of each. The employers who attend DAV events are on the lookout for job-seeking vets, and they encourage participants to bring resumes for immediate consideration. The DAV also runs the Patriot Boot Camp for entrepreneurs, an intensive program that connects vets and their spouses to mentors, educational programming, and other important resources related to owning your own business. You don't have to be a member of the DAV to participate, nor do you have to be disabled — but you do have to apply to be accepted into the program.

VFW employment services

Veterans of Foreign Wars (www.vfw.org/) has a number of tools that help vets find employment, including the Veteran Employment Tools Program. You're eligible if you're transitioning out of the military or have separated within the last year, want to become an automotive technician, and have (or will have) an honorable discharge. Other than the VET Program, the VFW offers resume and interview tips, plus connections with other services and resources that can help you find your next job.

Wounded Warrior Project's Warriors to Work

The Wounded Warrior Project (www.woundedwarriorproject.org/) specializes in career transition and development for injured veterans through its Warriors to Work program. If you're enrolled in the program, which is completely free to you, you get access to career counseling and job placement opportunities based on your qualifications and assistance writing a resume. Furthermore, you get help preparing for interviews, learn about salary negotiation, and access to networking opportunities to further your career. The program is also available to family support members who are older than 18. You must be registered with the Wounded Warrior Project to participate.

Scouring State Employment Services

All 50 states, Puerto Rico, Guam, American Samoa, and the U.S. Virgin Islands have American Job Centers, and those centers provide all kinds of assistance to job seekers. As a veteran, you get *priority of service*, which means you get first access to new job listings (typically 24 hours before they're visible to the general public), skills assessments, and resume assistance. You even get interview coaching so you can impress prospective employers.

A number of American Job Centers also have outreach programs for disabled veterans (particularly those who have service-connected disabilities). Additionally, local veterans' employment representatives work within most American Job Centers to reach out to employers, hold workshops, and coordinate with unions, apprenticeship programs, and businesses to help vets find successful employment.

Every state also has a state job bank, which is typically run by the state's Department of Labor. Employers typically post jobs to their state job bank, and you may be able to submit your resume when you register at your state's. Registration is free, and you can browse jobs and, in many cases, apply directly with employers. You can find yours by searching your state at www.careeronestop.org/, the federal Department of Labor's employment assistance website.

IN THIS CHAPTER

» **Capitalizing on veterans' preference**

» **Zeroing in on the jobs you want**

» **Putting together a federal resume**

» **Understanding assessment and selection**

» **Earning credit toward retirement through military service**

Chapter **11**

Transitioning from the Military to More Government Employment

Lots of veterans make a beeline for federal, state, or local government employment after leaving the military, and it's no wonder: The government offers benefits you're unlikely to find elsewhere. From taking your Thrift Savings Plan with you to your next job to getting all the free healthcare you can handle, transitioning out of the military and diving right back into government employment may make sense. Government agencies love hiring veterans, and sometimes they even give vets preference over other candidates. Even if you've been out of the military for a while, you have a handful of advantages thanks to your veteran status, which this chapter explains.

Eyeing the Types of Government Jobs

You can find federal government jobs in two places: USAJobs and on specific agency websites. If you know you want to get into a civil service career but aren't sure where to start, use USAJobs (www.usajobs.gov/). It's Uncle Sam's official hiring website, so just about every federal agency advertises job openings there. However, specific agency websites sometimes contain job opportunities that aren't listed on USAJobs.

REMEMBER

The three types of federal government jobs are competitive service, excepted service, and senior executive service. The type of job determines whether you qualify and how the hiring process works. Here's a bit more about each:

>> **Competitive service:** These jobs are those subject to civil service laws passed by Congress that ensure all candidates and employees are treated fairly during the hiring process. People send in resumes and participate in interviews before being hired.

>> **Excepted service:** These include any federal or civil service jobs that aren't in the competitive service or the senior executive service. Excepted service jobs aren't subject to the same pay, appointment, or classification rules that competitive service jobs are, which means government agencies offering them may choose to do things like hire people only from their own organization.

>> **Senior executive service:** These jobs are leadership positions, such as managerial, supervisory, and policy positions. Generally, these jobs are just below presidential appointees, and they serve as the link between the appointees and the federal workforce. Job titles such as executive director, senior executive leader, and chief of staff typically fall into this category.

Each state — as do localities — has its own system for classifying government jobs, but many operate the same way the federal system does. You can visit your state's employment website to see what positions are open.

Using Your Veterans' Preference

Your service in the military gave you the right to claim *veterans' preference* in some situations. The government applies veterans' preference in a few ways that I cover in the following sections. Some states even offer absolute preference to veterans.

Claiming veterans' preference points

The most common form of veterans' preference is the point system. In the point system, you're awarded zero, five, or ten points based on the circumstances of your military service and discharge.

The point system doesn't move you to the front of the hiring line (though a special hiring authority called *Veterans Recruitment Appointment* does, which I explain in the section, "Getting in the door with a Veterans Recruitment Appointment"). Preference points are only applicable when an agency uses a numerical category rating or ranking system to find the best-qualified applicants for a position.

Here's how it works:

1. Before a government agency puts a job announcement online, the hiring manager and the agency's HR department define the levels of qualification that they intend to use to group applicants.

That makes the whole hiring process more manageable.

EXAMPLE

If the job announcement says a bachelor's degree is required, all applicants whose applications don't mention a bachelor's degree are removed. The applications that do note a bachelor's degree move on to the next round. It's like that with every minimum qualification; applications end up in the recycle bin if they fail to show that the applicant is qualified for the job.

2. The HR personnel assigned to the job announcement decide whether each remaining applicant is best-qualified, well-qualified, or just plain qualified.

They may sort them based on exam scores (if the job application process requires applicants to take a civil service exam) or based on a questionnaire that the agency has developed to weed out people who aren't qualified (often considered an *experience and education evaluation*).

If fewer than three names are in the best-qualified category after scoring is complete, HR can combine them with the names in the well-qualified category. Then, HR sends a certification list to the hiring manager for the position. Veterans are put at the top of the list for each category, above those who aren't veterans. There's one exception, though: If the job is a professional or scientific position at Grade GS-09 or higher, HR doesn't have to put a veteran at the top of the list. (Eligible vets still get their points, though — they're just listed above other applicants who have the same rating.)

Veterans who have a 10 percent or higher disability rating are put into the best-qualified category — but remember, this step occurs after HR has already determined they meet at least the minimum qualifications for the job. In other words, this isn't a shortcut to getting a job you're not qualified to perform. It's just a shortcut to the top of the entire resume pile. If two or more veterans are in the best-qualified category, HR settles it the only reasonable way they can: a trial by combat. (Just kidding. They simply forward all the best-qualified applications to the hiring manager, who's then responsible for conducting interviews to sort it out.)

TIP

If you find a job announcement listed twice (one open to the public and one open to veterans), apply to *both*. Hiring managers often receive lists of qualified candidates from both announcements, and they can choose to use one or the other (or both) when choosing which candidates to interview. If a hiring manager uses a list that comes from a job that's open to the general public and you only applied to the announcement for veterans, your name won't be on it.

The following sections break down veterans' preference points and how they help you land a government job.

WARNING

Retirees only qualify for veterans' preference if they're disabled or retired below the rank of major (or its equivalent). Otherwise, you don't get an edge in hiring.

0-point preference

If you're a *sole survivor*, you qualify for preference without points if you served in the armed forces and were released after August 29, 2008. That means your sibling (or more than one sibling) was in the military and was killed; died as a result of wounds, accident, or disease; is in a captured or missing in action status; or is permanently 100 percent disabled or hospitalized on a continuing basis (and isn't employed because of the disability or hospitalization).

Though no points are awarded, if you're 0-point preference eligible, you're still entitled to be listed ahead of people who aren't preference-eligible, but who are in the same quality category or who scored the same as you did on an examination.

5-point preference

You're eligible for 5-point preference if you served on active duty in any of the following:

>> For more than 180 consecutive days (not counting training), and any part of that service occurred between September 11, 2001 and August 31, 2010.

>> For any length of time between August 2, 1990 and January 2, 1992.

>> For more than 180 consecutive days (not counting training) between January 31, 1955 and October 15, 1976.

>> Between April 28, 1952 and July 1, 1955.

>> For any length of time in a war, campaign, or expedition for which a campaign medal or badge has been authorized.

10-point preference

You may claim 10-point veterans' preference if you served at any time and have a service-connected disability or received a Purple Heart. If you claim 10-point preference, you must fill out and file Form SF-15 and include it with your application.

Getting in the door with a Veterans Recruitment Appointment

Veterans Recruitment Appointment (VRA) enables government agencies to directly appoint veterans for jobs without the vet having to compete against anyone else. However, it only applies to jobs in Grade GS-11 and below, so you're not going to become the chief of staff of a government agency right off the bat. And if you apply for a job under VRA, you still have to qualify for the job.

You may be able to score a job under VRA if you meet any of the following:

>> You have a campaign badge for service during a war or in a campaign or expedition.

>> You're a disabled veteran.

>> You have earned a medal for participation in a military operation.

>> You separated from the military within the past three years under honorable or general conditions.

These types of jobs are considered *excepted service appointments*. That means federal agencies aren't required to list them on USAJobs. You may only find them on individual agencies' websites or hear about them through word-of-mouth.

TIP

If you apply for a job that's eligible for VRA and others as well, annotate "VRA" on your application (possibly in your cover letter) or otherwise point out that you're a veteran. Doing so won't guarantee that you get the job, but it will let the hiring official know that they can fast-forward the process to hire you.

WHAT ABOUT THE VETERANS OPPORTUNITY TO WORK ACT?

Thanks to the Veterans Opportunity to Work Act (VOW), you can apply for government jobs before you're even discharged from the military. Signed into law by President Barack Obama, this act enables people who are almost out of the military to apply for jobs using veterans' preference, even without having a discharge document on-hand. In fact, under the VOW Act, federal agencies are required to treat active-duty servicemembers as veterans and preference eligibles, provided that they turn in a certification saying that they expect to be discharged or released from active-duty service under honorable conditions within the next 120 days and receive the same veterans' preference they would if they had their DD-214.

TIP

If you want a job at a specific agency but can't find one online, contact that agency's hiring office. Tell them that you want to be considered for any VRA–eligible positions and see what they tell you to do next.

Having the law on your side with VEOA

The Veterans Employment Opportunities Act (VEOA) of 1998 lets veterans apply to merit promotion job announcements they wouldn't ordinarily be eligible to apply for. *Merit promotion jobs* are those that are only open to people who are current and former federal employees. To be eligible for VEOA, your latest military discharge must be under honorable or general conditions, and you must either be considered a preference eligible or a veteran who completed three or more years of active service.

REMEMBER

You don't get to use veterans' preference points when applying for a job that accepts applications from VEOA candidates. The fact that you're allowed to apply is your veterans' preference.

Applying as a 30 percent or more disabled vet

Federal agencies can noncompetitively appoint any veteran who has a 30 percent or greater service–connected disability. If that's you, you can be tapped for any term position in any grade without competing with other people for the job. You're eligible if you meet one of these qualifications:

>> You're retired from active-duty service with a service-connected disability rating of 30 percent or more.

>> You have a rating from the VA showing a compensable service-connected disability of 30 percent or more.

Having absolute preference

A few states are so serious about hiring veterans that they've instructed their governments to give vets *absolute preference*. If a veteran meets the minimum qualifications for a job and passes qualifying exams, they're placed higher on the list of eligibles than everyone else is. That's how it works in Massachusetts, New Jersey, South Dakota, and Pennsylvania. Some of these states extend absolute preference to spouses and surviving spouses, and New Jersey even extends it to the parent of any veteran who died in service.

Putting Together a Government Resume

Dozens of great books go into detail about putting together a government resume (one of them is *Military Transition For Dummies* by yours truly — John Wiley & Sons, Inc.), as well as plenty of online resources. USAJobs even has a federal resume builder you can use as you apply for positions, so I won't bore you with a list of do's and don'ts here.

TIP

The single-most important thing you can do to get your resume noticed is to tailor it to each job you apply for using keywords from the job announcement. That means if the job announcement says that you need to do things like adjust standardized recipes for large-quantity cooking, prepare special-diet entrees, and work with an agitating kettle, you should address each of those things in your resume (as long as you're truthful).

TIP

Create your basic resume in a Word document. Then, when you apply to federal jobs, use USAJobs' resume builder by copying and pasting the appropriate information to the right places. That way, you can easily edit your resume to match each job description without having to start from scratch.

Your resume is the only way to get past the HR specialist and into a hiring manager's purview. Putting together a federal resume that gets noticed takes a long time because you have to go back-and-forth between the job description and your document, but the payoff (a shiny, new government job) can be tremendous.

Weighing Government Pay Scales

Like the military, the government pays based on a person's pay grade. Different agencies use different pay systems, though the *General Schedule (GS)* is most common. The GS system, like many other pay systems, operates on grades. Each grade has ten steps, each with a pay increase. Salaries under the GS system are two-part: your base pay and locality pay, which helps offset the cost of living in the area.

Other pay systems in the government are the *Federal Wage System (FWS)*, *General Law (GL)*, *Foreign Service (FS)*, and the SES pay schedule. You can find all these pay tables online if you're interested in how much you may make (just make sure to enter the locality when you search).

Understanding Assessment and Selection

You were in the military, so you know that the government operates in weeks, not days. That's true when it comes to hiring, too. The Office of Personnel Management sets the rules on how agencies evaluate and select candidates, and it requires government agencies to be extremely careful in hiring. I suspect that's because it's so tough to fire government employees — a bad hiring decision can stick around for decades. With that said, it takes a long time because the process requires several steps, which I discuss here.

Making the grade on assessment

Government agencies use all kinds of tools to assess applicants before hiring managers invest time in any one candidate. One of those tools is the *occupational assessment questionnaire*, which is a self-assessment of your special circumstances (such as whether you're using veterans' preference) and your qualifications. You may also be required to take a civil service test as part of your application.

Landing an interview

If your application makes it past the HR gatekeeper, the hiring manager for the position will review your resume and may call you for an in-person or video interview. Sometimes it's one-on-one, and other times, it's with a panel. You may have to go through more than one interview.

REMEMBER

Many government agencies use structured situational or behavioral interviews. These interviews include questions that begin with "Tell me about a time you . . ." or "What would you do if . . ." The interviewer asks you several questions and scores your responses, then ranks your scores against other interviewees' scores.

Winning your spot after an interview

If you're the hiring manager's first choice after your interview — or if you're their second, third, or subsequent choice and everyone ahead of you has declined the position — you receive a tentative job offer, or TO.

When you receive a TO, which comes from HR (not the person you interviewed with), it may be verbal or written. At that point, *ask to negotiate your step or grade* (both of which determine your salary). You may negotiate on one of two bases:

>> **Your current salary:** If you currently make more than the position pays, you can let HR know that you want salary-matching.

>> **Your superior qualifications for the job:** If you don't make more but you *want* to, and if your resume supports it, you can negotiate based on superior qualifications.

The HR rep you work with is on your side. They know the hiring manager wants you, and they want to help you maximize your earnings. And don't worry — they won't rescind your TO just because you asked for a higher salary. They expect you to negotiate. Also, hiring managers and HR must provide a valid reason for rescinding a TO after it's been issued, and a request to negotiate isn't it.

WARNING

Don't pass up the chance to negotiate your grade or step because you won't get it again. You may only negotiate the first time you enter federal service (and the military doesn't count). It's exactly like asking a military recruiter to put you in as an E-4 rather than an E-1. The one exception is when you switch government jobs; you may ask your new agency to match what your former agency paid you.

Untying the attached strings

A tentative offer comes with strings attached. You must usually complete several tasks, and if you fail to do so, you don't get the job. These tasks might include going through a credit or background check, obtaining a security clearance, or providing additional information (such as proof of your credentials). After you jump through Uncle Sam's hoops, you receive a formal job offer, or FO.

Getting Credited for Military Service

If you left the military before retirement, you may benefit from the Military Buy-back Program, which credits you for your active-duty service. This program gives you credit for your prior service so you can retire earlier. It also lets you earn a little bit more in your retirement checks — the government adds 1 percent for every year of creditable service to your High-3 salary, which is how federal retirement pay is calculated (see Chapter 8 for a detailed explanation of how that system works).

REMEMBER

There's a price, though: To take advantage of the Military Buyback Program, you must make a deposit totaling 7 percent of the military basic pay you earned on active duty, plus interest. You can make a lump-sum payment or set up an installment plan where payments are deducted from your paycheck. Your agency's HR department can give you the skinny on this valuable program for veterans.

Chapter **12**

Building Your Own Business with Veterans Benefits

What do Nike, FedEx, GoDaddy, Sport Clips, Esurance, and ID.me have in common? They were all founded by veterans — and if you have the desire, resources, and abilities to join their ranks, your veteran status can help you get started. Whether you're interested in setting up a simple side hustle, you're on the verge of inventing the next big thing, or you want to build a Fortune 500 company from the ground up, you're not alone.

Somewhere in the neighborhood of 2.4 million veterans own their own businesses, and those businesses employ about 6 million people. According to the Small Business Administration (SBA), veterans are 45 percent more likely than nonveterans to be self-employed. And who can blame them? After working in lockstep for years (sometimes decades), the thought of working for yourself is refreshing. As a business owner, you can follow your passions, achieve financial independence, control your schedule, and use your creativity to get ahead. This chapter looks at all the government programs (and some on the civilian side) you can take advantage of as a business-minded veteran.

Stepping through the Veteran Entrepreneur Portal

The Veteran Entrepreneur Portal (www.va.gov/osdbu/entrepreneur/index.asp), run by the Office of Small and Disadvantaged Business Utilization (OSDBU), is a one-stop shop for accessing federal services that can help you launch a business and keep it running smoothly. The services you find through the portal can help you cut to the chase and find financing, apply for federal contracts, and even teach you how to do business with federal agencies.

REMEMBER

The Veteran Entrepreneur Portal includes information and resources that come directly from the VA, the SBA, and a few other agencies. You can use the portal to do the following:

>> Discover how to build a business from the ground up.

>> Find funding to support your start-up or grow a business you've already started.

>> Explore leadership training and learn how to manage daily operations.

>> Get connected with customers.

>> Locate contracting opportunities with the federal government.

>> Apply for certification as a veteran-owned business.

>> Dive into networking and partnership programs.

>> Find and apply for training and employment programs designed specifically for veterans.

You don't have to sign up for an account to access the portal, though you may need to apply for certain benefits or to use certain resources.

Visiting the SBA's Office of Veterans Business Development

The SBA's Office of Veterans Business Development (OVBD) has a huge number of resources available to vets. I cover them in the following sections.

TIP

The SBA can directly connect you with local resources to kick-start your business. Visit www.sba.gov/local-assistance and enter your ZIP Code to get access to resources near you.

Boots to Business program

Transitioning service members, veterans of all eras, and their spouses are entitled to use the SBA's Boots to Business program (www.sba.gov/sba-learning-platform/boots-business). This program centers on its "Introduction to Entrepreneurship" course, which teaches you the fundamentals of starting and running your own business. It even covers tips on how to develop a business plan and gives you an inside track to SBA resources you can use along the way. Some sessions are in person, and some are online. After you complete the cornerstone course, you may choose to further your entrepreneurship education through additional classes — and it's all completely free.

Dog Tag Fellowship program

Funded and supported by the SBA and the Wounded Warrior Project, the Dog Tag Fellowship program is a five-month course where fellows — people selected to participate in the program — explore career paths, find out about potential resources, and develop plans for their future businesses. You don't need your GI Bill or any other military benefits to participate; in fact, you receive a monthly stipend and don't pay anything for program related expenses.

After you complete your fellowship, you receive a certificate from Georgetown University or Loyola University–Chicago (depending on where you're located). You may be eligible to apply for the program if you're a Post-9/11 veteran with service-connected disabilities, an active service member within six months of transition, or a Guard or Reserve member. (All military-affiliated spouses are eligible, regardless of the servicemember's disability rating.)

Entrepreneurship Bootcamp for Veterans

The Entrepreneurship Bootcamp for Veterans (EBV) is a 39-day learning experience run by a number of big-name universities. It kicks off with a 30-day online and instructor-led business fundamentals course that's followed by a nine-day residency at one of the eight EBV schools. You also get 12 months of continuing support focused on the creation and growth of your small business. The best part? It's *free*, including travel and lodging for your short residency. (Your residency may take place at one of eight consortium schools.) You must apply for acceptance; EBV is only open to Post-9/11 veterans with honorable discharges. Find out more about this program (and others) at https://ivmf.syracuse.edu/programs/entrepreneurship/start-up/ebv/.

The EBV has a sister program, too. The Entrepreneurship Bootcamp for Veterans Families (EBV-F) offers small business training to first-degree family members (spouses, parents, siblings, and adult children) of post-9/11 veterans and those who have service-connected disabilities, as well as surviving spouses of deceased military members.

Hiring Our Heroes program

Designed to help veterans find meaningful employment opportunities, the U.S. Chamber of Commerce Foundation's Hiring Our Heroes program offers workshops, virtual community meetings, and in-person networking events that veteran business owners can use to make connections. The organization's hiring events are open to all veterans and their spouses (as well as to active-duty troops). If you can't make it to an event, don't stress — you can use the Virtual Job Scout at www.virtualjobscout.org/ and find out more about other resources at www.hiringourheroes.org/.

LiftFund

Based in San Antonio, Texas, the LiftFund offers learning resources through the Women Veterans Entrepreneurship Training (WVET) Program. The organization's in-person workshops and training sessions all take place in Texas, but they offer webinars on running a business remotely, how to plan your transition into entrepreneurship, and what women vets need to know about accessing capital. The WVET Program also runs LiftLearn, a free online learning platform that gives you tools to start or grow your company. You can find out more at www.liftfund.com/wvet/.

Riata Center for Entrepreneurship's Veterans Entrepreneurship Program

Oklahoma State University's Spears School of Business runs the Veterans Entrepreneurship Program (VEP), which is completely free (including instructional materials, travel expenses, lodging, and meals). This three-phase boot camp covers concept development, an eight-day trip to Stillwater, Oklahoma, and five months of advising from entrepreneurs and subject-matter experts. The first and third phases are entirely virtual.

REMEMBER

Honorably discharged vets (and those currently separating from active duty) are eligible regardless of prior educational experiences, and preference is given to those with service-connected disabilities. Applicants are required to turn in two letters of recommendation, a list of military honors (read: awards and decorations), and a personal statement that explains why they want to participate. You have to sell yourself to qualify; the application also asks you about your personal characteristics, qualifications, and long-term goals. You can discover more at `https://business.okstate.edu/riata/vep_eligibility.html`.

SCORE

The SBA partners with SCORE, is the largest network of volunteer business mentors in the United States. Though not only open to veterans, this program can connect you with free, area-specific advice in your community through email, phone, and video chats. It also provides free training, on-demand courses, webinars, online workshops, and a packed online library full of resources that can help you launch a new venture. Find out more at `www.sba.gov/local-assistance/resource-partners/score-business-mentoring`.

Small Business Development Centers

The SBA's Small Business Development Centers (SBDCs) are local community resource centers. Though they're not exclusively for veterans, you can use SBDC programs to get individualized business advising and technical assistance, help solving problems, access capital, and just about every other aspect of entrepreneurship. You can find an SBDC near you: `www.sba.gov/local-assistance/resource-partners/small-business-development-centers-sbdc`.

Veteran Institute for Procurement

The Veteran Institute for Procurement (VIP) is an in-depth training program for owners, principals, and certain executives of service-disabled and veteran-owned small businesses. The training is completely free and covers federal procurement — the process by which the federal government obtains the goods and services it needs from commercial businesses. If you intend to get government contracts in the future, this program can give you the tools you need to do so. You can get more information at `https://nationalvip.org/`.

Veterans Business Outreach Center program

The SBA's Veterans Business Outreach Center (VBOC) program caters to vets, Guard and Reserve members, transitioning servicemembers, and their spouses. It offers pre-business plan workshops that help you use online resources, concept assessments that give you a clear picture of your entrepreneurial needs, business plan development and preparation, and even a *feasibility analysis* that helps you evaluate how likely your business plan is to succeed.

You can also use the VBOC to access free entrepreneurial training and counseling with other SBA resource partners (including programs designed especially for service-disabled vets, women veterans, and veterans interested in procurement). Like many other programs, VBOC connects veterans with qualified mentors and offers special training in areas such as international trade, Internet marketing, accounting, franchising, and more. You can discover more about at `www.sba.gov/local-assistance/resource-partners/veterans-business-outreach-center-vboc-program`.

Veteran Women Igniting the Spirit of Entrepreneurship

Veteran Women Igniting the Spirit of Entrepreneurship (V-WISE) is a training program in entrepreneurship and small business management designed for women veterans, as well as women military spouses and partners. It receives some funding from the SBA and some from corporate partners, and it's run by Syracuse University's D'Aniello Institute for Veterans and Military Families.

This three-phase program features a 15-day online course, a three-day residency experience, and 12 months of ongoing support focused on small business creation and growth. It's not free, but the registration fee is pretty reasonable and includes educational materials, two nights of lodging during the residency (and most meals while you're there). However, participants are responsible for getting to and from the conference. It's open to honorably discharged women veterans of any military branch or service era, including the Guard and Reserves; active-duty women servicemembers; and veterans' women spouses and partners. The Phase II residency events take place at various locations across the United States throughout the year, and about 65 percent of V-WISE graduates have started or grown their businesses. You can get more information on this program at `https://ivmf.syracuse.edu/programs/entrepreneurship/start-up/v-wise/`.

VetNet

Run by Syracuse University, VetNet offers free, regular webinars on topics that help veteran entrepreneurs, such as marketing, project management, and accounting. They also work with experts to create videos on personal branding, research, and a wide range of other topics that can help you launch a successful startup. You can watch the webinars at your own pace, and there's no requirement to complete any of them. Check out this program at `https://ivmf.syracuse.edu/programs/entrepreneurship/resources/vetnet/`.

Women's Business Centers

The SBA's Women's Business Centers provide free and low-cost counseling and training to women who want to start, grow, or expand small businesses. Their services aren't limited to veterans, but vets can make use of the tools and training available to launch new businesses and ensure those businesses are competitive. You can take training programs on accessing federal contracts as well as getting credit and capital. Find your nearest WBC at `www.sba.gov/local-assistance/resource-partners/womens-business-centers`.

Miscellaneous resources for veterans

The federal government has a number of miscellaneous programs designed to help veterans in unique situations. Here are a few that can give you a hand up when you need it:

>> **Surplus Personal Property for Veteran-Owned Small Businesses:** This program lets veteran-owned small businesses access federally owned personal property that the government is no longer using. The General Services Administration donates property to states that then can distribute it to veteran-owned small businesses for free. The only catch is that you must use it; you can't sell it for a specific period of time.

>> **EEOC Small Business Center:** The Equal Employment Opportunity Commission (EEOC) maintains a Small Business Resource Center that gives you information on how to keep records regarding employment, post information about discrimination laws, and handle special requests from employees to keep your company on the right side of the law.

>> **Military Reservist Economic Injury Disaster Loan Program:** This program lends up to $2 million to businesses that can't meet necessary and ordinary operating expenses because they lost an essential employee to an active-duty call-up. These loans come from the SBA.

>> **National Veteran Small Business Coalition:** This organization isn't free to join, but it does deliver some free resources to individuals, such as training events jointly hosted with reps from major corporations (including those that do business with the federal government).

Eyeing Labor Department Programs

The U.S. Department of Labor (DOL) has a handful of programs designed to help veterans start their own businesses (as well as a number of programs that assist veterans in getting to work for other people at any point after leaving military service — many of which I cover in Chapter 10). I explain these programs in the following sections.

DOL VETS Veteran Trucker resources

Thanks to the DOL, vets who choose to be truck drivers — whether working for themselves or someone else — are eligible for a waiver on the commercial driver's license (CDL) skills test at the state level. Some states also waive knowledge tests for qualified veterans, which I explain in Chapter 26. In addition to the test waivers, the DOL runs the 90-Day Trucking Apprenticeship Challenge, which encourages employers to expand their existing trucking apprenticeship programs and accelerate the time-to-hire necessary to bring in qualified drivers.

Off-Base Transition Training program

The DOL's Off-Base Transition Training (OBTT) program is open to veterans and their spouses. Comprised of workshops that let you combine the skills you learned in the service with the skills you need in the private sector, some aspects of the program can help entrepreneurs. For example, workshops cover employment rates, LinkedIn profiles, and marketing yourself. You can find out more at www.dol.gov/agencies/vets/programs/tap/off-base-transition-training.

Exploring the VA's OSDBU

The VA's Office of Small and Disadvantaged Business Utilization (OSDBU) hosts a number of events each month to help vets dive into entrepreneurship. The events include conferences, live training sessions, and webinars on a wide range of topics, including things like how to create an effective capability statement, how to work through the procurement process, how to use social media to grow your business, and what makes a website resonate with customers and clients. Workshops cover a range of topics from teaming and subcontracting, risk mitigation, and more.

The OSDBU also runs the Direct Access Program (DAP), which offers opportunities for veteran small business owners to build partnerships, network, and meet procurement decision-makers — the people who choose which businesses the federal government should work with. You can sign up for live or virtual events using the VA's VetBiz website at `www.vetbiz.va.gov/events`.

The same office gives you resources and tools to figure out how to do business with the VA itself. Small business liaisons work at the VA who can give you all the information you need to throw your company's hat in the ring for VA contracts. You can also access *learning sessions* online covering topics such as the process for submitting required business documents to get a VA contract, becoming a prime government contractor, and more. You can dive right into these learning sessions at `www.va.gov/osdbu/outreach/soc/learning-sessions.asp`.

Treating Yourself to VETRN

The VETRN (`https://vetrn.org/`) program is free to participants, but to qualify, you must be prior service or a family member of a vet. Your company must have already been in business for at least a year and have a minimum annual revenue of $75,000 to apply for this 14-session training curriculum, which lasts 28 weeks and is based on the NXLevel Guide to Growing Your Business. You get assigned to a mentor at the beginning of the program, and many sessions feature guest speakers from the legal, marketing, and finance communities.

Shoring Up Your Skills with Bunker Labs

Bunker Labs (`https://bunkerlabs.org/`) is a 501(c)(3) nonprofit organization that connects vets and military spouses with a thriving support community. They have programs and courses for vets at all stages of entrepreneurship:

- **Veterans in Residence:** This business incubator is for startups in their earliest days. The program puts business-owning vets in shared coworking and virtual spaces together so they can make connections and hold each other accountable for success. When you participate, you're required to attend weekly huddles with your cohort (which comprises the same group of people from start to finish) as well as attend monthly masterclasses in business topics. It's all free.

- **CEOcircle:** This free program is an executive cohort of people running growth-stage companies that are ready to scale. Founders and execs of companies that have significant revenue and a little traction in the market participate in virtual monthly meetings and, sometimes, quarterly in-person meetings, for a year.

- **Launch Lab:** This gamified entrepreneurship education platform helps you evaluate your readiness to start a business, figure out who your target customers are, and zero in on your unique value proposition (as well as how to share the information with the people who can buy your products or services).

- **Finances for Military Founders and Families:** This partnership with USAA teaches you how to budget, manage debt and accrue savings, and reach your business financial goals. The free course covers three sessions about stepping into entrepreneurship.

- **Business Basics Course:** This is a path forward for people who are certain they want to start a business and already have an idea. This five-part course covers everything from creating a business structure to getting your first ten customers.

Making Corporate Connections

The VA maintains connections with commercial companies all over the United States that promote veteran-owned and other small businesses. These companies tend to give significant discounts to veterans businesses and often give vets priority on specialized contracts. Some of the companies that the VA works with in this capacity include General Dynamics, Northrop Grumman, and AT&T. You can get a full list and information on the companies that partner with the VA to provide veterans with special opportunities on the OSDBU's website (`www.va.gov/OSDBU`).

Finding Franchising Opportunities

If you've ever seen or eaten at a restaurant with a plaque that says something like, "This store owned and operated by Joe Snuffy," you've patronized a franchise — and for some business owners, franchising is the way to go. The VA and the SBA both have online resources to teach vets about franchising opportunities, including complete rundowns on how franchising works.

If your curiosity is piqued after you take a peek at these agencies' educational materials on franchising, visit VetFran (www.vetfran.org/). This free directory lists vet-friendly franchising opportunities, and it offers all kinds of guidance that goes far beyond what the VA and SBA have to say. You can use the VetFran website to browse more than 600 member companies that are specifically looking for veterans to set up their franchises, search by industry or company name, or sort companies by how much money they require to franchise. They even list home-based franchise opportunities. The best part? Many of the companies listed in VetFran's directory offer tens of thousands of dollars (!) off initial franchise fees to qualified veterans.

Chapter **13**

Bringing Receipts: Using Your GI Bill

When you go to school after leaving the military, whether you've been in for 3 years or 30, you're probably going to feel like you and the instructor are the only grown-ups in the room. Fortunately, during your time in the service, you learned a lot of the skills that are going to make you successful in college, a trade school, or just about any other educational program. And even better, you now know how to stay awake during a boring lecture. Nobody's going to tell you to do cherry-pickers or pushups when you get sleepy, and civilians don't usually care if you have to stand up and stretch your legs in the back of the classroom. (It *is* a little bit of a culture shock when you see other students dozing on their desks, though!)

Because you're a veteran, the government will pick up the tab for your tuition (and a few other expenses). Your blood, sweat, and tears prepaid for your higher education. You don't even have to think about student loans. This chapter gives you the inside scoop on the GI Bill, the perks that come with it, and how to use other programs to supplement your tuition, fees, and expenses so you can join the ranks of thousands of veterans who performed military service before pursuing more education.

Identifying Your Own GI Bill

Generally speaking, when you joined the military determines which type of GI Bill you have, and some people were given the option to choose one type or another. You can use your GI Bill to pay for any of the following:

>> Correspondence courses

>> Degree training

>> Flight training

>> Licensing and certification

>> National testing programs

>> Noncollege degree training

>> Tutorial assistance

>> Work-study programs

You can start and stop using your GI Bill whenever you want. As long as you're within your window and you have benefits left, the VA doesn't care whether you attend school for a semester, wait two years, and start back up again before taking another break.

This education benefit dates back to 1944, when it was called the Servicemen's Readjustment Act, and it has evolved quite a bit since then. Today, veterans may be eligible for four types of GI Bills:

>> The Post-9/11 GI Bill (sometimes called *Chapter 33*)

>> The Forever GI Bill

>> The Montgomery GI Bill – Active Duty (sometimes called *Chapter 30*)

>> The Montgomery GI Bill – Selected Reserve (sometimes called *Chapter 1606*)

I explain each of these in the following sections.

Post-9/11 GI Bill

The Post-9/11 GI Bill provides a pretty robust selection of benefits, but you're only eligible if you meet at least one of these four requirements:

>> You served at least 90 days on active duty, which may have been all at once or with breaks and service, on or after September 11, 2001.

>> You received a Purple Heart on or after September 11, 2001, and were honorably discharged after any amount of service.

>> You served in the military for at least 30 continuous days with no break in service on or after September 11, 2001, and were honorably discharged with a service-connected disability.

>> You're a dependent child using benefits transferred by a qualifying veteran or service member.

TIP

If you're a reservist who lost your education benefits when the Reserve Educational Assistance Program (REAP) ended in 2015, you may be able to have your benefits restored under the Post-9/11 GI Bill. You should get in touch with the VA to find out how to get your benefits back.

Under the Post-9/11 GI Bill, you can get up to 36 months of education benefits. Some people, such as those who qualify for Veteran Readiness and Employment (VR&E) benefits, can get up to 48 months of education benefits using this program. The percentage of the benefit you're entitled to is based on the amount of time you spent in the military as shown in Table 13-1.

TABLE 13-1

Post-9/11 and Forever GI Bill Percentages

Time Served	Percentage of GI Bill Benefit You Receive
0 to 90 days	No education benefit
90 days to 6 months	50%
6 to 18 months	60%
18 to 24 months	70%
24 to 30 months	80%
30 to 36 months	90%
36 months or more	100%

These percentages don't affect the number of months for which you qualify; they affect the amount the VA will pay toward your tuition and fees.

The Post-9/11 GI Bill gives you a substantial stack of cash. If you qualify for the maximum benefit, the VA will cover the full cost of public, in-state tuition, and fees. (Rates for private and foreign schools have a cap that adjusts every year; the VA has current rates on its website.) You also get money for housing if you're in school more than half time. The monthly housing allowance (MHA) you receive is based on the cost of living where your school's main campus is located.

This version of the GI Bill also gives you up to $1,000 per school year for books and supplies, which the VA deposits right into your bank account. And if you need to move from a rural area to go to school, you may be eligible for a $500 payment to help you with your relocation — but when I say rural, I mean *rural* (fewer than six people per square mile and located more than 500 miles from the school you're attending).

You may qualify for a couple additional benefits, such as the Yellow Ribbon Program, which I cover in the later section, "Tying Things Up with the Yellow Ribbon Program." You may be able to transfer your unused benefits to a spouse or child, too.

WARNING

The Post-9/11 GI Bill expires 15 years from your last separation date from active-duty service. If you don't use all your benefits by that time, you lose the rest. The Forever GI Bill, which I discuss in the following section, doesn't expire.

Forever GI Bill

If you were last discharged or released from active duty on or after January 1, 2013, you qualify for the Forever GI Bill benefit, which is still the Post-9/11 GI Bill (but on steroids). This new-and-improved version went into effect in 2018 as a result of the Harry W. Colmery Veterans Educational Assistance Act. The biggest deal about the upgrade is if you qualify for the Forever GI Bill, you don't have to use your benefit within 15 years of discharge; it's yours for the taking until you die.

The benefit amount you're entitled to depends on how long you served. Check out Table 13-1 for the specifics. However, if you served at least 30 continuous days on active duty and were discharged due to a service-connected disability or if you received a Purple Heart, you get 100 percent of your GI Bill benefits.

This version of the GI Bill also lets schools give veterans priority enrollment, which means you may have the chance to enroll in courses earlier than other students. You're allowed to pass this benefit onto a dependent, who can then pass it on to another eligible dependent if they don't want it after you die. The Forever GI Bill also gives you the opportunity to earn an additional educational assistance allowance while you're performing qualifying work study activities, such as providing hospital and home healthcare. Your MHA is based on where you attend most of your classes, rather than the school's location (like the Post-9/11 GI Bill), and you can use it for technical education or a postsecondary vocational education. Here are other perks this version offers:

>> Restoration of your benefits if your school closes or if a course of study was disapproved (in some cases)

>> Additional benefits for enrolling in a STEM (science, technology, engineering, and mathematics) program

>> Limited charges for certain licensure and certification tests, such as GMAT, GRE, and CLEP, or state licensing, which is in contrast to the Post-9/11 GI Bill, which charged you for an entire month of entitlement to pay for these tests

TECHNICAL
STUFF

Harry Walter Colmery is the "father" of the original GI Bill, having authored the Servicemen's Readjustment Act of 1944 (popularly called the G.I. Bill of Rights). Though he passed away in 1979, Congress named the act that improved the Post-9/11 GI Bill after him.

Montgomery GI Bill – Active Duty

If you're a more seasoned servicemember or veteran (read: if it takes you more than two tries to get out of bed in the morning, you remember shark attacks, and you've worn more uniform styles than you can count), you may have joined the military when the Montgomery GI Bill Active Duty (MGIB–AD) was a thing. The MGIB–AD has four different qualification categories based on when you entered active duty and a few other factors.

You may be able to use up to 36 months of education benefits under the MGIB–AD, which the VA pays directly to you each month. The VA updates the payment rates annually, but they're based on your training, how long you served, and your qualification category. I explain each qualification category in the following sections.

REMEMBER

The MGIB–AD expires if you don't use it within 10 years of your separation.

Category I

You're in Category I if you served at least three years (unless your agreement when you enlisted was for two years), or at least four years if you entered the Selected Reserve within a year of leaving active duty, which was called the *2 by 4 Program*. You must also meet all of the following requirements:

>> You have a high school diploma, high school equivalency certificate, or 12 hours of college credit.

>> You entered active duty for the first time after June 30, 1985.

>> You had your military pay reduced by $100 a month for the first 12 months of your service.

Category II

You fall into Category II if you meet all the following:

>> You have a high school diploma, high school equivalency certificate, or 12 hours of college credit.

>> You entered active duty before January 1, 1977, or before January 2, 1978, under a delayed enlistment program that you signed up for before January 1, 1977.

>> You served at least one day between October 19, 1984, and June 30, 1985, and you remained on active duty through June 30, 1988 (or through June 30, 1987, if you entered the Selected Reserve within one year of leaving active duty and served a total of four years).

>> You had at least one day of entitlement left under the Vietnam Era GI Bill (also known as *Chapter 34*) as of December 31, 1989.

Category III

You're eligible for this category if you meet all the following:

>> You have a high school diploma, high school equivalency certificate, or 12 hours of college credit.

>> You don't qualify for Categories I or II.

>> You had your military pay reduced by $1,200 before separation.

Additionally, one of the following must be true about you:

>> You were on active duty on September 30 1990, and involuntarily separated from the military after February 2, 1991.

>> You involuntarily separated on or after November 30, 1993.

>> You voluntarily separated from the military under the Voluntary Separation Incentive (VSI) program or the Special Separation Benefit (SSB) program.

Category IV

To qualify for this iteration of the MGIB–AD, you must meet the following:

>> You have a high school diploma, high school equivalency certificate, or 12 hours of college credit, plus had your military pay reduced by $100 a

month for 12 months or made a $1,200 lump-sum contribution toward your MGIB-AD benefit.

TIP

>> You must have been on active duty on October 9, 1996, and had money left in a Post-Vietnam Era Veterans Educational Assistance Program (VEAP) account on that date and chose the MGIB-AD before October 9, 1997.

If your VEAP benefits expired before you had a chance to use them, the government should have automatically returned to you the money you contributed to the fund. However, if you were enrolled in VEAP and you never got your money back, complete VA Form 22-5281 and return it to the VA. That starts the refund process.

>> You may also qualify under this category if you entered full-time National Guard duty under Title 32, USC, between July 1, 1985, and November 28, 1989, and chose the MGIB-AD between October 9, 1996, and July 9, 1997.

What if, like me, you opted-in to the MGIB-AD and later chose the Post-9/11 GI Bill when it became available? You could be entitled to a refund of the $1,200 contribution you made. However, you can only get a refund if you entered active duty after June 30, 1985, or you served a combination of at least two years on active duty and four years of Selected Reserve service after June 30, 1985. Additionally, *all* of the following must be true:

>> You paid the $1,200 MGIB buy-in when you joined the military.

>> You chose the Post-9/11 GI Bill instead of the MGIB-AD.

>> You had unused MGIB-AD benefits when you started using your Post-9/11 GI Bill.

>> You've used all your Post-9/11 GI Bill benefits.

>> You were receiving a Post-9/11 GI Bill MHA on the day your entitlement ended.

Unless you meet all these conditions, you can kiss your $1,200 contribution good-bye. However, if you're eligible for this refund, the VA will automatically give it to you in your last MHA payment from your Post-9/11 GI Bill. But mistakes happen, and if you believe that the VA still owes you your refund, you can contact a representative through the VA website or the GI Bill hotline at 888-442-4551.

Unfortunately, if you participated in the Buy-Up program, which required you to pay an additional $600 in exchange for higher MGIB benefits, you can't get that money back.

Montgomery GI Bill – Selected Reserve

The Montgomery GI Bill – Selected Reserve (MGIB-SR) is a bit less complicated than any of its counterparts. As long as you're in the Selected Reserve, which means you're part of a Troop Program Unit (TPU), working in the Active Guard Reserve (AGR) or serving as an Individual Mobilization Augmentee (IMA), and as long as you meet all the program's requirements, you can use your MGIB-SR benefits. The benefit is simple: You get a few hundred dollars a month to attend school for up to 36 months. The current payment rate is available on the VA's website.

You must have agreed to a six-year service obligation, or you must be an officer in the Selected Reserve and have agreed to serve an additional six years (on top of your initial service obligation). However, your obligation must have started after June 30, 1985, or for some types of training, after September 30, 1990, and you must meet all of the following:

» You complete your initial active duty for training (IADT).

» You earn a high school diploma or high school equivalency certificate before you finish your IADT.

» You stay in good standing while serving in an active Selected Reserve unit.

The catch is that as soon as you leave the Selected Reserve, you lose your entitlement to this benefit. (So why's it in here? It's technically a GI Bill.)

Comparing all four GI Bills

You can't use more than one GI Bill at a time, so if you're eligible for more than one, you have to choose which one you want to use. For example, if you're eligible for the Post-9/11 GI Bill and the MGIB-SR, you have to pick one or the other. But don't worry — using one doesn't make you ineligible to use the other at a later date. You could use your MGIB-SR now and save the Post-9/11 GI Bill for later (or vice versa). Table 13-2 gives you a quick visual rundown of the qualifications and usage of all four types.

TECHNICAL STUFF

Although the GI Bill comes from the federal government and pays for your education, it's not considered financial aid — at least not in the traditional sense. It's an entitlement that you earned, so it doesn't count against you when you're applying for other types of financial aid, such as scholarships, Pell Grants, or student loans.

TABLE 13-2   # GI Bill Comparison Chart

Benefit/Requirement	Post-9/11	Forever	MGIB-AD	MGIB-SR
Minimum length of service required	90 days of active or aggregate service after September 10, 2001, or 30 days of continuous service if discharged for a service-connected disability	90 days of active or aggregate service if discharged after January 1, 2013, or any number of days if discharged for a service-connected disability or as a Purple Heart recipient	2 years of continuous service of a 3-or 4-year contract, or separated before that due to a service-connected disability after 0 days of service	6 years after June 30, 1985
Maximum number of months to receive benefits	36 months (unless another family member has also transferred their GI Bill benefits to you, or you have another special circumstance)	36 months (unless another family member has also transferred their GI Bill benefits to you)	36 months or less (if you don't complete your full contract, you get fewer months)	45 months
Monthly housing stipend (MHA, Basic Allowance for Housing, or something similar)	Paid to you for greater than half-time training at the E-5 with dependent's rate for your school's locality; paid at a percentage if you're not attending school full-time; paid at half-rate if all your classes are online; paid at set amount for foreign schools	Paid to you for greater than half-time training at the E-5 with dependent's rate for the locality where you take most of your classes; paid at a percentage if you're not attending school full time; paid at half the rate if all your classes are online; paid at set amount for foreign schools	None	None
Tuition and fee payments	Paid directly to school	Paid directly to school	Paid directly to student	Paid directly to student
Duration of benefits	15 years from last release from active-duty date	Forever	10 years and one day from the last day of the most recent active-duty service period	Ends the day you separate from your Selected Reserve component

Getting Familiar with How the GI Bill Pays Out

The Post-9/11 GI Bill and the MGIB pay out in different ways, as you can see in Table 13-2 in the previous section. With the Post-9/11 GI Bill, tuition payments go directly to your school; with the MGIB, you get the money from the VA and are responsible for making your tuition payments yourself. As an MGIB user, you're likely to get your payments within a couple of weeks after completing your monthly enrollment verification.

The Post-9/11 GI Bill (whether yours is the original or Forever GI Bill version) also pays you an MHA if you're eligible, and it gives you a stipend for books and supplies. When you sign up for your GI Bill benefit, the VA asks you to provide your direct deposit information; the VA then deposits the appropriate amount in your account.

The following sections describe the different types of funding that benefit you (and whose bank account they end up in) when you use your GI Bill.

Paying the rent with your MHA

The VA sends out MHA payments at the beginning of the month, but it isn't required to put the money in your account on any specific date. Your MHA payment may be prorated in some cases, such as when you aren't actually attending classes for the entire month. (For example, if the last day of the semester is on the 18th of the month, you'll only be paid MHA from the 1st through the 18th.) The VA pays MHA after a month of school attendance, not before, which means if you start school on January 1, the soonest you can get your MHA is February 1. And don't forget — the payments are prorated for the time you're actually in school, so if you start school in the middle of the month, your first MHA payment will be for the prorated amount.

If you use the Post-9/11 GI Bill, your MHA is based on the E-5 with dependents' Basic Allowance for Housing (BAH) rate for your school's locality. That means if you attend Howard University, which is located in Washington, D.C., you'll get more in MHA than you would if you attended Michigan State University; the BAH rate is higher in D.C. than in East Lansing, Michigan. (Just for the record, the DOD and each military branch work together to review local median housing costs and determine new BAH rates each year.) If you use the Forever GI Bill, which is the Post-9/11 GI Bill for those who were discharged after January 1, 2013, your MHA is based on the location where you take most of your classes. For example, if you attend Michigan State University but go to most of your classes in Michigan's

Upper Peninsula, you'll get *more* MHA under the Forever GI Bill than you would have under the standard Post-9/11 GI Bill; that's because locality pay is higher in the Upper Peninsula than in East Lansing. (Sometimes it also works out that you earn less in MHA with the Forever GI Bill.) When BAH rates change, MHA changes with them.

Some people don't get the full MHA rate. The VA cuts MHA by 50 percent if you only attend school less than half time, and if you take online classes of your own volition (in that case, you receive an MHA that's half the national BAH average). During the COVID-19 pandemic, when many colleges and universities switched to online-only classes, the VA continued to pay full MHA because it wasn't the students' choice. They'd do the same if it happened again.

There's one minor catch, though: If you want to receive your MHA (or kicker payments, which I cover in the later section, "Kickin' with the Guard's GI Bill Program"), you must verify your school enrollment each month in order to continue receiving your payments. You can opt into text message verifications, or you may verify by email; as a last resort, you can verify by phone on the GI Bill Hotline (it's 888-GIBill-1 so it's easy to remember).

WARNING

If you fail to verify your enrollment two months in a row, the VA will put your MHA and kicker payments on hold. You then have to call the GI Bill Hotline to get the VA to release your payments to you.

Paying for books and supplies

One of the perks of the Post-9/11 GI Bill is that you may be eligible for up to $1,000 per year to help pay for books and school supplies. This cash is put directly into your bank account, and you receive an amount that's directly proportional to the number of credit hours you enroll to take. (If you enroll in one class, you're not getting a grand.) It's paid in installments around the beginning of each term.

Defining a month in the GI Bill's terms

GI Bill benefits pay out monthly, and they're calculated in months, too. You generally max out at 36 months of benefits from each GI Bill benefit (except the MGIB-SR, which I cover in the section, "Montgomery GI Bill – Selected Reserve," earlier in this chapter). A *month* is 28, 29, 30, or 31 days — except when you attend classes for only a portion of a month. In that case, the VA assumes a month is 30 days long. For example, if you attend classes from May 1 through May 15, the VA gives you a half month of benefits (although there are 31 days in May, so it works out in your favor by just a smidge).

Identifying Survivors' and Dependents' Assistance

Some survivors and dependents are eligible for VA education benefits. The survivors' and dependents' assistance program, commonly called Chapter 35, may be available to the child or spouse of a veteran or servicemember if one of the following is true:

>> The servicemember died in the line of duty after September 10, 2001.

>> The servicemember is missing in action or was captured in the line of duty by a hostile force.

>> The servicemember was detained by force while in the line of duty by a foreign government or power.

>> The servicemember is in the hospital or receiving outpatient treatment for a service-connected permanent and total disability and is likely to be discharged.

Additionally, you may be eligible for these benefits if you're the child or spouse of a veteran who is permanently and totally disabled due to a service-connected disability or who died on active duty or as a result of a service-connected disability. (If you're a dependent who doesn't meet any of these criteria, you don't qualify for education benefits unless the veteran transferred some or all of their Post-9/11 GI Bill benefits to you while they were still serving on active duty.)

If you qualify for these benefits, you can get money for education and training, tuition, housing, and books and supplies. However, you must apply for them. (You might also consider applying for the Fry Scholarship or the Survivors' and Dependents' Educational Assistance program, both of which I discuss in Chapter 14.)

Tying Things Up with the Yellow Ribbon Program

Some schools participate in the Yellow Ribbon Program, which helps veterans pay for fees, out-of-state tuition, and additional costs for programs at private, foreign, and graduate schools — all things that your GI Bill may not cover. You may be eligible for this program if you qualify for the full Post-9/11 GI Bill and at least one of the following is true about you:

>> You served at least 36 months on active duty and received an honorable discharge.

>> You received a Purple Heart on or after September 11, 2001, and you were honorably discharged.

>> You served for at least 30 continuous days on or after September 11, 2001, and you were discharged or released from active duty because of a service-connected disability.

>> You're a dependent child or spouse using benefits that your veteran parent transferred to you.

>> You're a Fry Scholar.

If you qualify, your school — if it participates in the program — will contribute a set amount of money to your tuition and fees through a scholarship, grant, or similar program, and the VA will match your school's contribution.

You need to turn in your GI Bill Certificate of Eligibility to your school as soon as possible and ask to apply for the program. Usually, enrollment in the Yellow Ribbon Program is on a first-come, first-served basis, which means that if you're too late, you may miss out on the opportunity. Your school decides how much funding you receive based on how much your Post-9/11 GI Bill pays toward tuition as well as any scholarships and grants you have that offset your costs.

REMEMBER

You don't need to reapply if you continue to attend the same school year after year. As long as your school keeps participating in the program, and as long as you make acceptable progress toward completing your program, remain enrolled without a break, and have money left on your Post-9/11 GI Bill, you're automatically re-enrolled in the program.

The VA maintains a list of schools that participate in the Yellow Ribbon Program on its website at www.va.gov/education/yellow-ribbon-participating-schools.

Kickin' with the Guard's GI Bill Program

If you're in the National Guard, the GI Bill Kicker program is right up your alley. If you're qualified, part of a critical military occupational specialty (MOS) and have the MGIB (either the AD or SR version, which I explain earlier in this chapter in the section, "Identifying Your Own GI Bill,"), you can receive additional funding from the Guard to go toward tuition and fees. These tax-free payments only last as long as your MGIB does, though; when that expires, so does your Kicker. Here are the three Kicker categories:

>> **Enlisted Accessions (EA):** EA is for those with an ASVAB score of 50 or higher. (And hey, if you need to retake the ASVAB, I happen to know that *ASVAB For Dummies* is the best possible resource available — I know the author!) You must meet other criteria to qualify, as well, and you may need to reclass and/or reenlist.

>> **Re-Enlistment/Extension (RE):** This category is for people who re-up or extend for at least six years at certain points in their careers.

>> **Officer Commissioning (OC):** This category is for people who have an enlisted MOS and have completed Phase 1 of Officer Candidate School but haven't yet commissioned, for those in the Reserve Officer Training Corps, warrant officer candidates, and officers who have commissioned within the past year.

Your state's GI Bill manager has information on current rates, eligibility, and status changes. You can also talk to your state Education Services Officer (ESO) or your unit's readiness NCO to find out more about using your GI Bill Kicker benefit.

Using Your GI Bill for Other Programs

You may use your GI Bill for a wide range of educational programs that help you get ahead — you're not limited to colleges and universities. The following sections explain how your benefit applies in a variety of scenarios.

Taking off for flight school

You probably already know that your GI Bill covers the cost of degree programs related to flying, but you may not have known that it also covers the cost of flight training itself. As long as you qualify for the Post-9/11 GI Bill or the MGIB, you have a private pilot's license, and you have a second-class medical certificate valid for second-class privileges (or a first-class medical certificate, in some cases), you can participate in a vocational program at a Part 141 pilot school.

REMEMBER

This benefit amount has a yearly limit, and you aren't eligible for a housing allowance or books and supplies, but you can earn qualifications for rotary-wing, B747-400, dual-engine, or flight engineering.

Getting your hands dirty with OJT

If you qualify for the GI Bill and work in an industry or job that has on-the-job training (OJT — such as firefighting or plumbing), you may be able to get money for books and supplies, as well as money for housing if you're covered under the Post-9/11 GI Bill. The MHA depends on where you are in your training. You get 100 percent of your MHA entitlement during your first six months of training, and from there, it decreases. You get 80 percent during your second six months, 60 percent during your third six months, 40 percent during your fourth six months, and 20 percent during the rest of your training period.

WARNING

OJT payments work differently if you have the MGIB. When you enroll, you receive 75 percent of your full-time GI Bill rate for the first six months of training, 55 percent for the second six months of training, and 35 percent of the full-time rate for the rest of your training period.

Pursuing noncollege-degree programs

The GI Bill can pay for hyper-specific training programs, such as those designed for emergency medical technicians (EMTs), HVAC repair, truck driving, beautician or barber school, and more. In addition to tuition, you may also get money for books and supplies. The amount you get depends on whether you have the Post-9/11 GI Bill or the MGIB. For the Post-9/11 GI Bill, the VA pays in-state tuition and fees up to the national maximum; for the MGIB, the VA pays a monthly rate that depends on the program and the amount of time you served in the military.

Being repaid for licensing and testing

You can use your GI Bill benefit to cover the cost of tests you need to take to become a licensed or certified professional in your field. The VA maintains a comprehensive list of all the tests and certifications that are eligible for fee repayment, such as real estate licenses and tattooing licenses, on its website. You can use your GI Bill to apply for as many approved licenses or certifications as you'd like, and the VA will pay even if you don't score high enough to get the license or certification you need. You can take the same test over and over if necessary, and your GI Bill covers the cost of retaking tests to get recertified or retain a license you already have, too.

Your GI Bill also reimburses you for national testing, including registration fees, costs of specialized tests, and mandatory administrative fees. The VA will pay you afterward for taking the SAT, ACT, TOEFL, or other approved tests, such as AP and CLEP exams, such as the GMAT, GRE, LSAT, MAT, MCAT, PCAT, and OAT. All you need to do is apply and provide the VA with receipts.

Stepping on the gas with accelerated payments for high-tech programs

Available only to active-duty servicemembers and those using the MGIB-SR or REAP benefits, the accelerated payment program gives you 60 percent of tuition and fees if you're enrolled in a high-cost, high-technology program that costs more than 200 percent of the GI Bill you'd otherwise qualify to get. If you don't have enough entitlement to cover 60 percent of the program's tuition and fees, VA will pay you a percentage based on the entitlement you *do* have. Some programs that may qualify you for accelerated payments include engineering, mathematics, biotechnology, and aerospace. These accelerated payments can pay for expensive programs, but they replace the monthly benefits you'd ordinarily get through the GI Bill.

Mastering the GI Bill Application

Wouldn't it be nice if the VA chased you down after you left the military and said, "Here, take this money and go to school!"? But the VA doesn't do that, and it's up to you to apply for your GI Bill benefit. If you're eligible, the VA requires you to pull together the following information:

>> Your Social Security number

>> Your direct deposit information

>> Your educational transcripts and military history information

>> Some basic details about the school or training facility you want to attend or that you currently attend

You can apply for your GI Bill benefits online, through the VA's website, or by mail or in person at a VA regional office. You can also get help from an accredited representative from a VSO — I discuss those in Chapter 3. The benefit to applying online is simple: You don't have to print anything, and the VA guides you to the right forms for your situation. You can submit your form online and wait for the VA's response.

Waiting on the VA's determination

The VA takes about 30 days to process education claims, and they're pretty straightforward unless there's a question about your eligibility. After the VA approves your claim, you receive a certificate of eligibility (COE) or award letter in the mail. Bring the letter to the VA certifying official at your school and let them take it from there.

Applying to schools

You can apply to any school you want, even if it's not the one listed on your GI Bill application. You should apply to schools and for your GI Bill benefit at the same time — that way, you have the COE in your hot little hands when it's time to talk about tuition payments.

TIP

Many schools have application fee waivers for veterans (and for active-duty servicemembers) if you're applying as part of your pre-separation preparation). Ask the veteran liaison at your school about their program.

Chapter **14**

Staking Your Claim on Other Education Programs

The U.S. government wants veterans to pursue an education, even if that means using programs other than the GI Bill, which I explain in great detail in Chapter 13. A lot of the education benefits available to veterans come directly from the U.S. Department of Veterans Affairs, though they're also available through other government agencies, as well as state and local governments. In many cases, these benefits come in extra-handy when your GI Bill runs out, but your thirst for knowledge doesn't. Though this book isn't nearly long enough to explain every state education benefit available to veterans, I do have enough space to tell you about the VA's (and other government agencies') programs for veterans and their dependents, scholarships you may be eligible for, and how to access state education benefits set aside for you in this chapter.

Getting on Track with VR&E

Veteran Readiness and Employment (VR&E), also known as *Chapter 31*, is for veterans who have a service-connected disability that limits their ability to work or prevents them from working entirely. (This program used to be called Vocational Rehabilitation and Employment, and the services it provided were a little different.) Today, VR&E gives service-disabled veterans an edge on getting education and training, finding and keeping a job, and living as independently as possible. Some family members also qualify for benefits under this program. I cover it in more detail in Chapter 20, where you can find even more resources and programs for disabled veterans, but the gist of it is this: You can participate in one of the following five VR&E tracks to get the education and training you need to reenter the workforce or start your own business:

>> Rapid access to employment track

>> Self-employment track

>> Employment through long-term services track

>> Reemployment track

>> Independent living track

Studying High-Speed Skills in VET TEC

When you decide you want to gain computer experience so you can kick off a thriving career in the high technology industry, you may be able to use the VA's Veteran Employment through Technology Education Courses (VET TEC). This program matches you with one of the country's leading training providers to help you develop the skills you need to launch your new career. Eligibility requirements say that you must be out of the military (or within 180 days of separating from active duty), qualify for the GI Bill, have at least one day of unexpired entitlement, and be accepted by a VA-approved training provider.

VET TEC training doesn't count against your GI Bill entitlement, and because you only need one day of unexpired GI bill benefits to participate, you can use it if you've already begun attending courses or certification programs through other institutions.

REMEMBER

The VA can connect you with a training provider to study skills in a high-demand area, such as computer software, computer programming, data processing, information science, or media applications. Your tuition is fully paid through VET TEC, and you may even be eligible for money for housing during your training. If you attend your training program in person, you'll receive a housing stipend that's equal to the monthly military basic allowance for housing (BAH) for an E-5 with dependents. If your training program is entirely online, you'll receive half the national average BAH for an E-5 with dependents.

Applying for the VET TEC program on the VA's website takes about ten minutes. You need your direct deposit information, information on your highest level of education, and your previous experience in the high-tech industry (if you have any). Also, if you have any information on the training provider you want to work with or the program you want to participate in, keep it handy.

The VA will review your application within about 30 days. If the VA needs more information from you, it'll send you a letter in the mail to ask for it; it'll also send you its determination by mail. If you're eligible, you'll receive a certificate of eligibility.

The VET TEC program is only open to participants while funding is available; after the funding runs out, the VA may cancel the program or ask for more funding from the government to continue it.

Planting Some Roots with the Rogers STEM Scholarship

The Edith Nourse Rogers STEM Scholarship (I know — that's a big name, but it's a big benefit, so they're a good match) is available to some veterans and dependents. Veterans who qualify for the Post-9/11 GI Bill may be eligible to use it, and so can dependents who use the Fry Scholarship, which I cover in the later section, "Exploring Educational Benefits for Dependent Family Members."

This scholarship helps pay for undergraduate degree programs in subject areas such as agricultural science, biomedical science, computer and information science (and support services), and mathematics or statistics. It also goes toward healthcare, physical science, and science technology programs. You can find a full list of eligible STEM degree programs on the VA's website (as well as the current education benefit rates available under this scholarship).

To qualify for this scholarship as a GI Bill extension or as a complement to the Fry Scholarship, you must meet any of the following:

>> You're currently enrolled in an undergraduate STEM degree program or qualifying dual-degree program.

>> You've already earned a postsecondary degree or graduate degree in an approved STEM degree field, and you're currently enrolled in a covered clinical training program for healthcare professionals.

>> You've already earned a postsecondary degree in an approved STEM degree field and are working toward earning a teaching certification.

The list of qualifications you must meet is on the VA's website, where you can apply. Typically, it takes the VA about 30 days to make a decision on these scholarship applications; it awards these scholarships on a monthly basis.

Answering the National Call to Service

If you enlisted under the National Call to Service program, you don't qualify for the Montgomery GI Bill (unless you reenlist again at a later date for an additional period of service). However, you do qualify to apply for a cash bonus of $5,000 or repayment of a qualifying loan (under the amount of $18,000). Or you may qualify for educational assistance equal to the three-year monthly MGIB rate for 12 months or equal to half the less than three-year monthly MGIB rate for 36 months.

If you completed your initial entry training, continued to serve on active duty for 15 months in a certain military occupational specialty designated by the Secretary of Defense, and served an additional period of active duty or a period of 24 months in active status in the Selected Reserve, you may qualify to apply. You must not have had a break in service, and you must have spent the remainder of your obligation on active duty, in the Selected Reserve, in the Individual Ready Reserve, or in AmeriCorps (or another domestic national service program). If you're interested in this benefit and you believe you qualify, you can apply on the VA's website.

Cashing in on VEAP or Getting a Refund

Though this is a little-used benefit these days, people who entered the service for the first time between January 1, 1977, and June 30, 1985 (except those who joined the Air Force during that time) and who put money into a Veterans'

Educational Assistance Program (VEAP) account before April 1, 1987, may qualify to use the VEAP program. But to qualify, you must also have put in at least $25 on your own, as well as finished your first period of service without getting a dishonorable discharge.

If you served in the Air Force, you must have entered the service for the first time between December 1, 1980, and September 30, 1981 — and you must have enlisted on one of only a handful of Air Force specialties from a specific location.

You can use your VEAP tuition benefits for up to 10 years after you leave the military; after that, the VA automatically refunds it to you. However, if you were due a refund and haven't received it, you can fill out VA Form 22-5281 to let the VA know it needs to send your cash back. After it's complete, mail the form to your nearest VA regional office for processing.

Scouting for Scholarships and Grants

Grants and scholarships are gifts to you; you never have to pay them back. Some are merit based, which means you can earn them by meeting certain standards (such as a certain grade point average). Others are need based, and still others are for specific groups of people (such as members of the Paralyzed Veterans of America, which I cover in the following section). Several veterans' and civilian organizations provide grants and scholarships specifically to veterans, and you can find many of them by searching "veteran scholarships" online. You can also talk to the financial aid office at your school or use the Department of Labor's free scholarship finder at www.careeronestop.org/.

TIP

When you find a scholarship you're interested in, check its deadline to make sure the organization offering it is currently accepting applications. Scholarships and grants each have their own eligibility requirements; some require essays. Here are a few of the most notable scholarships and grants you, as a veteran, may be eligible for. (Scholarships for your dependents are listed in the later section, "Earning scholarships and grants for your dependents based on your service.")

American Legion Auxiliary scholarship

The American Legion Auxiliary (ALA) offers scholarships to members of the American Legion, Auxiliary, and Sons of the American Legion who are current on dues for at least two years. The organization awards one nontraditional student scholarship for $2,000 per year to qualified applicants who are pursuing training in a trade, professional, or technical program, or in a two- or four-year degree program.

AMVETS scholarship

To qualify for an AMVETS scholarship, you must be currently serving or have served in the U.S. military, including the National Guard or Reserves, and you must demonstrate financial need. You have to complete an essay for AMVETS to be considered for this scholarship, as well as provide a copy of your DD-214 and send in your official college transcripts (or your high school transcript, if you haven't attended college yet). This scholarship awards between $4,000 and $12,000 to recipients.

Paralyzed Veterans of America scholarship

Paralyzed Veterans of America awards scholarships ranging from $1,000 to $2,500 to its members who attend colleges and universities. You're eligible to apply if you're a member of the PVA, a U.S. citizen, and have been accepted and enrolled as a part- or full-time student in an accredited U.S. college or university.

Veterans of Foreign Wars scholarship

The VFW sponsors the Sport Clips Help a Hero Scholarship to provide veterans with financial assistance so they're less likely to need student loans. The scholarship is worth up to $5,000 and is only available to retired or honorably discharged servicemembers or to active-duty servicemembers, National Guard members, or members of the Reserves who separated with or currently hold a military rank of E-5 or below. You must demonstrate financial need for this scholarship.

REMEMBER

The VFW also offers a Student Veteran Support Grant designed to help support specific events aimed at vets. Applicants must be VFW members and may receive up to $500 to support each veterans event, up to twice a fiscal year.

Exploring Educational Benefits for Dependent Family Members

Some dependent family members of veterans with service-connected disabilities qualify for educational assistance through the VA. Several types of support, which I outline in the following sections, are available. (For noneducational programs available to some dependents, flip to Chapter 21, where I explore benefits for spouses, kids, and caregivers, as well as Chapter 23, where I cover benefits for survivors.)

REMEMBER

Dependents sometimes qualify for the Edith Nourse Rogers STEM Scholarship, which I cover in the section, "Planting Your Roots with the Rogers STEM Scholarship," earlier in this chapter.

Packing it in with PCPG for Dependents

If your dependent is eligible for the Post-9/11 GI Bill or either version of the Montgomery GI Bill, they can get educational and career counseling through Personalized Career Planning and Guidance (PCPG — sometimes called Chapter 36). This program offers one-on-one counseling with an expert that helps your spouse or child explore their skills, abilities, and interests. It also helps them plan the best use of their VA benefits and map out a path to employment. Your dependents can apply for counseling through the PCPG program online on the VA's website or apply by mail or in-person at the nearest VA regional office or VetSuccess on Campus counselor.

Checking out Survivors' and Dependents' Educational Assistance

Designed for the children and spouses of disabled veterans, servicemembers who are missing in action or have been captured, or a deceased veteran or servicemember, the Survivors' and Dependents' Educational Assistance (also called DEA or Chapter 35) program can provide help paying for school or job training. This benefit may help dependents cover the costs of college or graduate degree programs; career training certificate courses; educational and career counseling; apprenticeships; or on-the-job training. Eligible parties can receive benefits for up to 36 months. I cover the DEA program more extensively in Chapter 21.

Using the Fry Scholarship to pay for school, supplies, and housing

The Fry Scholarship (technically, the Marine Gunnery Sergeant John David Fry Scholarship) is for the children of servicemembers who died in the line of duty on or after September 11, 2001, while serving on active duty; servicemembers who died in the line of duty while not on active duty on or after September 11, 2001; or members of the Selected Reserve who died from a service-connected disability on or after September 11, 2001.

This benefit, which can last up to 36 months, includes money for school tuition (full in-state tuition costs and up to a certain amount for private or out-of-state schools), money for housing, and cash for books and supplies. I cover the Fry Scholarship in greater detail in Chapter 23.

Earning scholarships and grants for your dependents based on your service

Several veterans service organizations provide scholarships for veterans' dependents, including the American Legion, AMVETS, ANAVICUS, Paralyzed Veterans of America, and Veterans of Foreign Wars — and a number of civilian organizations provide them, too. Have a quick look at what's available only to dependents in the following sections.

Air Force Aid Society Education Grants and scholarships

The Air Force Aid Society (AFAS) General Henry H. Arnold Education Grant Program is available to eligible Air Force dependents, including some dependents of retirees and widows or widowers, who may qualify for this need-based grant that ranges in value from $500 to $4,000.

AFAS also offers merit scholarships worth $5,000 to dependent children and spouses of retired Airmen or Guardians (Space Force) who demonstrate outstanding academic potential based on grade-point average.

American Legion scholarships

The American Legion offers several scholarships to family members, which you can read more about at www.legion.org/scholarships, including:

>> **Samsung American Legion Scholarship:** Established by Samsung to express its appreciation to the U.S. veterans who helped Korea during the Korean War, this scholarship is available to students between their junior and senior years of high school who are a direct descendant of a wartime U.S. military veteran who served on active duty during a period of war that qualifies the veteran for membership in the American Legion. The student also must attend the current session of an American Legion Boys State or American Legion Auxiliary Girls State program. (The veteran who served during a wartime period doesn't need to be a member.)

>> **Legacy Scholarship:** The Legacy Scholarship offers college funding to the children of post-9/11 veterans who died on active duty as well as those who have a combined VA disability rating of 50 percent or greater. This needs-based scholarship provides up to $20,000 in aid.

>> **Baseball Scholarship:** The American Legion Baseball Scholarship is nominative; a team manager or head coach of an American Legion (post-affiliated) team may nominate a player; awards range from $500 to $5,000.

- **National High School Oratorical Contest Scholarship:** This scholarship is awarded to the three finalists in the National High School Oratorical Contest that the American Legion puts on each year. Awards range from $2,000 for first-round winners who don't qualify for the finals to $25,000 for the first-place winner. (Second- and third-place winners receive $22,500 and $20,000, respectively.)

- **Eagle Scout of the Year Scholarship:** This scholarship awards up to $10,000 to Eagle Scouts nominated for it. The nomination starts in local posts; packets go to the state level, and then to the national level for awards determinations.

- **Junior Shooting Sports Scholarship:** The winners of the annual American Legion 3-Position Junior Air Rifle Championship get $5,000 in college scholarships; second-place winners receive $1,000.

AMVETS scholarships

AMVETS provides a number of scholarships to students each year, which you can apply for at `https://amvets.org/scholarships/`. These scholarships are available to veterans' spouses, and their children and grandchildren:

- **AMVETS Spouse Scholarship** is available to spouses or widows of U.S. veterans who served on active duty, in the National Guard, or in the Reserves. It's only open to those who have a high school diploma or high-school equivalency certificate who demonstrate academic promise and financial need. Hopeful recipients need to write an essay for consideration and provide the veteran's DD-214 (and some other information). The organization gives out one of these $4,000 scholarships per year.

- **AMVETS Children and Grandchildren Scholarship** is awarded to four recipients per year with awards ranging between $1,000 and $4,000. It's open to applicants who are children or grandchildren of veterans who are about to enter college at the next fall semester. Based on academic promise and financial need, this scholarship also requires an essay, the veteran's DD-214, and transcripts.

American Legion Auxiliary Scholarships

The American Legion Auxiliary (ALA) offers three scholarships to the children and other descendants of veterans, which you can find more about at `www.legion-aux.org/scholarships`:

- **Children of Warriors National Presidents' Scholarships** are worth $5,000 and are given to veterans' kids, grandkids, and great-grandkids, provided the veteran served in the Armed Forces between April 6, 1917, and November 11, 1918, or any time after December 7, 1941.

>> **Spirit of Youth Scholarships** go to officer members of the American Legion Auxiliary Girls Nation in amounts between $2,500 and $5,000.

>> **Junior Member Loyalty Scholarships** are for junior members of the ALA in the value of $2,500.

ANAVICUS Scholarships

ANAVICUS (that's short for Army, Navy and Air Force Veterans in Canada and the United States) is a part of ANAVIC, a Canadian veterans organization. This organization provides a number of scholarships, each with different qualification criteria, in honor of former National Commander Harry W. Colmery (whose name you may recognize from the act that established the Forever GI Bill [see Chapter 13]). Students may apply for these $1,500 scholarships through their schools:

>> **E. Roy Stone, Jr. ROTC Scholarship** goes to a "worthy and deserving" full-time student at Furman University in South Carolina.

>> **Father Edward J. Carney Scholarship** is awarded to a sophomore or junior student attending Merrimack College in Massachusetts.

>> **General Frank R. Schwengel Scholarship** goes to a sophomore or junior at Iona College in New York who's in financial need.

>> **General Lewis B. Hershey Scholarship** is based on financial need and goes to a sophomore or junior at Trine University in Indiana.

>> **James F. O'Neil Scholarship** is for outstanding sophomore or junior students attending Saint Anselm College in New Hampshire.

>> **Judge Daniel F. Foley Scholarship** is for direct descendants of members (or deceased members) of ANAVETS (the Army, Navy, and Air Force Veterans in Canada).

>> **Rev. Jerome D. Fortenberry Scholarship** is an annual award that goes to living and current ANAVICUS members' direct descendants (children, grandchildren, and great-grandchildren).

>> **Reverend Frank L. Harrington Scholarship** goes to an outstanding sophomore or junior student at Carroll College in Montana.

>> **Richard M. Pedro Memorial Scholarship** is available to students participating in the ROTC program who have financial need.

Paralyzed Veterans of America scholarships

The Paralyzed Veterans of America (PVA) invests in its members' families' education with scholarships ranging between $1,000 and $2,500. You qualify if you're the spouse or unmarried child (under the age of 24) of a PVA member and are considered the member's dependent. You must also be a U.S. citizen and have been accepted and enrolled as a full- or part-time student in an accredited U.S. college or university. You can apply at `https://pva.org/find-support/scholarship-program/`.

Veterans of Foreign Wars scholarships

The Veterans of Foreign Wars (VFW) awards Voice of Democracy scholarships to high-schoolers, and they range in value from $1,000 to $30,000. The VFW pays the recipient's school directly. To qualify, a student between ninth and twelfth grade must complete an audio essay on the year's topic. The competition is open to students enrolled in public, private, and parochial schools, as well as home-schoolers in the United States, and to dependents of military or civilian personnel in overseas schools. To enter, contact your local VFW chapter.

REMEMBER

Though it's not technically a scholarship, the Patriot's Pen is a cool essay contest for kids (and nobody's stopping you from putting their winnings in a savings account for college). This contest is open to kids in sixth through eighth grades and requires an essay on the year's topic. Prizes range between $500 and $5,000.

Passing your GI Bill on to your family

The DOD is in charge of deciding whether a person can transfer their GI Bill benefits to their dependents — and you can only transfer your benefits while you're still on active duty or in the Selected Reserve. Generally, you need to put in a Transfer of Entitlement (TOE) request with the DOD. If the DOD grants your request, which comes with strings attached (usually you have to reenlist before gaining approval), your beneficiary must apply for the benefit.

You may be able to redistribute your benefits (or give them back to yourself). But for the record, if a veteran dies with unused GI Bill benefits, those benefits can't be transferred to a spouse, child, or other dependent. However, some dependents are eligible for the other education benefits listed in this section.

Getting Your State to Kick in for Tuition

Most states offer special veterans education benefits of their own, which you can use in addition to your GI Bill (or as an alternative to it). Texas is a great example: If you were a Texas resident at the time you joined the military, and if you're currently a resident for tuition purposes, served at least 181 days on active duty, and have exhausted your GI Bill, the state exempts you from paying tuition and some fees at public colleges and universities.

Many states have additional benefits for members of the National Guard, including waived (or reduced) tuition and grants. The best list I've seen is from the American Legion (you can access it at www.legion.org/education/statebenefits). Alternatively, you can contact your state's Department of Veterans Services or Department of Education to discover what's available to you — and your nearest VA office can also provide you with guidance.

» **Making the grade for approval**

» **Showing lenders you're good to go**

» **Understanding the extra perks associated with a VA loan**

Chapter **15**

Buying into Post-Military Life with Your VA Loan Benefit

B ack when my Grandpa Charlie returned from World War II in 1945, veterans benefits weren't as robust as they are now — but in those days, you could use your GI Bill to help fund a house. (Well, vets could borrow up to $2,000 toward the purchase of a house; the average home price was somewhere around $5,150 at that time.) I may never know if my grandpa used his GI Bill benefits to buy his first home, but I do know that the current home-buying benefits afforded to veterans are a lot more significant than they used to be.

Today, you can borrow hundreds of thousands of dollars against a new home (a condo, a townhome, a single-family home, or even a multi-family home), all backed by the Department of Veterans Affairs. In turn, that makes lenders more likely to approve you for a mortgage — even if you wouldn't ordinarily qualify. VA loans' interest rates are typically lower than they are with other loans, which leaves you more breathing room after making your monthly mortgage payments, and you can pay off your home early without a penalty. Even better, you can buy a home with nothing down (and skip private mortgage insurance) when you use this program.

But for some reason, only about 24 percent of veterans who currently own homes used this long-term, reusable benefit. (For a frame of reference, there are about 18 million living veterans, and somewhere between 75 and 80 percent of veteran households are homeowners.) After almost a century of evolution, the VA home loan benefit is bigger and better than it's ever been; you can even use this benefit for more than meets the eye. This chapter explains how VA loans work, where (and how) you get the money to buy a home, and all the extra perks associated with this long-term, reusable benefit.

Living the Dream with a VA Home Loan

For most people who want to buy a home, there's a standard operating procedure: They brush up their credit, scrimp and save for a down payment totaling about 20 percent of a home's purchase price, find a lender that's willing to work with them, and sign the dotted line. But the VA-Guaranteed Home Loan program is a fast-track for veterans.

TECHNICAL STUFF

Although it's often referred to as a *VA loan*, the money doesn't usually come from the VA. It most commonly comes from private lenders — think banks, credit unions, and mortgage companies — and a portion of the loan is guaranteed by the Department of Veterans Affairs.

REMEMBER

VA backing means that if you default (fail to pay) on your mortgage, the VA will swoop in and ensure that the lender gets at least some of its money back. This guaranty benefits you because lenders assume less risk by letting you borrow than they would, say, a civilian with no government backing. And because the VA offers this promise, which makes you a more attractive candidate for a home loan, you get the ability to buy a home with no down payment, competitive interest rates, an exemption from private mortgage insurance, and lower closing costs.

The VA also requires lenders to look at your whole financial picture, not just your credit score, to determine whether you qualify for a loan. That means even if you wouldn't ordinarily qualify, or if you'd only qualify for a loan with higher interest rates, you have a better shot at getting this type of loan.

You can do more than just buy a house with a VA loan, though. The rest of this chapter focuses on VA loan benefits for several scenarios (and how they work).

Understanding VA Home Purchase Loans

VA home purchase loans may be the most well-known types of VA loans. The U.S. government backs these loans, which means that the VA guarantees a portion of the loan; if you go into foreclosure, your lender can ask the government to cover some (or all) of its losses.

TIP

Not all real estate agents are well-versed in VA loans and how they work, so it's in your best interest to look for one who does. Search for agents who have special designations, such as Military Relocation Professional (MRP), or who focus on working with veterans. And if a real estate agent tries to discourage you from using your VA loan benefit, find another agent.

The following sections explain the nuts and bolts of VA purchase loans, giving you a peek at how they work and how they may benefit you.

Scouting out what you can buy

You can buy more than a single-family house with a white picket fence with your VA loan benefit. In fact, you can use it to purchase any of the following:

>> Single-family home, duplex, triplex, or fourplex

>> Condominium or townhouse

>> Single-family home that needs improvements

>> Manufactured home or lot

>> New construction home (meaning you can use your VA loan benefit to build a home)

You may also use your VA-backed purchase loan to make changes or add new features to your home to make it more energy efficient.

Looking at credit requirements

The VA doesn't specify a minimum credit score required to use your VA loan benefit, but individual lenders usually do. Even if your credit isn't perfectly polished, though, you may still be able to qualify for a VA loan. That's because the VA requires lenders to look at your entire financial picture, rather than just at your credit score, when making a loan determination. Some lenders will extend loans to people with credit scores in the 580 range, but remember: The lower your credit score is, the higher your interest rate is likely to be.

WHY WOULD YOU BUY A MULTIFAMILY HOME?

You can purchase a duplex, triplex, or fourplex using a VA loan, as long as you agree to live on the property until you meet VA home occupancy requirements. Lenders are typically free to determine how long they may require you to use the home as your primary residence.

Though multifamily homes may be more expensive than single-family homes, purchasing one of these types of properties has a significant advantage: Under the VA's occupancy requirements, you're allowed to live in one unit and rent out the rest. Experts say that if you play your cards right, your tenants will provide you with a steady stream of passive income that's enough to cover your mortgage payments (and then some). If you have enough money and don't mind living in a shared property, this may be a great way to make your real estate investment a little more powerful.

Note: Most lenders say that you must agree to live in just about *any* home you buy with this benefit for at least a year (sometimes longer). After you meet the occupancy requirement, you're free and clear to move and rent the entire property.

Offering zero down payment with no PMI

According to the VA, around 90 percent of these loans are made without a down payment. That means you don't have to save a dime for your down payment (though you may have to pay some out-of-pocket costs). The caveat is that the home's sales price can't be higher than the home's appraised value. If it is, you need to pay the difference between the sales price and the appraised value (but in a situation like this, you may be able to negotiate the price down).

Most people who get a mortgage loan with less than a 20 percent down payment must purchase private mortgage insurance (PMI). This insurance protects the lender, not the borrower. It's there in case the borrower defaults on the loan. The borrower pays for it, usually until they've built 20 percent equity in the home; that's when lenders feel like the borrower has some skin in the game. However, when you use a VA loan, lenders aren't allowed to require you to buy PMI — the government is already backing the loan, so it's unnecessary.

And about potential out-of-pocket costs: You have to pay a VA funding fee, as well as some closing costs (the costs of doing business, such as your loan origination fee, hazard insurance, real estate taxes, and title insurance). You may also have to pay for inspections (including a termite inspection). The good news is that when you use a VA loan to purchase a home, the seller is allowed to pay some or all of your closing costs. Also, you may be able to roll your closing costs into your total loan amount; that way, you don't need any cash at closing. Talk to your real estate agent about closing costs and what you can ask the seller to pay.

Though you're not required to make a down payment to use your VA loan benefit, pulling together some cash may be in your best interest. That's because the less you borrow, the lower your monthly mortgage payments will be.

Providing competitive interest rates and no prepayment penalty

People who use VA purchase loans may get better terms and interest rates than they would on other types of loans. That's because government-backed loans assure lenders that they'll recoup at least some of their money if you default on your payments. Additionally, lenders aren't allowed to charge you a penalty fee if you pay off a VA loan early. (Sometimes lenders charge these prepayment penalties to help them recoup the loss of future interest payments.) That means if you hit the lottery next year and want to pay off your home, you don't have to worry about extra charges from your lender.

Recycling benefits through reusable and assumable loans

Contrary to popular belief, you can use your VA loan benefit more than once. In fact, you may use it as many times as you want, provided that each loan is satisfied before you open another. A loan is considered *satisfied* when it's paid in full — it doesn't matter whether you paid it off yourself or you sold the home and the new buyer's lender paid off your lender. As soon as your previous VA loan is satisfied, you can reuse your benefit.

VA loans also are *assumable*, which means if another person comes along and wants to buy your home, they can simply take over payments for you. If another veteran who qualifies assumes your loan, they can substitute their entitlement for yours on that mortgage. However, if someone who doesn't qualify for a VA loan takes over yours, you can't reuse your benefit until they've fully repaid the loan. You should always consult with a financial professional before you even think about letting someone assume your VA loan; if they screw it up (such as by defaulting on payments), you could be on the hook for the repercussions, and the VA could terminate your ability to use your benefit in the future.

TIP

Make sure you always work with a real estate agent, especially when you're buying a home. As a buyer, you don't pay a real estate agent's commission (the seller does). That means a buyer's agent's services are completely free to you, and your agent has a fiduciary responsibility to represent your best interests. Your agent negotiates pricing, manages all the technical aspects of the sale, and makes the magic happen on closing day. And here's another pro tip: Don't work with a seller's or builder's real estate agent when you're buying. That agent represents the seller or builder's best interests. You're better off getting your own agent.

Using your VA loan benefit — The how-to

Any home purchase, with or without a VA loan, has many steps, but the first thing to do if you want this benefit (and why *wouldn't* you?) is to get a certificate of eligibility (COE) from the Department of Veterans Affairs. You can kick off this crazy-easy process at www.benefits.va.gov/homeloans/ or go straight to your eBenefits account (I walk you through the process of creating that in Chapter 3). You can also request one by mail, though it takes longer; if that's the route you want to take, you need VA Form 26-1880, *Request for a Certificate of Eligibility.*

After you have your COE, bring it to the lender of your choice to get mortgage preapproval. When a lender preapproves you, you know exactly how much home you can afford; you can use that information to start your house-hunt. After you find a home you want to buy, your lender will request an *appraisal* (an assessment of the home's value). If the appraisal says the home is worth what you want to pay for it, and if your credit and income information get a thumbs-up from the mortgage underwriters working on your case, your lender will spring into action (I use that term loosely, having used two VA loans myself) to put your benefit to work.

The VA has regional loan centers on many VA campuses as well as a helpline you can call if you have questions. You can find your nearest loan center and the most recent helpline number on the VA's website.

Considering Other Types of VA Loans

The VA offers other home loan programs to eligible veterans, including Native Americans whose tribal or other governing body have entered into a Memorandum of Understanding (MOU) with the VA and vets who want to buy a farm and live off the land. The VA also has special loans for vets who want to refinance existing VA loans to snag a lower interest rate and those who need to get cash out of their home equity. And though they're not technically VA loans, the VA offers special grants to veterans who need to adjust their homes to make life easier. I cover each of these loans (and grants) in the following sections.

Native American Direct Loan Program

The Native American Direct Loan (NADL) program can help you buy, build, or improve a home on federal trust land if you qualify. You may be eligible for an NADL if you meet all of the following:

>> You're a Native American veteran or a non-Native American veteran married to a Native American.

>> You received a discharge that's other than dishonorable.

>> Your tribal government has an agreement or Memorandum of Understanding with the VA detailing how the program works on its trust lands.

>> You have a valid COE from the VA.

>> You meet the VA's credit standards.

>> You can prove that you make enough money to cover the mortgage payments and other, associated costs.

>> You intend to live in the home you're using the loan to buy, build, or improve.

These loans offer several benefits, just like VA-backed purchase loans do. In most cases, you don't need to come up with a down payment, and the VA won't make you buy PMI, either. Closing costs are limited, and you get a low-interest, 30-year fixed-rate mortgage. Currently, the VA interest rate for NADLs begins at 4.5 percent, but your state's VA regional loan center can tell you what your interest rate will be. Like other VA loans, this benefit is reusable. You may also refinance it for a lower interest rate if the opportunity arises. Keep in mind that you may need to pay a one-time VA funding fee, too.

To use your NADL benefit, contact your nearest VA regional loan center. You can find a list of regional loan centers on the VA's website.

Farm loans

You may use your VA loan benefit to buy a farm, but only if the land has a home on it *and* you intend to live in the home as your primary residence. You can't use a VA loan to purchase a farming business, though; the VA will only back a home loan. The VA doesn't limit the number of acres the property can have, but it does require a property appraisal. The appraisal may include improvements such as barns, sheds, and stables, but it can't include crops, livestock, farm equipment, or supplies. If you intend to qualify for the loan using income you'll generate from operating the farm, the VA will verify your ability and experience as a farm operator.

The application process to buy a farm using your VA loan is just like it is with any other purchase loan. You need to bring your COE to your lender, and your lender will preapprove you so you know how much farm you can afford. Then, work with a real estate agent to find a property you want.

Interest rate reduction refinance loans

If you already have a VA-backed loan, you may be able to refinance it using an interest rate reduction refinance loan. Commonly called IRRRLs, these loans let you replace your current loan with a new one that has different terms. In order to use this type of loan, you must certify that you currently live in, or used to live in, the home.

REMEMBER

Like VA purchase loans, the money for an IRRRL doesn't come from the VA. You work with a private bank, credit union, or mortgage company for refinancing. You have the option of comparison shopping, so use it to find out what lender is offering you the best terms and interest rates. When you find a lender you want to work with, follow its processes for closing on the loan; you'll most likely need to provide your lender with the COE you used to get your original loan as well as other documentation that proves you're in good enough financial standing to qualify.

Cash-out refinance loans

VA-backed cash-out refinance loans let you replace your current loan with a new one. You may use this type of loan if you want to take cash out of your home equity or if you want to replace a non-VA–backed loan with a VA-backed loan (such as when you purchased a home prior to military service or didn't know you could use a VA loan as a veteran). To use this benefit, you must qualify for a VA loan and obtain a COE from the VA. You must also meet the VA's and your lender's requirements for credit and income and certify that you plan to live in the home you're refinancing with the loan.

REMEMBER

This loan allows you to take cash out of your *home equity* — the difference between what your home is currently worth and what you owe on it. You can use the cash for anything you want. For example, if your home is currently worth $300,000 and you owe $250,000 on it, you have $50,000 in home equity. Using a VA cash-out refinance loan means that you can get 100 percent of your home equity in cash (unlike most other cash-out refinance programs). But these loans have closing costs, and in some cases, they total thousands of dollars. You may also need to pay a VA funding fee. Make sure you crunch the numbers before you decide whether a cash-out refinance loan is the right choice for you.

WARNING

If a refinance offer you receive in the mail (or your email) seems too good to be true, it probably is. If you intend to use a cash-out refinance loan, make sure it's from an approved VA lender. Any offer that claims you can skip mortgage payments or get unbelievably low interest rates (or makes any other claims that seem fishy) may be part of a misleading offer that you should ignore.

Specially Adapted Housing Grants

Though not technically a VA loan, specially adapted housing grants come from the VA and allow you to buy, build, or change your home. You may be eligible for one of these grants if you have a qualifying service-connected disability, which I discuss in Chapter 9. A limited number of these grants are available each fiscal year, so if you think you may qualify, you should apply as soon as possible.

THE VA VENDEE LOAN PROGRAM

The VA Vendee Loan Program exists because sometimes people who use VA loans default on them; that is, they don't make their mortgage payments. When that happens, the lender takes possession of the home — and with VA loans, the lender has the option of asking the VA to buy it. When the VA does buy one of these properties, it becomes what's known as a VA real-estate owned (REO) property.

The VA lists the property for sale, and anyone from the public may purchase it using a guaranteed loan or by using the VA Vendee Loan Program, which is administered through a third-party lender. If you use the VA's program, you have to pay a VA funding fee of 2.25 percent, but you can purchase the home with little or nothing down; credit requirements are flexible, and you don't need to buy PMI if you have less than 20 percent of the sales price to put down.

You can't finance closing costs, and you must use your personal credit (not your business's credit). A lot of times, these properties are fixer-uppers; that's because the people who owned them didn't have the money for the mortgage payments, so they likely didn't have the cash for maintenance and repairs. If you're interested in the homes listed through this program, you can search "VA Vendee Loans" on the VA's website.

Applying for Your COE

To participate in the VA home loan program, you must meet basic requirements. Typically, the requirements are based on your time in service (which varies by time period and whether you were active duty or in the National Guard or Reserves). The minimum service requirements do have some exceptions, such as when you were discharged due to a service-connected disability. Some surviving spouses also qualify for the VA loan program. If you're not sure about your eligibility, get in touch with your VA regional loan center; the professionals there can talk to you about your situation.

You don't have a VA loan benefit if you received a dishonorable discharge.

To get your COE, visit the VA's website or log into your eBenefits account (I explain that process in Chapter 3). You need a copy of your discharge documents or separation papers to apply for your COE. After you're logged in, you simply answer a few questions, and the VA will review your documents. If you qualify, the VA will provide you with a letter that says so. You may take that letter to your lender to show that you're eligible for a VA-backed loan.

Chapter **16**

Enjoying Your Golden Years in a Military Retirement Home

The United States government has operated military retirement homes in one form or another for more than 200 years, and today's evolutions are more like resorts than you might imagine. But you don't have to pin your hopes on getting a spot in a military retirement home run by the feds. You may be eligible to move on a military installation to live alongside current military servicemembers, or you may be able to join a military-only retirement community in your local area. You may even be able to find your place in a state veterans' home or VA retirement home. This chapter outlines your options for living your best life in one of these places, what you need to do to get in, and what's possible after you've unpacked your framed discharge document.

Living in an AFRH

The Armed Forces Retirement Home (AFRH) is an independent government agency under the executive branch of government. It provides living quarters and related services for some retired and former members of the U.S. armed forces, regardless of branch. Many vets feel right at home in the company of other former servicemembers, and they enjoy the safety, security, and convenience that these residences provide. The following sections examine what AFRHs offer and who's eligible to live in one.

Checking out what AFRHs offer

The two AFRH residences are in Gulfport, Mississippi, and Washington, D.C. Table 16-1 lists their offerings and specifies which services are (and aren't) included with your resident fees.

REMEMBER

All the rooms at AFRH facilities are nonsmoking, but each campus does have smoking areas. And in case you were wondering, pot is never permitted on federal property.

Your spouse may live with you in a married couple suite at an AFRH facility, even if they aren't a veteran. However, your spouse must be enrolled in the Defense Enrollment Eligibility Reporting System (DEERS), and you must be able to prove that you were married before you became eligible for retired pay and benefits. You're responsible for paying for your spouse's accommodations, too. If your spouse is also a qualifying veteran, they can live with you in a married couple suite without having to prove that you were married before retirement.

TIP

In both facilities, couples may choose two single beds or a full or queen-sized bed in a double-occupancy apartment.

Pets aren't allowed in AFRH facilities, and neither are emotional support animals. However, medical service animals may live with you.

Here's a quick overview of the two sites:

>> **AFRH Gulfport:** Located on the Mississippi Sound, this facility was destroyed following Hurricane Katrina. It has since been rebuilt, and it's designed to mitigate the effects of a Category 5 hurricane. In addition to the standard AFRH amenities, it has an outdoor swimming pool, rooms with ocean views, a walking bridge directly to the beach, an art studio, and oversize parking for RVs.

TABLE 16-1   AFRH Services

Available Services	Part of Resident Fee	At Your Own Expense
Private rooms with private bathrooms	X	
On-site medical services, including dental, podiatry, and vision care		X*
Three meals a day	X	
Daily recreational activities	X	
Special events each month	X	
Resident day trips	X	
State-of-the-art fitness centers	X	
Movie theaters, bowling centers, and craft and hobby shops	X	
In-room cable and Internet		X
Full-service libraries	X	
24-hour-a-day security and emergency alert system	X	
Shuttle services to military and VA healthcare facilities	X	
Access to religious services	X	
Access to 24-hour laundry rooms	X	
Housekeeping		X
Parking for one vehicle	X	
Other personal services, such as dry cleaning, haircuts, and linen service		X
Assisted living services, memory support, and long-term care		X

Health insurance may pay for these services.

Each apartment in Gulfport is furnished with a single or double bed, armoire, and TV stand, and you can bring a comfortable chair or loveseat, shelves, and artwork of your own. You may also bring your own comfort items, such as a TV, computer, and personal items. Space is limited, though, so you may need to downsize your belongings.

>> **AFRH Washington:** Created in 1851 and originally called the Old Soldiers' Home, AFRH Washington was a popular visiting spot for President Abraham

Lincoln (as well as presidents before him). Lincoln even had a cottage on the grounds, and he spent about a quarter of his time in it; he wrote the Emancipation Proclamation while staying there. Back then, there was a 300-acre dairy farm on the property that veterans worked to earn their keep — but that changed in the 1900s, when it became a more leisurely place to live. What were once cow pastures are now part of the 9-hole golf course and resident gardens, scenic walking trails, and stocked fishing ponds. Residents can also enjoy an art studio and several recreation rooms in the facility.

The rooms in D.C. come with a single bed, dresser, and nightstand, but there's enough room to bring a comfortable recliner and some other small furnishings. Because the apartments aren't penthouse-sized (they're fairly modest in size, more like studios), you may need to downsize before moving in.

Determining eligibility and cost

You may be eligible to live in an AFRH if you served more than 50 percent of your career as an enlisted member, warrant officer, or limited-duty officer. If you're a retiree, you must have served 20 or more years on active duty in a regular component, served in the Guard or Reserves with at least 20 years of creditable service, or qualified for an early retirement (if you receive retired pay and benefits). You may also be eligible if you have a service-connected disability rated at 50 percent or more, served during a period of conflict and received hostile fire pay, or served in a theater of war during a time of war.

You must be able to live independently at the time you move in. That means you must be able to manage your own daily personal needs, navigate the campus on your own, and have full mental competency. However, if your health status changes, you won't be required to move out. And if your spouse outlives you, regardless of their health condition, they'll be permitted to stay after you're gone.

WARNING

Your spouse, widow, or widower can't apply to live in an AFRH facility without you if they don't qualify in their own right.

WARNING

If you have an active substance use disorder, you can't live in an AFRH facility. If you had alcohol or drug issues in the past, you must turn in a completed mental health evaluation form and show that you've been sober for at least one continuous year.

REMEMBER

The AFRH doesn't have an application or entry fee. However, you do have to pay a monthly fee for the level of care you require; that fee is based on a percentage of your gross income. There's a cap on the amount you can be required to pay, though. *Note:* The percentages and caps are subject to change every year and adjust with inflation.

Moving Back on a Military Installation

Looking for a gated community that's close to the commissary, PX, troop clinic, and other amenities? You may be able to move to a military installation. Though not all bases have housing for retirees, and you'll likely be on the bottom of the waiting list, it's a sweet deal: Lots of security, utilities bundled into your monthly rent (depending on the installation), dog parks, free lawn care, and home maintenance usually come standard with living on post. Contact your nearest base or post's housing office to find out whether there's room for you (and how much it costs) if you're seriously considering this option.

Getting Back to Your Roots in a Military-Only Retirement Community

If you served as an officer and want to be surrounded by other vets, consider a military-only retirement community. Some of the most popular around the country are as follows:

» Falcon's Landing in Potomac Falls, Virginia (www.falconslanding.org/)

» Indian River Colony Club in Melbourne, Florida (https://colonyclub.com/us-military/)

» Knollwood Military Retirement Community in Washington, D.C. (https://knollwoodcommunity.org/)

» The Army Residence Community in San Antonio, Texas (https://armyresidence.com/about-us)

» Vinson Hall Retirement Community in McLean, Virginia (www.vinsonhall.org/)

Each of these communities has its own admission requirements (but they all require you to have been a commissioned officer with the exception of Indian River Colony Club, which allows warrant officers). Some communities cater to military retirees but are open to the general public, such as The Fairfax at Belvoir Woods (Fort Belvoir, Virginia), Blue Skies of Texas (San Antonio, Texas), and Patriots Landing (DuPont, Washington).

Living in a State Veterans Home

State veterans homes typically provide nursing home care, domiciliary care, or adult daycare. Some, but not all, state veterans homes have the ability to provide long-term healthcare for people who are chronically ill, disabled, and incapacitated. These residential facilities are managed by state governments, and some states have more of them than others. Every state determines its own eligibility criteria for admission to one of these homes.

Accommodations in a state veterans home are available to most veterans, but it'll cost you. Like eligibility criteria, the costs vary depending on the home; your costs also vary based on the level of care you need and whether you have insurance. If you receive benefits from the VA, such as Aid and Attendance, you may be able to use them to defray your costs of living in a state veterans home.

Living in a CLC Home

Community Living Centers (CLCs) are VA nursing homes, and there are more than a hundred of them across the country. Usually, they're located on VA medical center campuses, though some are nearby. These facilities provide apartment-style living with plenty of amenities, such as planned activities and special visiting spaces. Even better, pets are allowed to live in many of these facilities.

Your eligibility is dependent on whether you need the services a CLC can provide, as well as whether space is available. You must also meet other criteria, such as a certain level of disability and income requirements.

These nursing homes provide

- » 24-hour skilled nursing care
- » Restorative care
- » Access to social work services
- » Geriatric evaluation and management

Some also provide mental health recovery care, memory care, respite care, and palliative and hospice care for end-of-life situations.

4

Burial and Memorial Benefits, Survivor Benefits, and More

IN THIS PART . . .

Get access to special benefits for homeless, unhoused, and indigent veterans.

Find out what benefits are available to incarcerated veterans (and how to use them, wherever you are).

Check out programs and benefits for women, minority, and LGBTQ+ veterans.

Discover benefits that are only available to vets of specific wars, former prisoners of war, and disabled veterans.

Explore your eligibility for benefits as a spouse, dependent child, or veteran's caregiver.

Uncover burial and memorial benefits you may be entitled to as a veteran or dependent, as well as how to apply for a plot in Arlington, a VA national cemetery, or another resting place.

Find out what benefits survivors are entitled to claim.

Analyze your shopping benefits and extend your purchasing power as a card-carrying veteran.

Investigate travel benefits you may be eligible to use, including how to fly Space-A and get coveted spots at Armed Forces Resorts.

Study up on state benefits that may be available to you as a veteran.

Chapter **17**

Accessing Benefits for Homeless Vets

According to the U.S. Department of Housing and Urban Development (HUD), about 40,000 veterans in the United States are homeless at this very minute — but over the course of a year, about twice that many vets experience homelessness. Out of all adults who are unhoused, homeless, or temporarily unsheltered, about 13 percent are veterans. Although these numbers have gone down over the past ten years, the only acceptable number is zero.

Ending veteran homelessness is one of the VA's top priorities, but it can only do so much with the resources it has. The good news: As a result of the VA's work with other federal, state, and local partners, veteran homelessness has been reduced by 50 percent over the past decade.

The VA defines *homelessness* as not having a full-time or adequate nighttime residence, having a nighttime residence that's not intended to be a place for people to sleep (such as a car, an abandoned building, or campground), living in a shelter (or hotel or motel), or being at imminent risk of losing housing. It also considers people who are fleeing or attempting to flee domestic violence and other dangerous situations to be homeless. If you or a veteran you care about is in any of those situations, or something similar, call the National Call Center for Homeless Veterans at 877-424-3838 (877-4AID-VET) for immediate help. Other resources are also available to provide help, which I cover in the following sections.

Dialing in to the National Call Center for Homeless Veterans

The National Call Center for Homeless Veterans (877-4AID-VET) helps vets who are homeless or who are at risk of homelessness as well as family members, friends, and others who reach out in support of veterans. If calling isn't an option, you can chat online with someone from the Call Center through the VA's website. All the help and guidance you receive from the helpline is free and confidential; you get to talk to a trained VA counselor 24 hours a day, 7 days a week. You can use the hotline to get information on all the VA's homeless programs, healthcare (including mental healthcare), and other services you may find useful. You can also get connected with resources and services through the VA's website at www.va.gov/homeless/.

REMEMBER

When you call the National Call Center for Homeless Veterans, a VA staff member will ask you a few questions to determine who can help you. Then, your call will be transferred to that person.

Getting Expedited Benefits

Your nearest VA regional office, which you can find on the VA's website, has trained professionals on staff to help you apply for veterans benefits. Every VA office and medical center also has a homeless coordinator who can help expedite your claims. And if you don't have a fixed address or bank account, that's okay; your coordinator can help ensure that you receive your benefit payments anyway.

Unlocking Access to the VA's Housing Assistance Programs

The VA offers a handful of housing assistance programs, including those that feature domiciliary care (see the later section, "Finding Healthcare Services," to discover more about them). Domiciliary care is usually tied into some type of healthcare, whether it's substance abuse treatment, behavioral health treatment, or other medical treatments — but if you don't need that type of care or treatment, the VA has other programs that can help.

All the VA's housing assistance programs are focused first on housing and then services. This model means that the VA's main priority is to get veterans into a safe, stable place to live before anything else. After you're housed, the VA can help you access the services and benefits you need.

To access most of the following programs, you need to get in touch with the National Call Center for Homeless Veterans or speak to the homeless coordinator at your local VA medical center or regional office.

Housing Choice Rental Vouchers

The VA works with HUD to provide supportive housing to eligible veterans by way of housing vouchers in a program known as HUD-VASH (that's short for HUD plus VA Supportive Housing). The way it works is simple: HUD provides homeless veterans with rental assistance vouchers for privately owned housing. These vouchers, also called housing choice vouchers (HCVs), go toward paying rent in what you may know as *Section 8* housing. Homes that are considered Section 8 are privately owned and may be apartments, condominiums, single-family homes, or duplexes. If you receive these vouchers, you may choose to rent anywhere that accepts them.

The only way to get into this program is to work with the VA. The VA refers veterans who need the program to the local Public Housing Agency (PHA), which then determines a veteran's eligibility as well as administers the program moving forward. That means the PHA will explain the program's rules, issue the voucher, approve the home, make housing assistance payments to the owner, and ensure that everyone sticks to the rules.

REMEMBER

PHAs aren't allowed to conduct criminal background checks on HUD-VASH recipients except to determine whether a household member is on a state sex offender registry. If a family member is a sex offender, you may still be eligible for the program — but that person won't be permitted to live with you. If you, the veteran, are a registered sex offender, you and your family are ineligible for this program.

Safe Haven

Safe Haven is the VA's program to provide transitional supportive housing — that is, temporary housing — and access to programs that can help veterans suffering from severe mental illness or substance use disorders. Admission to a Safe Haven doesn't have a sobriety requirement, and you don't have to comply with mental health treatment, either. However, there are only established Safe Havens in a handful of cities, which are listed on the VA's website.

If you think you may qualify for temporary housing in a Safe Haven, or if you want to find out whether there's one near you, call 877-4AID-VET or visit a VA medical center or regional office; ask to talk to the homeless coordinator for help. You must be referred to a Safe Haven facility. You can't just walk in and ask to stay a while.

Drop-in centers

Some cities have drop-in centers that veterans can use to take a shower, change and launder clothes, get haircuts, and access food. These centers are only for veterans (though your city or town may have a similar drop-in center that's open to the public). When you visit a veterans drop-in center, you may be able to talk with the staff to get help accessing other resources — and in many cases, even receive help applying for veterans benefits you're entitled to receive. Drop-in centers don't provide overnight accommodations; they only provide a safe place to be during the day. Not all cities have veterans drop-in centers (or many homeless programs at all), so if you need help, reach out to the National Call Center for Homeless Veterans to find out what's available in your area.

Finding Healthcare Services

The VA has a number of healthcare programs specifically designed for homeless, unhoused, and at-risk veterans. You can access some of them by calling the National Call Center for Homeless Veterans. You may also visit your nearest VA Medical Center to find out what type of healthcare services you may be eligible to receive. Three of the main programs the VA has in place are related to domiciliary care, and the other two are Health Care for Homeless Vets and the Homeless Veterans Dental Program. I explain each in the following sections.

Domiciliary Care for Homeless Vets

The biggest thing to know about the Domiciliary Care for Homeless Veterans (DCHV) program is that sobriety or compliance with treatment isn't required. That means if you're struggling with alcohol or drug use or dependence, you don't have to get treatment right away; you can still take advantage of the DCHV program. The program provides supportive housing to veterans who have had a tough time staying compliant with other homeless programs (such as those that require sobriety or compliance with mental healthcare).

Domiciliaries (the housing and treatment facilities involved in the DCHV program) are there to provide a structured, supportive residential environment 24 hours a day, 7 days a week. To get access to a domiciliary program, contact the VA's homeless veteran helpline at 877-424-3838 or a homeless coordinator at your local VA hospital or regional office.

Residential Rehabilitation Treatment

The VA's Domiciliary Residential Rehabilitation Treatment Program (DRRTP) provides a residential level of care that may include treatment for medical and psychiatric conditions, posttraumatic stress, and substance abuse issues for homeless veterans.

DRRTP can give you a chance to live within a community of other vets while learning special skills to help you avoid homelessness in the future. You can get addiction counseling, spiritual guidance in your chosen faith, behavioral counseling, and even dietary counseling. You have the opportunity to participate in vocational and occupational therapy, including the Compensated Work Therapy program, which I cover in more detail in Chapter 10. To find out whether you're eligible for DRRTP, talk to the homeless coordinator at your local VA hospital or regional office, or call the National Call Center for Homeless Veterans.

Domiciliary PTSD and Domiciliary SA

Like other domiciliary programs the VA runs, the Domiciliary PTSD (Dom PTSD) and Domiciliary Substance Abuse (Dom SA) programs provide residential care to veterans suffering from either of these conditions. You may be eligible to use these programs if you're homeless or at risk of becoming homeless and you suffer from posttraumatic stress or a substance abuse issue. Both offer residential treatment that can help you get back on your feet. Typically, the only way to get into one of these residential treatment programs is to call the National Call Center for Homeless Veterans or talk to a homeless coordinator at your nearest VA facility.

Health Care for Homeless Vets Program

The Health Care for Homeless Veterans (HCHV) program may be able to help you get the medical care you need, at the VA's expense, as well as assign you a case manager who can connect you with healthcare providers and housing intervention services. You can get treatment for chronic conditions, checkups, and other medical services through this program. This program conducts outreach events when possible, and you can access the same or similar services by calling the National Call Center for Homeless Veterans.

Homeless Veterans Dental Program

The Homeless Veterans Dental Program (HVDP) provides dental care to some veterans who are in certain VA-sponsored rehabilitation programs such as those listed in this section. The program offers free, focused care to treat conditions that are affecting you at the time you're enrolled in the program, including care that's medically necessary. The treatment you receive is the same that's generally available to newly discharged veterans, such as treatments that are necessary to help you overcome dental issues to gain or regain employment, alleviate pain, or treat moderate, severe, or complicated conditions.

Though you may not qualify for routine dental care through this program, you may be eligible to apply for dental benefits based on your service, income, or other factors. If you're not sure whether you qualify, a VA rep or case manager can help you explore your options; sometimes, reps from the VA can connect you with other resources, such as local and state programs, that may be able to help you get dental care.

Getting Mental Healthcare

The VA provides special treatment to some homeless veterans who are experiencing mental health issues, including substance abuse, posttraumatic stress, and the effects of military sexual trauma (MST). See the earlier sections, "Residential Rehabilitation Treatment" and "Domiciliary PTSD and Domiciliary SA" for more information on inpatient help — but if you don't need or want inpatient help, you may benefit from the outpatient treatment programs, which I discuss here.

Substance Use Disorder Treatment Enhancement Initiative

Under its Substance Use Disorder Treatment Enhancement Initiative, the VA provides a number of substance use treatments. Depending on your level of need and program availability, you may be able to access cognitive behavioral therapy that helps you manage cravings, refuse opportunities to use substances, and use problem-solving approaches to help you stay clean and sober. The VA also uses motivational interviewing to help you find your focus and motivational enhancement therapy to help you strengthen your personal motivations for change.

REMEMBER

In some cases, substance abuse disorders are successfully managed with medication. When you're in treatment, your VA healthcare or mental healthcare provider may be able to prescribe medications such buprenorphine, injective naltrexone, or methadone for opioid use disorders; acamprosate, disulfiram, naltrexone, or topiramate for alcohol use disorders; or nicotine replacement therapy, bupropion, and varenicline for tobacco use disorders.

If you need these types of treatment, the first step is contacting the National Call Center for Homeless Veterans, visiting your local VA healthcare facility, or checking out a Community Resource and Referral Center (see the later section with the same name for more information on finding those). You can also check the VA's website for a Substance Use Disorder (SUD) program near you or call the VA's main information hotline at 800-827-1000. You don't need to qualify for VA healthcare benefits to apply for help.

Readjustment Counseling Service's Vet Center Program

Vet Centers are community-based counseling centers that offer individual, group, marriage, and family counseling (though some Vet Centers have more complete lists of services than others do). You're eligible for help through a Vet Center if any of the following are true, whether you served on active duty or in the National Guard or Reserves:

>> You served in any combat theater or area of hostility, including Iraq, Afghanistan, and many others.

>> You experienced military sexual trauma, regardless of gender or service era.

>> You provided mortuary services or emergency medical care to treat casualties of war while serving on active duty.

>> You performed as a member of a UAV crew that provided direct support to operations in a combat theater or area of hostility.

>> You received care at a Vet Center prior to January 2, 2013, and are a Vietnam-era veteran.

>> You served on active duty in response to a major disaster or national emergency declared by the president, or under orders of the governor or chief executive of your state in response to a disaster or civil disorder in that state.

>> You're a former member of the Coast Guard who participated in any drug interdiction operation.

>> You're a member of the Reserves or National Guard and have a behavioral health condition or psychological trauma related to military service that adversely affects your quality of life or adjustment to civilian life.

REMEMBER

Accessing these services has no time limit; even if you were discharged from the military 50 years ago, you can still get counseling at a Vet Center if you meet eligibility requirements. You may be eligible for readjustment counseling regardless of your discharge characterization.

If you don't want to visit your local Vet Center, you can still get free, confidential help by calling the Vet Center Call Center at 877-927-8387. You can talk about your military experience or any other issue you're facing with combat veterans from several war eras or with vets' family members who are trained to talk about important issues.

Working toward Employment

The VA has a handful of programs to help homeless veterans find and retain employment. Two of the most notable are the Homeless Veteran Community Employment Services and the Compensated Work Therapy program, which I cover in the following sections. Don't forget that you may also qualify for other employment programs and resources, which I cover in Chapter 10, as well as your GI Bill (Chapter 13) and disability benefits (Chapter 20).

Homeless Veteran Community Employment Services

The VA's Homeless Veterans Community Employment Services program has vocational development specialists who serve as Community Employment Coordinators (CECs) in most VA medical centers. These CECs can pre-screen you to determine what skills you have that would be useful in the workforce, refer you to open job positions, and help you through the hiring and onboarding process. Though this program doesn't provide housing, it's open only to homeless and at-risk veterans.

Compensated Work Therapy

Compensated Work Therapy (CWT) is a clinical vocational rehabilitation program that I cover in more detail in Chapter 10. In plain English, CWT is a work program for disabled vets and those with barriers to employment; it helps match vets with employers who are ready to hire right now. CWT can provide you with the basic work skills you need to get and keep a job, including information on appropriate workplace attire, navigating workplace relationships, and meeting your employer's expectations.

Getting the Veterans Pension

The veterans pension is available to wartime vets who meet certain criteria. To be eligible for this monthly cash payment, your net worth must fall below a certain limit and you must have any discharge characterization other than dishonorable; you must also be over the age of 65 or be permanently and totally disabled. I cover the full eligibility requirements and how this program works in Chapter 8.

Accessing Community Resource and Referral Centers

You may be able to walk into a Community Resource and Referral Center (CRRC) to find out what services you're eligible for. CCRCs can provide you with temporary shelter and connect you with services such as mental healthcare, job development programs, housing options, and other benefits you may qualify for.

CCRCs are located in several major cities, including Washington, D.C., Atlanta, Philadelphia, Detroit, Chicago, Milwaukee, New Orleans, Denver, and Dallas. You can find a complete listing of CCRCs and their contact information on the VA's website or by searching "VA Community Resource and Referral Center" online.

URGENT HELP THROUGH SSVF

The Supportive Services for Veteran Families (SSVF) program provides case management and supportive services that may help you prevent the imminent loss of your home. The program can help you identify a new, more suitable housing situation and rapidly re-house you and your family, as well as provide case management, healthcare, transportation, housing counseling, and legal services. This program is reserved for very low-income veterans and their families. If you're in danger of losing your home or are living in an unsuitable location (such as your car or a park), reach out to the National Call Center for Homeless Veterans (877-4AID-VET) to find out whether you qualify for immediate help through this program. The only way to get help through this program is by getting a referral from a VA professional.

Participating in Stand-Downs

From time to time, local VAs hold *stand-downs*. These one- to three-day events rely on VA staff and volunteers to provide food, clothing, and healthcare screenings to homeless and at-risk vets. During a stand-down, you can get help finding a place to stay or live, healthcare referrals, and employment help; you can also access substance use treatment and mental health counseling.

The VA also distributes excess government property to homeless veterans at these events, including things like sleeping bags, footwear, coats, and hats. Find upcoming stand-downs in your area by contacting your nearest VA medical center or regional office, or by visiting www.va.gov/homeless/events.asp.

Exploring State Programs for Unhoused Veterans with NRD

Most states have a variety of programs for homeless veterans, and your local VA medical center, Vet Center, or campus has information on what's available near you. So does the National Call Center for Homeless Veterans. You can also find information on local programs by using the National Resource Directory (https://nrd.gov/). When you're there, type in your city and state, and choose "Homeless Assistance" from the dropdown menu. You'll receive a list of vetted organizations that may be able to provide you with the help you need.

IN THIS CHAPTER

» Figuring out which benefits you still have

» Exploring healthcare when you get out

» Connecting with Veterans Justice Outreach

Chapter **18**

Using Benefits While Incarcerated

ncarcerated veterans — who make up about 8 percent of the federal and state inmates in the United States — face unique challenges and are at risk of losing earned benefits. More than 65 percent of justice-involved veterans were in some form of combat, and of those, around 55 percent deal with posttraumatic stress or a traumatic brain injury. (*Justice-involved veterans* are former service-members who have been detained by or are under the supervision of the criminal justice system, which includes everything from arrests to prison sentences.)

In 2016, the U.S. Department of Justice conducted a study on vets in prison, finding that about 74 percent of veterans in state prisons and 77 percent of those in federal prisons received honorable discharges or general discharges under honorable conditions; only 6 and 5 percent, respectively, received dishonorable or bad conduct discharges. And among incarcerated vets, around 30 percent have a history of homelessness.

Several studies have linked traumatic experiences and posttraumatic stress to criminal justice involvement, which may explain the reason why military servicemembers are more likely to end up in jails and prisons than their civilian counterparts. Although I can't begin to speculate what will happen in the future, I can say that recent changes in legislation, a more widespread acceptance of Veteran Treatment Courts (special courts designed to help eligible vets stay out of jail while providing treatment for mental health issues, addiction, and other conditions), and a small number of VA programs are available to justice-involved veterans. Many organizations are fighting to change the way the legal system handles vets who are convicted of crimes.

This chapter addresses those VA programs and outlines what happens to your benefits if you find yourself behind bars (or otherwise involved in the criminal justice system).

Exploring How Incarceration Affects Your Eligibility for Benefits

The Department of Veterans Affairs is bound by laws passed by Congress, which means Congress is in charge of whether justice-involved vets are entitled to benefits. Under current laws, the VA is allowed to pay you some benefits if you're incarcerated — but often, the benefits are dependent on the reason for incarceration.

If you're in jail or prison, or if you're on parole, extended supervision, or a similar program, you may be eligible for disability compensation, education and training benefits, healthcare benefits, insurance, vocational rehabilitation and employment, and burial benefits. The following sections outline the main types of VA benefits and what happens to them when you're imprisoned.

Receiving disability compensation

If you receive VA disability compensation payments and you're convicted of a felony and imprisoned for more than 60 days, the following happens:

» If you have a 20 percent or greater VA disability rating, your disability rating is bumped down (only for the purposes of financial calculations, though) to 10 percent.

» If you have a 10 percent VA disability rating, your payments are reduced by one-half.

» If you receive any increased compensation, it's subject to reduction.

When you're released from prison, you may ask to have your compensation payments reinstated. However, your service-connected disabilities will be reevaluated, which may result in a lower compensation rate.

REMEMBER

If your family depends on your disability payments to live, you may be able to ask the VA to give all or part of them to your spouse, children, or dependent parents instead. You must file a claim to ask the VA to do this — it's not automatic. The VA will look at your income and living expenses, how much compensation you normally receive, and whether your family members have special needs to determine whether it can apportion your payments to your dependents. If your dependents are incarcerated, they aren't eligible.

The VA won't reduce your compensation if you're participating in a work-release program, living in a halfway house, or living under community control, which is different in each state that uses it. (In some states, *community control* is like probation; in others, it's more like house arrest with some privileges to leave for work, school, and emergencies.) It also won't reduce your compensation if you're jailed for a misdemeanor — just a felony when your imprisonment lasts more than 60 days.

TIP

You may apply for disability benefits while you're incarcerated. Though you won't receive more than the rate for a 10 percent disability if your application is granted, you'll receive the full amount you qualify for after your release. The exception is when you're rated at 10 percent disabled; in that case, you can't qualify for more than 5 percent while you're in jail or prison for more than 60 days.

Looking at other benefits

Here are some other benefits that are affected if you're incarcerated:

>> **Disability pension:** If you receive a disability pension from the VA, which is usually only for wartime vets aged 65 or older who meet certain income requirements, you lose it if you're convicted of a crime and sentenced to more than 60 days in jail or prison. That goes for a misdemeanor or a felony. You're required to let the VA know if you're incarcerated; if the VA overpays you, you're responsible for repaying the benefits you receive. You must reapply after your release if you want your disability pension reinstated.

>> **GI Bill:** You may use your GI Bill if you're incarcerated — but if you're in prison for committing a felony, you won't receive the housing stipend. You're only entitled to the cost of tuition, fees, and books and supplies. If you're in a halfway house, in jail for committing a misdemeanor, or participating in a work-release program, you're still entitled to your full GI Bill benefits. But if another program kicks in to pay for any aspect of your education (such as a state program for incarcerated veterans), the VA won't pay them.

>> **VA healthcare services:** Being in jail or prison doesn't cancel your VA healthcare benefits if you receive care from a VA medical facility (or with VA payments to another provider). But the VA can't provide any hospital or outpatient care to you when the facility you're in has a duty to provide care or services. That means that if the jail or prison you're in is responsible for your medical care, a VA provider can't see you. (In the vast majority of cases, correctional facilities *are* responsible for providing medical care — even those that charge inmates copays for medical services.)

REMEMBER

When you're released from a correctional institution, the VA can begin providing your medical care again. That's true whether you're living in a halfway house or another facility, you're under supervision, or you're living in your own home.

>> **Retirement pay:** For the most part, retirees who receive retirement pay may continue to receive it while in jail or prison. The government will continue to direct deposit your earnings into your bank account. However, some convictions make a pension null and void, such as those related to treason, espionage, sabotage, and other crimes against the United States. If you're convicted of any of those types of crimes, you can kiss your retired pay goodbye.

Keeping TRICARE Active for Your Family

You're eligible to maintain TRICARE for Life coverage for your family if you're incarcerated, though as part of that plan, you must maintain Medicare Part A and Medicare Part B coverage. That means you have to continue paying your Medicare Part B premiums. (I cover TRICARE and how it works with Medicare in Chapter 6.) Your TRICARE benefits under this plan are only available to your family, not you. If you're younger than 65 and receive Social Security Disability Insurance (SSDI), you remain eligible for Medicare.

TECHNICAL STUFF

The Health Insurance Portability and Accountability Act (HIPAA) normally requires healthcare providers and insurance companies to protect your personal health information. Under HIPAA rules, people have to consent to the release of their own medical information. However, if you were covered by TRICARE before you were locked up, TRICARE may share your personal health information with the jail or prison you're in without your consent.

Eyeing the Health Care for Re-entry Veterans Program

The Health Care for Re-entry Veterans (HCRV) program provides services to help vets when they're released from prison. This VA program's main goals are to prevent homelessness and ensure that veterans have the right access to medical care and mental healthcare upon release. Thanks to this program, you're eligible to a pre-release assessment, and you can get referrals to medical, mental health, and social services. You can also take advantage of employment services after you're released, as well as get short-term case management help so you can stay organized and get the medical treatments you need after you're out.

Somewhere around 1,000 state and federal prisons across the country have connections with HCRV specialists, but if yours doesn't, you can ask to be put in touch with one or reach out to the specialist from your state. (The VA keeps a list of HCRV specialists at www.va.gov/homeless/reentry.asp).

Getting with Veterans Justice Outreach

The Veterans Justice Outreach (VJO) program reaches out to justice-involved vets all over the country, but if they haven't reached out to you, ask to talk to a Veterans Justice Specialist (VJS) or VA representative in your institution. These experts work at every VA medical facility and can get you access to valuable programs that you can use while you're incarcerated and after you get out. A VJS can connect you with mental health treatment and medical care, job training and other employment resources, and even help you reapply to reinstate your benefits after your release. (I cover reinstatement of benefits in the later section, "Resuming Benefits after Incarceration.")

The VA can't provide you with legal services. However, your VJS may be able to connect you with community legal assistance resources. In fact, many VA facilities host free legal clinics for veterans (though they're operated by non-VA legal service providers).

FELONY WARRANTS COST YOU YOUR BENEFITS

The government will automatically cut off all your VA benefits if you have a felony warrant. It's not just about you, either — if your benefits are going to your dependents, they're out of luck until your warrant is resolved. (The same is true for beneficiaries; if they have an outstanding felony warrant, they don't receive any VA benefits.) That means no healthcare, no medications, and no disability benefits; you get nada until you turn yourself in, get your warrant recalled, or otherwise resolve the situation. As long as you're out on bond, you're entitled to your full benefits; whether you lose access to some benefits depends on whether you're convicted and sentenced to more than 60 days of imprisonment. (You won't lose your benefits until your 61st day of imprisonment, so if you're sentenced to less than that, you're still entitled to everything you currently have.)

Finding Help through Justice for Vets

Justice for Vets is a national organization that helps incarcerated and formerly incarcerated veterans get the services and help they need. Though the organization can't provide legal help, substance abuse help, or mental health services, it can refer you to professionals in each field.

It also runs the National Mentor Corps (https://justiceforvets.org/mentorcorps/), a network of mentors who can provide vet-to-vet support to vets reentering society after incarceration. Mentors can help you find housing, employment, and transportation, navigate disability compensation claims, and even contest your discharge status. They know how to connect you with valuable services that are available to you locally and federally.

Checking out Programs for Legal Help

Several organizations connect veterans with the legal help they need. In addition to your state's Legal Aid office, which provides access to free legal help to qualified vets (and others), you may find the following helpful:

>> **Stateside Legal** (www.statesidelegal.org/) is designed to help members of the military, vets, and their families with legal matters. With a huge library of self-help resources on all kinds of legal issues ranging from civil rights and

immigration to criminal and family law as well as connections to free legal assistance just for veterans, it's a tremendous resource you can use at any time (even if you're not involved in the criminal justice system).

>> **The American Bar Association's Home Front program** (`www.americanbar.org/groups/legal_services/milvets/aba_home_front/`) gives you lists of attorneys who provide free legal help as well as veteran-specific programs available to you.

>> **The National Organization of Veterans' Advocates, Inc.** (`www.vetadvocates.org/cpages/sustaining-members-directory`) provides lists of attorneys who regularly work with veterans on a wide range of issues, including criminal defense, appeals, and more.

Resuming Benefits after Incarceration

You must apply to reinstate your benefits after you're released; the VA doesn't simply give them back to you. If you received VA disability payments before your incarceration, you need to be reevaluated for your service-connected disabilities after your release. Your new VA disability rating will be based on the severity of your disabilities *at the time of your release*, so it may be different than it was before you were locked up.

A VJS from the VA can help you line up reinstatement while you're still incarcerated, but if you haven't had the opportunity to talk to one, that's okay. You can visit your nearest VA medical center and ask to speak to a VJS about resuming your benefits. You may also choose to work with a VSO such as the Veterans of Foreign Wars, American Legion, or Disabled American Veterans, which I cover in Chapter 3.

Chapter **19**

Applying for Benefits for Women, Minority, and LGBTQ+ Vets

Every qualifying veteran — today, that is — is eligible for all available VA benefits. But that wasn't always the case. In the not-so-distant past, millions of veterans were denied access to the GI Bill, VA-backed home loans, and other benefits because of their skin color, sexuality, and a number of other discriminatory reasons. And even in cases where the U.S. government didn't deny minorities benefits, the service branches sometimes did; in other cases, private organizations (such as lenders and homebuilders) often refused to help minorities use their earned benefits.

For example, after World War II, more than 1.2 million Black Americans were denied the use of their GI Bill benefits because of the way the Servicemen's Readjustment Act of 1944 was structured. (I strongly encourage you to look up what happened when Black Americans attempted to use their GI Bills following the war.) In another example, LGBTQ veterans were given other than honorable discharges and denied their military benefits before the repeal of the "Don't Ask, Don't Tell" policy in 2011.

But fortunately, denying benefits (or the use of benefits) for discriminatory reasons is illegal, provided that the person claiming them falls into a protected category. To help prevent discriminatory practices and to encourage minority veterans to get the benefits they deserve, the VA established the Center for Minority Veterans and the Minority Veterans Program. Though very few specialty benefits are available exclusively to minority vets, this chapter covers important things you should know about navigating the benefits available to you and working with the VA to get them.

TECHNICAL
STUFF

Established in 1994, the VA's Center for Minority Veterans is relatively new in the grand scheme of things. It was established in response to more than a century of unfair treatment and poor outreach related to minority veterans, and today, one of its primary purposes is to connect with previously underserved vets and encourage the use of benefits. But most of its work takes place behind the scenes, including advising the VA Secretary, conducting research, and analyzing and evaluating complaints from minority veterans.

Getting Acquainted with the Minority Veterans Program

The VA defines veterans who are minorities as those who are identified as African American, Asian American/Pacific Islander, Hispanic, Native American/Alaska Native, and Native Hawaiian. The program helps connect minority veterans with services and benefits through the use of minority veterans program coordinators (MVPCs).

Every VA regional office, healthcare facility, and national cemetery has an MVPC; that person can serve as your direct contact when you want to learn about what benefits you qualify for. The MVPC can help you apply for those benefits, and they can also refer you to other organizations and resources that can meet your needs.

Enlisting the Help of Women Veterans Programs

Currently around 1.6 million female veterans (and almost 16 million male veterans) live in the United States. The government has come a long way in recognizing women's service since the days of Mary Ludwig Hays McCauley (known as "Molly Pitcher" in popular folklore), Deborah Sampson (most likely the first woman to join the U.S. Army in 1781), Loretta Walsh (the first woman to lawfully enlist in the military, who joined the Navy in 1917), Opha May Johnson (the first woman to join the Marine Corps in 1918), twins Genevieve and Lucille Baker, as well as Myrtle R. Hazard (the first women to join the Coast Guard in 1918), Esther McGowin Blake (the first woman to serve in the U.S. Air Force in 1944), and countless 18th-century women who successfully disguised themselves as men to enlist.

REMEMBER

Today, the VA's Center for Women Veterans puts women veteran coordinators (WVCs) in every regional office. These WVCs can be your primary point of contact for questions, women's issues, and comprehensive assistance in getting your benefits. They can also help you get access to related non-VA benefits, as well as claims intake, development, and processing of military sexual and personal trauma claims.

TIP

If you're interested in sharing your story, the Center for Women Veterans encourages you to participate in the Veterans History Project as part of its "I Am Not Invisible" campaign. You can get information on how to participate through the Library of Congress at www.loc.gov/vets/kit.html.

Navigating Benefits through Native American Veterans Programs

Although only two VA benefit programs are exclusively for Native American veterans, the VA has an Office of Tribal Government Relations (OTGR). The OTGR coordinates and consults with American Indian and Alaska Native tribal governments to develop partnerships that enhance access to benefits and services for these populations. The OTGR also sponsors regional training sessions for tribal leaders and veteran service organizations to help increase veterans access to VA healthcare and other benefits.

The two benefit programs exclusive to Native American veterans are as follows:

>> **The Native American Direct Loan Program (NADL):** I cover this benefit in Chapter 15.

>> **The Alaska Native Veterans Land Allotment Program of 2019:** The Alaska Native Veterans Land Allotment Program of 2019 is designed for eligible Vietnam-era veterans and their heirs to select between 2.5 and 160 acres of free federal land in Alaska. Veterans (or their heirs) must select and apply for

land by December 29, 2025. You can find out more about this program and find out whether you qualify at the VA's website or through the Bureau of Land Management's website at www.blm.gov/.

Leveraging LGBTQ+ Benefits

The military's somewhat checkered past dealing with LGBTQ+ servicemembers and veterans laid the groundwork for LGBTQ+ veteran care coordinators. These coordinators are located in each VA healthcare system and are committed to delivering your healthcare services in an affirming and inclusive environment. They're also there to answer your questions, advocate for you, and handle complaints or concerns you have about your care, and they can help you get started with services designed for LGBTQ+ veterans.

TECHNICAL STUFF

The VA is allowed to offer gender-affirming hormone therapy, preoperative evaluation, mental healthcare, and post-operative and long-term care following gender-confirming surgery, but it can't perform or fund gender-confirming surgery as of this writing.

TIP

Veterans who were discharged from the military under the "Don't Ask, Don't Tell" policy or a preceding policy discriminating against LGBTQ+ servicemembers are eligible to apply for discharge upgrades, which I explain in Chapter 2. If that's you, contact the VA to check your eligibility for all the benefits you may be entitled to.

Chapter **20**

Zeroing In on Claims for Vets of Specific Wars, Former POWs, and Disabled Vets

According to the U.S. Census Bureau, not even *half* of vets use the benefits available to them; they just get out of the military and never look back. That may be because many aren't aware that they qualify — but the bottom line is that a lot of vets have been exposed to toxic chemicals and other hazards that may qualify them for healthcare, disability payments, and more. Though you may not qualify for some benefits (such as disability payments), you may qualify for others that are specific to when and where you served. This chapter outlines the benefits available to certain veteran populations, so search for the conflicts you participated in or the hazards you were exposed to in the military to determine what you may be eligible to apply for.

Exploring Benefits for Veterans Who Served in Specific Theaters

The U.S. military sends troops all over the world — some in large-scale operations and others on small missions — but in many places, servicemembers are exposed to environmental hazards and toxins that don't exist in the United States. Many of these exposures lead to long-term health conditions, and if you have any of them, the VA may be required to provide you with medical care. I discuss the most recent theaters of operations and related conditions in the following sections.

Iraq, Afghanistan, and the Persian Gulf

The VA knows that many veterans who served in Iraq, Afghanistan, and the Persian Gulf during Operation Desert Storm, Operation Enduring Freedom (OEF), Operation Iraqi Freedom (OIF), Operation New Dawn (OND), as well as on other missions in the Southwest Asia theater of operations, were exposed to environmental and chemical hazards that pose health risks. In addition to putting your name in the Open Burn Pit Registry, which I cover in the later section, "Getting on the Airborne Hazards and Open Burn Pit Registry," the VA says you should have a healthcare provider evaluate you if you have symptoms after being exposed to burn pits or any of the hazards I describe in the following sections.

Particulates, sand, and dust

Particulates are very tiny, fine specks of matter that can cause serious health problems because they make their way deep into the lungs and airways. They can come from acids, chemicals, metals, soil, or dust. *Particulate matter (PM)* levels in the Middle East are naturally higher than they are in the United States and many other countries; the particles come from dust storms, vehicle exhaust, farming, industrial emissions, and construction sites. So-called *moon dust,* the fine, shifting sand that covers the terrain in many Middle Eastern countries, is just one example of particulate matter that's been tested and found to cause lung illnesses in servicemembers.

The most common health concerns related to sand, dust, and particulates are respiratory and cardiopulmonary (involving your heart and lungs). In fact, a 2017 study discovered that servicemembers returning from the Greater Middle East experienced a number of lingering health effects, including new-onset asthma and *constrictive bronchiolitis* (a condition that causes the inflammation of small airways). Other common effects of sand, dust, and PM include cold- or flu-like symptoms, such as coughing, runny nose, and shortness of breath. Some types of particulate matter have been classified as carcinogenic.

Depleted uranium and toxic embedded fragments

The military uses depleted uranium (DU), a by-product of the uranium enrichment process, in tank armor and some armor-piercing rounds. It's called *depleted* because by the time the military uses it, it's lost about 40 percent of its radioactivity — but there's still 60 percent left, and it can be extremely harmful when it's inhaled, swallowed, or injected into muscle and soft tissue (such as during an explosion).

Veterans of the Gulf War, Bosnia, OEF, OIF, and OND may have been exposed to DU when they were entering or near burning vehicles, near fires involving DU munitions, salvaging damaged vehicles, or in, on, or near a vehicle hit by friendly fire. Depleted uranium can also contaminate drinking water and food.

Though the military says that DU is most likely cleared from the lungs after several years, fragments may remain embedded in the body for decades. Exposure to uranium can cause serious kidney problems (including kidney failure), and accumulated radioactive dust in the lungs can lead to lung, lymph, and brain cancers. Long-term exposure to DU may also cause genetic birth defects in exposed veterans' children.

REMEMBER

If you were based at the Karshi-Khanabad Air Base (K-2) in Uzbekistan, you're eligible for free DU testing through the VA because you may have been exposed to DU left behind by Soviet forces. Contact your nearest VA medical center for an evaluation.

Malaria pills

Malaria is a mosquito-borne illness, and because the military determined some servicemembers were at risk of contracting the potentially serious disease, it passed out the drug mefloquine. If the military gave you the brand Lariam, you need to know that the military recognizes its long-term neurologic and psychiatric side effects, which include anxiety, paranoia, depression, and hallucinations. In some cases, these side effects last for years after you stop using the drug.

Sulfur fire at Al-Mishraq, Iraq

In June 2003, a fire at the Mishraq State Sulfur Mine plant near Mosul burned for nearly a month, and sulfur dioxide levels from the blaze were high enough to be determined "immediately dangerous to health and life." The fire also released toxic hydrogen sulfur, and servicemembers in the area — particularly soldiers from the 101st Airborne Division — were exposed to the fumes. The chemicals the fire released are known to cause severe airway obstruction, low oxygen levels in the body, and pulmonary edema (fluid in the lungs). In some cases, short-term, high-level exposure can lead to constrictive bronchiolitis and reactive airway dysfunction syndrome (an asthma-like condition).

Chemical warfare agent exposure in Iraq

During OIF, some servicemembers demolished or handled explosive ordnance that may have contained chemical warfare agents such as sarin and mustard gas.

Also, in Khamisiyah, Iraq during the Gulf War, rockets filled with sarin and cyclosarin mixes were found at a munitions storage depot that U.S. Forces demolished after the 1991 ceasefire. Nobody knows how much of these nerve agents were released into the atmosphere, but the DOD determined that somewhere around 100,000 veterans may have been exposed. Since then, VA researchers have been studying the risk of brain cancer mortality in vets who were in Khamisiyah compared to other Gulf War vets. Even small exposures to these chemical agents may cause long-term effects on the nervous and respiratory systems. If you may have been exposed, you should contact the DOD's hotline at 800-497-6261.

Chromium exposure at Qarmat Ali in Iraq

Around 830 servicemembers may have been exposed to chromium in 2003 while guarding a water treatment facility in the Basrah oil fields at Qarmat Ali in Iraq. The facility was contaminated with chromium, a known carcinogen, through sodium dichromate dust. Servicemembers who worked at the port or transported supplies to and from Qarmat Ali weren't at risk for exposure; only those who may have breathed in the dust while working in the facility may have been exposed.

Chromium is known to cause lung cancer when the levels in the air are high. But any exposure may cause nasal irritations, nosebleeds, nasal ulcers, and holes in the nasal septum, as well as respiratory problems such as asthma. It can also cause skin irritation and skin ulcers. The VA has developed a Qarmat Ali Medical Surveillance Program for veterans who may have been exposed; if you enroll, you receive a complete physical exam with emphasis on your ears, nose and throat, and lungs and skin. You also receive a chest X-ray and a pulmonary function test, and if your physician finds any abnormalities, the VA refers you for specialty care. You can enroll in the program by contacting your nearest VA medical center.

Asbestos exposure

Though asbestos is no longer used in the United States, it's in many buildings and products in the Middle East — and many servicemembers have been exposed to it. The VA says you should be tested for illnesses that affect your lungs if you worked in mining, milling, shipyards, construction, carpentry, or demolition. You should also be tested if you worked with products such as flooring, roofing, cement, pipes, insulation, or friction products on vehicles. Additionally, if you were in or around old buildings damaged during the war, you should make an appointment for an evaluation.

Exposure to asbestos can lead to a wide range of illnesses, including *asbestosis* (scarring of lung tissue that causes breathing problems), *pleural plaques* (scarring in the inner surface of the ribcage and area around the lungs that causes breathing problems), and cancer — particularly lung cancer and mesothelioma.

Oil well fires during the Gulf War

Between February and November of 1991, huge clouds of smoke from oil well fires surrounded and engulfed servicemembers in the Persian Gulf; the clouds comprised soot, gases, liquids, and aerosols. The DOD determined that exposures were highest in winter encampments in Saudi Arabia. Although the VA says that research shows no long-term health effects from the smoke, you may have conditions related to your exposure.

TIP

Saudi Arabia isn't the only place subject to oil well fires; they also occurred in Iraq during OIF. If you have concerns about your exposure to smoke from oil fires, bring them up with your healthcare provider.

Gulf War Syndrome and other Gulf War-related illnesses

If you served in the Gulf War, which has been ongoing since August 2, 1990, you may have medically unexplained illnesses that many people refer to as *Gulf War Syndrome*. The VA presumes that some types of chronic, unexplained symptoms are related to your service in the Gulf, regardless of their cause, but the symptoms must have appeared while you were on active duty in the Southwest Asia theater of military operations or by December 31, 2026 — and they must be at least 10 percent disabling.

If you were diagnosed with one of the following illnesses or conditions while you were on active duty *or* before December 31, 2026, you can get benefits if you were ill for at least six months and your illness resulted in a disability rating of 10 percent or more:

>> Myalgic encephalomyelitis/chronic fatigue syndrome (ME/CFS), a condition that causes long-term and severe fatigue that doesn't get better with rest and isn't directly caused by another condition

>> Functional gastrointestinal disorders, which are disorders that cause any of the organs in your gastrointestinal tract to malfunction without causing structural damage, including irritable bowel syndrome (IBS), functional dyspepsia, and functional abdominal pain syndrome

>> Fibromyalgia, a condition known for causing widespread muscle pain, insomnia, stiffness in the morning, headaches, and memory problems

>> Other undiagnosed illnesses, including but not limited to cardiovascular disease, muscle and joint pain, menstrual disorders, fatigue, headaches, neurological and psychological problems, skin problems, respiratory disorders, and sleep disturbances

If you were diagnosed with brucellosis, *Campylobacter jejuni*, *Coxiella burnetii* (sometimes called Q fever), malaria, nontyphoid salmonella, shigella, or West Nile virus within a year of your date of separation, and if your illness caused a disability rating of at least 10 percent, you qualify to apply for disability benefits.

If your illness or condition was diagnosed at any time after you separated from the military and you have a disability rating of 10 percent or more, you may receive compensation and other benefits for mycobacterium tuberculosis or visceral leishmaniasis.

Additionally, the VA presumes a diagnosis of amyotrophic lateral sclerosis (ALS) to be connected to your service in the Gulf regardless of when you were diagnosed or discharged from the military.

TIP

If you served in the Persian Gulf during Operation Desert Shield, Operation Desert Storm, OIF, or OND, you're eligible for a free Gulf War Registry exam. You don't need to be enrolled in VA healthcare to qualify. Though it's not a disability compensation exam, it includes a complete rundown of your exposure and medical history, lab tests, and a physical exam. You'll meet face-to-face with a VA health professional who will discuss your results, which may lead to further exams and diagnoses that lead to VA healthcare benefits and disability compensation.

Cold War era

The Cold War era between 1945 and 1991 covers a lot of ground, and servicemembers were exposed to a lot of environmental and chemical hazards during that time. Vets who served during this time may have claims related to the exposures outlined in the following sections.

Ionizing radiation

Vets who participated in *radiation-risk activity* are eligible for a free Ionizing Radiation Registry health exam from the VA to identify long-term health problems, including cancer, tumors, and cataracts related to their exposure. These "atomic veterans"

>> Served at a gaseous diffusion plant in Paducah, Kentucky; Portsmouth, Ohio; or K25 in Oak Ridge, Tennessee, for at least 250 days before February 1, 1992

- » Cleaned up Enewetak Atoll between January 1, 1977 and December 31, 1980

- » Participated in underground nuclear weapons testing at Amchitka Island, Alaska, before 1974

- » Responded to a fire onboard the Air Force B-52 bomber carrying nuclear weapons near Thule Air Force Base in Greenland between January 21, 1968 and September 25, 1968

- » Cleaned up the Air Force B-52 bomber in Palomares, Spain, between January 17, 1966 and March 31, 1967

- » Participated in atmospheric nuclear weapons tests in Nevada, the Pacific Ocean, and a few other areas before 1962

- » Participated in the occupation of Hiroshima and Nagasaki

- » Were POWs in Japan during World War II

You also may have been exposed to ionizing radiation if you were near the Fukushima nuclear accident in Japan, the U.S. Air Force plutonium mission in Palomares, Spain, or you worked in a Long Range Navigation (LORAN) station between 1942 and 2010. Additionally, if you worked in the McMurdo Station nuclear power plant between 1964 and 1973, you may have been exposed.

Herbicide tests and storage

When the U.S. government wanted to test Agent Orange and other herbicides used in Vietnam, it did so in the United States and a few other countries. The government also stored and disposed of these toxic compounds in a variety of locations, and some Cold War veterans who didn't go to Vietnam may have been exposed. The VA has a complete list of the locations where the DOD tested, stored, and dumped them, but here's a quick rundown of the locations and dates to give you a general idea if you may have been exposed between 1945 and 1977:

- » Alabama (1965 to 1968)
- » Arkansas (1967)
- » Florida (1951 to 1969)
- » Georgia (1964 to 1968)
- » Indiana (1945)
- » Maryland (1946 to 1969)
- » Mississippi (1977)

- » Montana (1953)
- » New York (1959)
- » Tennessee (1964)
- » Texas (1970)
- » Utah (1963 to 1964)
- » Cambodia (1969)
- » Canada (1966 to 1967)

- » India (1945 to 1946)
- » Johnston Atoll (1977)
- » Korea (1968)

- » Laos (1965 to 1969)
- » Thailand (1962 to 1969)

If you were exposed to Agent Orange or another herbicide during these periods, you may be eligible for a free Agent Orange Registry health exam, healthcare, and disability compensation associated with exposure. Your dependents, as well as survivors of veterans who were exposed, may also be eligible for benefits.

Project 112/Project SHAD

Project 112/Project SHAD (Shipboard Hazard and Defense) was a classified testing program the DOD conducted from 1962 to 1973. The project subjected humans, animals, and plants to biological and chemical agents to see how they'd react. The tests took place on the open ocean in the North Atlantic Ocean, in the Pacific Ocean, and near the Marshall Islands, Hawaii, Puerto Rico, and California. The DOD conducted land-based tests in Alaska, Florida, Georgia, Hawaii, Maryland, Utah, and Panama.

Though the VA says no clear evidence of long-term health problems is related to the tests the DOD conducted, veterans who participated in these experiments may be eligible for healthcare based on conditions or illnesses related to exposure. The VA attempts to contact exposed veterans by mail as it receives names from the DOD, but it needs your correct address — so you may have missed your letter. If you think you were exposed or participated in the testing, contact the VA to schedule an exam.

Edgewood Arsenal/Aberdeen experiments

Between 1955 and 1975, the U.S. Army Chemical Corps was responsible for a number of classified medical studies at Edgewood Arsenal (located on Aberdeen Proving Ground) in Maryland. Somewhere in the neighborhood of 7,000 soldiers participated in the experiments, which included exposure to alcohol and caffeine, as well as more than 250 different chemicals, including:

- » Mustard agents
- » Irritants and riot control agents
- » Nerve agents, such as sarin, and nerve agent antidotes and reactivators
- » Psychoactive agents, such as LSD and PCP

FREE MEDICAL CARE FOR TEST SUBJECTS

The U.S. Army provides free medical care to veterans who served as chemical and biological agent test subjects if those veterans have an injury or disease resulting from testing. That includes chemical and biological substances, as well as medications and vaccines that are under Army review. It provides this treatment through military treatment facilities (MTFs).

To qualify, you must have your DD-214 or War Department discharge and separation forms (or a functional equivalent), and you must have served as a research subject in an Army program and have a diagnosed medical condition that you believe is a result of your participation in the program. If you were a test subject, call 800-984-8523 or visit the Army's research program website at https://armymedicine.health.mil/CBTP.

Mustard gas

Used heavily in the first two world wars and during the Iran–Iraq War in the 1980s, mustard gas can cause serious long-term health effects. If you were exposed to mustard gas, you should contact your physician or your local VA Environmental Health Coordinator.

Camp Lejeune water contamination

If you lived or worked at U.S. Marine Corps Base Camp Lejeune, North Carolina, you may have been exposed to drinking water contaminated with industrial solvents, benzene, and other chemicals. Even if you don't have one of the following health conditions associated with exposure, you may be entitled to free VA healthcare if you served at least 30 days on active duty there between August 1, 1953 and December 31, 1987:

>> Bladder cancer

>> Breast cancer

>> Esophageal cancer

>> Female infertility

>> Hepatic steatosis

>> Kidney cancer

>> Leukemia

>> Lung cancer

>> Miscarriage

>> Multiple myeloma

>> Myelodysplastic syndromes

>> Neurobehavioral effects

>> Non-Hodgkin's lymphoma

>> Renal toxicity

>> Scleroderma

The VA presumes that eight health conditions are related to exposure to the water contamination, so if you have any of them, you don't need to prove that they're service-connected when you file a disability compensation claim. They include adult leukemia, aplastic anemia and other myelodysplastic syndromes, bladder cancer, kidney cancer, liver cancer, multiple myeloma, non-Hodgkin's lymphoma, and Parkinson's disease. (You can still prove a service connection with other conditions; these are just the ones the VA automatically presumes are related to the water contamination.)

Family members of veterans who also lived on Camp Lejeune during that time are eligible for reimbursement for out-of-pocket medical expenses related to the 15 health conditions listed here. (You can apply for reimbursement by calling 866-372-1144 or visiting www.clfamilymembers.fsc.va.gov/.) That includes people who were in utero during that time — that is, if your mother was pregnant with you and lived on Camp Lejeune, you may be eligible for reimbursement for related medical conditions.

Atsugi Waste Incinerator

Between 1985 and 2001, servicemembers stationed at Naval Air Facility (NAF) Atsugi in Japan may have been exposed to environmental contaminants from the Shinkampo Incinerator Complex, which burned up to 90 tons of industrial and medical waste every day. The toxic smoke that came from its incinerators included a wide range of chemicals and other particulate matter. The U.S. Navy says there are potential long-term health effects from living and working near the incinerator, including cancer and other lung problems.

Fort McClellan

If you were stationed at Fort McClellan in Alabama prior to its closing in 1999, you may have been exposed to radioactive compounds, chemical warfare agents, airborne polychlorinated biphenyls (PCBs), and other environmental hazards. Although the VA doesn't automatically associate any adverse health conditions with living or working on Fort McClellan, each of these hazards poses serious long-term health risks. If you're suffering from any type of condition that may be associated with your service there, you should talk to a physician to determine whether it may be connected.

Vietnam

The Vietnam War lasted from November 1, 1965 through April 30, 1975, and the VA presumes that servicemembers from that era were exposed to three things: Agent Orange, hepatitis, and liver flukes. It says that conditions associated with these exposures are more likely than not caused by service during that era. These conditions, in addition to regular occupational hazards, may serve as the basis for a VA disability claim, so I outline them in the following sections.

Agent Orange and other herbicides

Agent Orange, known as a *tactical herbicide* the military used to control vegetation for strategic purposes, is now known to be exceptionally toxic to humans. The VA offers eligible veterans a free Agent Orange Registry health exam to help pinpoint long-term health problems related to exposure. The VA presumes that the following conditions are service connected if you served in Vietnam or other areas where Agent Orange was used, and you don't need to prove a connection to get disability benefits:

>> AL amyloidosis

>> Bladder cancer

>> Chronic B-cell leukemias

>> Chloracne or a similar acneiform disease

>> Diabetes mellitus Type 2

>> Hodgkin's disease

>> Hypertension (high blood pressure)

>> Hypothyroidism

>> Ischemic heart disease

>> Monoclonal gammopathy of undetermined significance (MGUS)

>> Multiple myeloma

>> Non-Hodgkin's lymphoma

>> Parkinsonism and Parkinson's disease

>> Peripheral neuropathy with early onset

>> Poryphria cutanea tarda

>> Prostate cancer

>> Respiratory cancers

>> Soft tissue sarcomas

The VA only recently added three conditions — bladder cancer, hypothyroidism, and Parkinsonism — to its presumptive conditions list for Agent Orange exposure, which means the list will most likely continue to grow. Check with your healthcare provider to determine whether any of your medical conditions may be connected to exposure.

TIP

If you see the name of an illness, injury, or disease that you're not familiar with, talk to your doctor. Because some of these conditions are rare, it's important that your doctor knows you were exposed to Agent Orange and that you may suffer from them — even if you don't know what the symptoms are. Your doctor can evaluate you for any symptoms you're experiencing and determine whether you have one of these conditions (or another condition entirely).

It's also important to note that the VA recognizes some birth defects among Vietnam-era veterans' kids, including spina bifida, are connected to Agent Orange exposure. These children may be eligible for compensation, healthcare, and other benefits.

Agent Orange wasn't only used in Vietnam. You may also have been exposed in one of these theaters:

>> In the Korean Demilitarized Zone (DMZ) between September 1, 1967 and August 31, 1971

>> On C-123 airplanes flown during and after the Vietnam War

>> On U.S. military bases or a Royal Thai Air Force base in Thailand between January 9, 1962 and June 30, 1976

>> On military installations in the United States and in other countries (see the section, "Herbicide tests and storage," in this chapter to determine whether you may have been exposed to Agent Orange in a stateside or allied location)

>> In Laos between December 1, 1965 and September 30, 1969

>> In Cambodia at Mimot or Krek, Kampong Cham Province between April 16, 1969 and April 30, 1969

>> In Guam or American Samoa (or in the territorial waters off either) between January 9, 1962 and July 30, 1980

>> In Johnston Atoll or on a ship that called there between January 1, 1972 and September 30, 1977

Hepatitis C

Hepatitis C (HCV), a virus that can cause serious liver damage, is more common in Vietnam veterans than it is among the general population. As many as one in ten are infected, and most people who have it show no symptoms. If you served in Vietnam or during that era, you should ask your healthcare provider to test you; HCV is curable.

Bile duct cancer and liver fluke infection

A common risk factor for bile duct cancer is past liver fluke infection. *Liver flukes* are parasitic worms that are found in the fresh waters of Southeast Asia, and you can become infected by eating raw or undercooked fish containing the parasites. The irritation and scarring liver flukes cause can lead to bile duct cancer, which you should have your doctor test you for if you experience symptoms such as jaundice, pain in the abdomen, dark urine, light-colored stool, or unexplained weight loss.

Recognizing Benefits for POWs

Every former POW is eligible for VA healthcare services, including hospital treatment, outpatient care, and nursing home care. Additionally, your dependents and survivors may be eligible for compensation, pension payments, healthcare services, education benefits, and VA home loan benefits. You may also qualify for disability compensation related to your service or your time in captivity. In fact, the VA presumes a service connection to all the following conditions, regardless of how long you were captive:

>> Osteoporosis (on or after October 10, 2008, if you have posttraumatic stress injury)

>> Neuropsychiatric conditions, such as psychosis, dysthymic disorder, or any anxiety states

>> Cold injury

>> Traumatic arthritis

>> Stroke

>> Heart disease

If you were in captivity for 30 days or more, these conditions are presumed to be service-connected:

>> Osteoporosis (on or after September 28, 2009)

>> Nutritional deficiencies, including avitaminosis, beriberi, malnutrition, and pellagra

>> Helminthiasis

>> Peripheral neuropathy

>> Digestive disorders, including chronic dysentery, irritable bowel syndrome, cirrhosis of the liver, and peptic ulcer disease

Thanks to the Purple Heart and Disabled Veterans Equal Access Act of 2018, former POWs have commissary and exchange shopping privileges, as well as MWR access with a Veteran Health Identification Card denoting former POW status. Survivors and dependents of former POWs may also be entitled to death pension benefits, home loans, education and training, healthcare services, and more. Some also qualify for Dependency and Indemnity Compensation (DIC), which I explain in Chapter 23.

Eyeing Benefits for Purple Heart Recipients

If you're a Purple Heart recipient, you're entitled to the following:

>> An automatic upgrade of your VA healthcare priority group; you're put in Group 3, regardless of the severity of your injuries or your income, unless you're entitled to be part of a higher group (see Chapter 5)

>> An exemption from the VA home loan funding fee

>> Full GI Bill benefits, regardless of your active-duty time

>> Automatic 10-point preference in federal hiring, which I cover in Chapter 10

>> Commissary, exchange, and MWR privileges with a Veteran Health Identification Card that denotes receipt of a Purple Heart

Many states extend special benefits to Purple Heart recipients, too, such as free or discounted license plates, in-state university tuition waivers, and scholarships.

Getting on the Airborne Hazards and Open Burn Pit Registry

Vets who served in the Southwest Asia theater of operations on or after August 2, 1990, or in Afghanistan or Djibouti on or after September 11, 2001, should put their names on the Airborne Hazards and Open Burn Pit Registry. (If you're not sure, these regions include Afghanistan, Bahrain, Djibouti, Egypt, the Gulf of Aden, the Gulf of Oman, Iraq, Kuwait, Oman, Syria, Qatar, Saudi Arabia, United Arab Emirates, Uzbekistan, and the waters of the Arabian Sea, Persian Gulf, and Red Sea.)

The VA established the registry in 2014 to research the potential health effects of airborne hazards, which are common in the regions listed here. Though you may not have any symptoms from being exposed to airborne hazards, it's a good idea to include yourself on the registry.

When you join the registry with your doctor's help or online at `https://veteran.mobilehealth.va.gov/AHBurnPitRegistry/`, you answer several questions about your possible exposure and your current health conditions. After you finish the questionnaire, you have the option of contacting a local Environmental Health Coordinator to schedule a free medical evaluation. This health evaluation isn't the same as a disability exam that can help you get benefits, but your care provider will note all your conditions in your file, and the VA will use the information it gathers (with your privacy intact) to conduct research.

TIP

If you deployed before 9/11, were part of a special forces group, or were redeployed within three months, you may see a warning that you're not eligible (even if you are) when you try to register. If you see the warning, click "Request Eligibility Review," and follow the instructions that pop up on your screen.

Filing a Claim Based on the PACT Act

The Sergeant First Class Heath Robinson Honoring Our Promise to Address Comprehensive Toxics (PACT) Act, signed into law by President Joseph R. Biden in August 2022, addresses dangerous exposures from burn pits and other toxins. Vets who served in the countries and time periods listed in Table 20-1 don't have to prove that the following conditions are connected to their service:

>> Asthma that was diagnosed after service

>> Brain cancer

>> Chronic bronchitis

>> Chronic obstructive pulmonary disease (COPD)

>> Chronic rhinitis

>> Chronic sinusitis

>> Constrictive bronchiolitis or obliterative bronchiolitis

>> Emphysema

>> Gastrointestinal cancer of any type

>> Glioblastoma

>> Granulomatous disease

>> Head cancer of any type

- >> Interstitial lung disease (ILD)

- >> Kidney cancer

- >> Lymphatic cancer of any type

- >> Lymphoma of any type

- >> Melanoma

- >> Neck cancer

- >> Pancreatic cancer

- >> Pleuritis

- >> Pulmonary fibrosis

- >> Reproductive cancer of any type

- >> Respiratory cancer of any type

- >> Sarcoidosis

TABLE 20-1 ## Dates and Locations for PACT Act

On or after September 11, 2001	On or after August 2, 1990
Afghanistan	Bahrain
Djibouti	Iraq
Egypt	Kuwait
Jordan	Oman
Lebanon	Qatar
Syria	Saudi Arabia
Uzbekistan	Somalia
Yemen	The United Arab Emirates
The airspace above any of these locations	The airspace above any of these locations

Veterans' survivors may also be eligible for Dependency and Indemnity Compensation (DIC) or a survivors pension based on a veteran's eligibility under the PACT Act. I cover each of these benefits in Chapter 23. Additionally, survivors may be entitled to a one-time accrued benefits payment if the VA owed the veteran unpaid benefits at the time of their death. You can apply for these benefits on the VA's website.

Identifying Benefits for Disabled Vets

In addition to disability compensation, which I cover extensively in Chapter 9, veterans with a disability rating may be eligible for additional benefits. Most of these benefits have very specific eligibility requirements, so I outline them in the following sections.

Getting Aid and Attendance or the Housebound allowance

Aid and Attendance is a bump in your VA pension (the money some vets get based on low income and age or disability, which I cover in Chapter 8) that you may qualify for if you already receive a VA pension and meet at least one of the following requirements:

>> You need help from another person to perform daily activities.

>> You're a patient in a nursing home because you've lost mental or physical abilities related to a disability.

>> You have to remain in bed, or at least spend a large portion of the day in bed, because of illness.

>> You have limited eyesight (even with corrective lenses, you have 5/200 vision or less in both eyes, or you have concentric contraction of the visual field to 5 degrees or less).

If you receive a VA pension and you're housebound — that is, you can't leave your home much because of a permanent disability — you may be eligible for the Housebound allowance. This allowance is also an increase in your VA pension amount. You can't collect Aid and Attendance at the same time you're collecting a Housebound allowance; it's one or the other.

You can apply for either of these benefits using VA Form 21-2680, which is available on the VA's website and at your nearest VA regional office or medical center. Your physician needs to fill out a section of this form. Mail the form to your Pension Management Center (PMC), which is based on the state where you live. You can get a complete list of which states each PMC serves on the VA's website, or you can ask someone at your local VA medical center or regional office to help you find the right information.

Applying for housing grants

Disabled veterans with certain service-connected disabilities are eligible for housing grants that provide money to buy or adapt a home to meet their needs. You may apply for one of the VA's disability housing grants, which I explain in the following sections, through the VA's website.

Specially Adapted Housing Grants

Specially Adapted Housing (SAH) grants are for people who need to buy, build, or change a permanent home. According to the VA, a *permanent home* is simply a home you plan to live in for a long time. This grant provides you with around $100,000, though the exact amount is subject to change annually. A very limited number of veterans may receive this grant each fiscal year.

REMEMBER

To qualify for this grant, you must already own or be planning to buy the home, and you must have at least one qualifying service-connected disability, such as:

>> The loss or loss of use of more than one limb

>> The loss or loss of use of a lower leg along with lasting effects of a natural disease or injury

>> Blindness in both eyes with 20/200 visual acuity or less

>> Certain severe burns

>> The loss or loss of use of one lower extremity (a foot or leg) after September 11, 2001, which forces you to use braces, crutches, canes, or a wheelchair to balance or walk

Special Home Adaptation Grants

Special Home Adaptation (SHA) grants are for people who need to buy, build, or change a permanent home. However, the grant amount is different; you can get up to a little more than $20,000 (and like SAH grants, the maximum amount is subject to change). You may qualify for an SHA grant if you or a family member owns or will own the home that needs to be adapted, and if you have a service-connected loss (or loss of use of) both hands, certain severe burns, or certain respiratory or breathing issues.

Temporary Residence Adaptation Grants

If you qualify for an SAH or SHA grant, discussed in the previous sections, you may qualify for a Temporary Residence Adaptation (TRA) grant. This grant is for adapting a family member's home when you live there temporarily. The amount of money you receive depends on whether you qualify for an SAH or SHA grant; the award is higher if you qualify for an SAH grant and can be upwards of $40,000. If you qualify for an SHA grant, you can get a little more than $7,000 to make adaptations. Both these amounts are subject to change as the VA receives new funding amounts each fiscal year.

Buying VA life and mortgage insurance

Disabled veterans are eligible for life insurance through the VA, which many people find to be a low-cost alternative to traditional life insurance plans. (Some civilian life insurance plans charge a premium for — or even refuse to cover — people with disabilities.) Your options, which I explain in greater detail in Chapter 7, may include Service-Disabled Veterans Life Insurance (S-DVI), VALife, and Veterans Mortgage Life Insurance (VMLI).

Signing up for an automobile allowance or adaptive equipment grant

The VA's automobile allowance and adaptive equipment is a one-time payment to help you buy a specially equipped vehicle or make modifications to an existing vehicle so you can use it (such as adding lift equipment that helps you get in or out or installing features like power steering). If you want this benefit, you must apply before you purchase the vehicle or adaptive equipment, and you must have one of the following:

» Loss or the permanent loss of use of one or both feet

» Loss or the permanent loss of use of one or both hands

» Permanent decreased vision in both eyes (20/200 vision or less in your better eye with corrective lenses, or greater than 20/200 vision but with a visual field defect that reduces your peripheral vision to 20 degrees or less in your better eye)

» A severe burn injury

» Amyotrophic lateral sclerosis (ALS)

» Ankylosis in one or both knees or hips

If you qualify for this benefit, you may receive money to help buy a vehicle or make modifications to an existing vehicle. The VA pays the seller directly if you're purchasing a new vehicle; if you're adapting a vehicle, the VA may pay you or the seller.

To apply for a one-time payment to help you buy a specially equipped vehicle, you need VA Form 21-4502. If you want the adaptive equipment grant, you need VA Form 10-1394. You can send either of these forms to your VA regional office to apply.

Picking up free hearing aids

Some veterans qualify for free hearing aids, replacement batteries, wax guards, and other hearing aid accessories through the VA. You may be eligible if you meet any of these requirements:

>> You have any service-connected disability.

>> You're a former POW.

>> You have a Purple Heart.

>> You're housebound or receive Aid and Attendance benefits.

>> You have a hearing impairment that interferes with daily living or your ability to participate actively in your own medical treatment.

You may apply for a hearing aid in person at a VA medical center or clinic, by filling out VA Form 10-10EZ on the VA's website, or by mailing the form to the VA. After you register with the VA, you may schedule an appointment with its audiology department, where a provider will determine your need for free hearing aids or other hearing-assistive devices and accessories.

Getting help with nonservice-connected blindness

When low vision or blindness is connected to your service, you're eligible to apply for disability and VA medical care. If it's the result of a service-connected disability (such as Type 2 diabetes, a medication you take for another condition, or traumatic brain injury), you're also eligible. But the VA may still help you with blindness or low vision even when it results from aging or another condition that's not related to your service. If you're eligible for VA healthcare, you can receive a free visual impairment exam and may qualify for rehabilitation services, aids that help you see (such as audiobooks or electronic devices), or other services. You can apply for these services through the VA or with the help of a VSO such as the Blind Veterans Association (https://bva.org/).

Receiving a clothing allowance

If your clothing has been damaged by a prosthetic or orthopedic device, or by the medications you take to treat or help a skin condition, you may be eligible for a clothing allowance from the VA. Your clothing allowance may be a one-time payment or an annual payment. The amount is subject to change, but you can find the current cap on the VA's website.

You're only eligible if your device or medication damages your clothing *and* you need the device or medication because of a service-connected condition. You may qualify for multiple payments if you have more than one prosthetic or orthopedic device, you have more than one skin medication, or your device or skin medicine affects more than one type of clothing.

You can apply for a clothing allowance by filling out VA Form 10-8678 and bringing it to the prosthetic representative at your nearest VA medical center.

Getting a guide or service dog

Guide and service dogs can be tremendous helps to disabled vets, so the VA may pay for you to get one if you need it. For the record, *guide dogs* are trained to help blind and visually impaired people by guiding them around obstacles; *service dogs* are trained to help people with physical or hearing disabilities by performing specific tasks.

If you're eligible for a guide or service dog, the VA will pay for the pup, all its veterinary care, and all the equipment you need so you and the dog can work together (such as harnesses and backpacks). The veterinary care the VA pays for includes office visits, prescription medications, vaccines, and some dental procedures.

TIP

To apply for a guide or service dog, you must go through your assigned VA primary care provider, who will request a referral to a specialist for you. The specialist will determine whether you need assistive devices (including a dog). If they decide you need a dog, the VA will refer you to an accredited agency to get one; the agency won't charge you for the dog or the dog's training. (If it were up to me, I'd say, "You get a dog! And you get a dog! And you get a dog!")

Scoping out VR&E services

If you have a disability that was caused or made worse by active-duty service and that disability prevents you from working or limits your ability to work, you may be able to access the employment support and services available through the Veteran Readiness and Employment (VR&E) program. You may apply for VR&E

benefits if you didn't receive a dishonorable discharge from the military and you have a service-connected disability rating of at least 10 percent from the VA.

Here are some of the VR&E services you may be eligible for:

>> A comprehensive evaluation that determines your abilities and skills, as well as your employment interests

>> Professional or vocational counseling

>> Rehabilitation planning for employment services

>> Employment services such as job training and resume development

>> Help finding a job

>> On-the-job training and apprenticeships, as well as nonpaid work experiences (such as internships) that may lead to employment

>> Postsecondary education and training at a college, vocational, business, or technical school

>> Rehabilitation services such as counseling and medical referrals

>> Independent living services

TECHNICAL STUFF

Your VR&E benefits don't take anything away from your GI Bill entitlement, but if you've already used *other* VA education benefits, your VR&E benefits may be limited. However, a vocational rehabilitation counselor (VRC) at the VA may be able to help restore your full VR&E benefits.

The VR&E program offers five support-and-services tracks to eligible veterans, which I explain in the following sections. And just a note: When I use the term employment handicap, I'm going by the VA's definition of the term. According to the VA, when you have an employment handicap, "your service-connected disability limits your ability to prepare for, obtain, and maintain suitable employment." (That's a job that doesn't make your disability worse, is stable, and matches your abilities, aptitudes, and interests).

Rapid Access to Employment track

The Rapid Access to Employment track helps disabled service members find jobs or careers that match well with their existing skills. You're eligible for this track if you have barriers to employment or an employment handicap *and* you already have experience, training, or education in your field of interest.

When you're on this track, the VA can give you tools to help with your job search, provide you with professional or vocational counseling, and help you with writing your resume and preparing for job interviews. The VA can also help you determine whether you're eligible for veterans preference in applying for jobs.

Self-Employment track

The Self-Employment track puts you on the path to business ownership. You may qualify for this track if you have a strong desire, the necessary skills, and significant motivation to run a business. As with other tracks, you must have an employment barrier or employment handicap to participate.

This track provides you with a big toolkit to launch your own company, including help with developing a proposed business plan, analysis of your business concept, and guidance in finding the resources you need to make it all happen. You receive specialized training in small business operations, marketing, and finances.

Employment through Long-Term Services track

The Employment through Long-Term Services track helps people who have service-connected disabilities that create employment barriers; that is, they face obstacles that differently abled people don't face due to a disability. You may qualify for this if you have an employment barrier or handicap, and your service-connected disability makes it hard for you to prepare for a job, get a job, and hold a suitable job. (In this case, *suitable* means a job that doesn't worsen your disability, is stable, and matches or comes very close to your abilities, interests, and skills.)

On this track, you get a complete skills assessment, career guidance, education and training in a professional or vocational field, and apprenticeship, on-the-job training, volunteer opportunities, and any other employment assistance you need.

Independent Living track

The Independent Living track is designed for people who can't get to work right away because they have a tough time performing the activities of daily living, such as bathing, dressing, interacting with others, and participating in their communities. You may be eligible for this track if you're living with a serious employment handicap, your disabilities stop you from looking for work or returning to work, and you need services to help you live as independently as possible.

This track provides evaluation and counseling that helps you identify your needs and goals, referrals to support resources you need, and an evaluation to determine whether you're eligible for the VR&E home adaptation grant (a grant that helps you improve your home so it's more accessible to you). It also gives you guidance on adaptive housing programs, which I cover in the section, "Applying for housing grants," earlier in this chapter.

Reemployment track

The Reemployment track is for veterans who need help going back to a job they held before a period of service, such as training or a deployment, and it provides support to the veteran and the employer in dealing with employment barriers or handicaps.

Cashing in on subsistence allowance

Some VR&E participants are entitled to receive a subsistence allowance while they pursue an educational or training program. The VA pays this allowance each month based on the rate of attendance (such as full-time or half-time attendance), the number of dependents the veteran has, and the type of training they're pursuing. The VA lists the most current subsistence allowance payment rates on its website.

If you have at least one day of entitlement remaining on a Post-9/11 GI Bill and you're within your GI Bill eligibility window, you may choose to be paid the GI Bill subsistence rate instead of the VR&E subsistence allowance rate. In many cases, the Post-9/11 rate is higher than the VR&E rate is, so have a look at the VA's website to crunch the numbers before you decide.

WARNING

If you were discharged from active duty before January 1, 2013, your basic period of eligibility for VR&E benefits ends 12 years from the date you received notice of your date of separation from active duty or the date you received your first VA service-connected disability rating, whichever comes later. Having your basic period of eligibility extended is possible if a vocational rehabilitation counselor finds that you have a serious employment handicap; that means you have extreme difficulty preparing for and obtaining or maintaining suitable employment. If you were discharged from active duty after that date, you don't have to worry about the 12-year period of eligibility; there's no time limit on eligibility for you.

Applying for VR&E benefits

You can apply for VR&E benefits on the VA's website, by visiting your local VA regional office, or with help from a veteran service organization (VSO — I go into detail on those in Chapter 3). Getting a VA disability rating is the first step, which you can find out more about in Chapter 9. If you already have a disability rating, you may apply immediately. The VA invites eligible applicants to an orientation at their nearest VA regional office.

TIP

If you were wounded, injured, or fell ill while serving and are found unfit for duty, you can access VR&E services through the Integrated Disability Evaluation System (IDES). Your care team must refer you to the program. The VA works with the DOD after IDES gives you a proposed VA disability rating, which makes you eligible for VR&E.

Getting Dependents' Educational Assistance

Dependents' Educational Assistance (DEA) is for the children and spouses of disabled servicemembers (as well as those who have been captured or are missing, or who have passed away under certain circumstances). This program is officially called *Chapter 35*, and it sends eligible dependents a monthly payment to cover the cost of college or graduate degree programs, career-training certifications, apprenticeships, on-the-job training, and career or educational counseling. I cover DEA in more detail in Chapter 21.

TIP

The Marine Gunnery Sergeant John David Fry Scholarship (usually just called the *Fry Scholarship*) is for the children and spouses of Selected Reserve veterans who pass away from service-connected disabilities, as well as the dependents of servicemembers who died on active duty. I cover it extensively in Chapter 23.

Social Security Disability Insurance

Social Security Disability Insurance (SSDI) is a government program available to some disabled veterans (and civilians). Under the Social Security Administration's (SSA) definition, a person is disabled when they have the "inability to perform substantial gainful activity due to a medically determinable physical or mental impairment," and that impairment is expected to last (or has already lasted) a year, or it's expected to cause the person's death. VA disability benefits don't affect your eligibility for SSDI (or vice versa), so you may apply for both. Note that each program has its own criteria; they're not related to each other, so you may qualify for one and not the other. You may apply for SSDI by calling 800-772-1213 or through the SSA's website at www.ssa.gov/applyfordisability/. The SSA's TTY number is 800-325-0778.

» Getting educational assistance

» Exploring the possibilities with career assessments

» Finding help through readjustment counseling

» Tapping into caregiver benefits

Chapter **21**

Diving into Benefits for Spouses, Dependents, and Caregivers

"Families serve, too" is a pretty common phrase in the military, so you may have heard it a time or two. Though spouses and dependent children don't put on the uniform every day, they play vital support roles that help servicemembers move forward in their careers — and those same family members are there playing supportive roles during and after the transition from Soldier, Airman, Sailor, Marine, Guardian, or Coast Guardsman to veteran.

The VA provides a handful of benefits for some qualifying dependents and caregivers, such as healthcare, education and training, help with employment, and financial help. But they're not automatic; like all VA benefits, you must apply for them. Sometimes these benefits are tied into the sponsoring veteran's disability rating, era of service, or the level of care they need, so this chapter gives you a peek at all of them.

TIP Each military branch permits spouses to attend transition assistance classes on a space-available basis, which is a great way to get a handle on possible benefits.

Using Survivors' and Dependents' Educational Assistance

Also known as *Chapter 35* benefits, the Survivors' and Dependents' Educational Assistance (DEA) program provides monthly payments to help pay for college or graduate degree programs, career training certifications, educational and career counseling, apprenticeships, and on-the-job training for up to 36 months. It's only available to specific dependents and survivors, though. Here I examine who qualifies and how you can apply.

Recognizing who's eligible

You must be the dependent child or spouse of a servicemember or veteran, and you qualify if the servicemember meets the following criteria:

>> They're permanently and totally disabled because of a service-connected disability.

>> They died on active duty or because of a service-connected disability.

>> They're missing in action or were captured in the line of duty by a hostile force.

>> They were forcibly detained or interned in the line of duty by a foreign entity.

>> They're in the hospital or receiving outpatient treatment for a service-connected permanent and total disability, and they're likely to be discharged from the military for that disability.

Children and spouses face different limitations on the ways they may use this benefit.

Limitations on children

If you're a qualifying veteran's child, you may only receive DEA benefits if you're between the ages of 18 and 26, with limited exceptions. If you receive Dependency and Indemnity Compensation (DIC), which I explain in Chapter 23, you can't use the DEA program at the same time; you have to choose one or the other. If you join the military yourself, you can't use this benefit while you're on active duty. And if you want to use DEA benefits after you get out of the military, you can't have a dishonorable discharge. However, your own military service can only extend your eligibility period until you turn 31 (though the VA does make a very small number of exceptions).

Limitations on spouses

If you're the spouse of a qualifying veteran or servicemember, your benefits start on the date that the VA decides you qualify and extends for 10 years. If your veteran sponsor is permanently and totally disabled and was rated that way with an effective date at least 3 years from their discharge from active duty, you can use these benefits for up to 20 years after the effective date. If your sponsor died on active duty, you're allowed to use these benefits for up to 20 years from their date of death. And unlike children of qualifying vets and servicemembers, you're allowed to receive DIC payments at the same time you use your DEA benefits.

Applying for DEA benefits

You can apply for all VA education benefits on the VA's website or by filling out and mailing to the VA Form 22-5490. You may fill out these forms and apply on your own, but if you're not sure what to do, you can ask the VA for help. Alternatively, you may work with a veterans service organization (VSO) for help. (I explain VSOs and what they provide in Chapter 3.)

If you're already enrolled in an educational program, you may still apply; you simply need to ask your school to fill out a VA enrollment certification (VA Form 22-1999) and file it with your application.

WARNING

You can't use DEA benefits and the Fry Scholarship at the same time. You must choose one or the other, even if you're eligible for both. However, you can use them back-to-back; the VA caps combined benefits at 81 months of full-time training. I cover the Fry Scholarship in Chapter 23.

Mapping Your Path with a Career Assessment and Counseling

If you're a dependent who's eligible for the Post-9/11 GI Bill, the Montgomery GI Bill Active Duty, or the Montgomery GI Bill Selected Reserve, which I cover in Chapter 13, you may be able to participate in the Personalized Career Planning and Guidance (PCPG) program, which is also known as *Chapter 36*. If you qualify, you get educational and career counseling, including help exploring your abilities and interests, identifying the right plan to find employment, and planning how to use the VA benefits available to you.

You may apply for the PCPG program online or by mail; if you apply by mail, you need VA Form 28-8832. Mail that form to your nearest VA regional office. If the VA determines that you're eligible, it'll invite you to an orientation session where you can get more information and start working through the program.

Getting Back on Track with Readjustment Counseling

Transitioning from a military lifestyle to a civilian one is tough — not just for servicemembers, but also for their families. The VA's Vet Centers provide readjustment counseling services for qualifying combat vets and their families (including kids). You qualify if your sponsoring veteran served in any combat zone and received a military campaign ribbon for their service. You can find your nearest Vet Center on the VA's website or by calling 877-WAR-VETS (927-8387). The counseling is free and confidential, and all Vet Centers have nontraditional appointment schedules so if you need to, you can swing by after normal business hours.

Working through VR&E Benefits that Extend to Spouses

The Veteran Readiness and Employment (VR&E) program is designed to help vets with service-connected disabilities find and keep jobs, but some of its benefits extend to family members, too. Though every case is different, you may qualify for

>> Education and career counseling (see the sections, "Using Survivors' and Dependents' Educational Assistance" and "Mapping Your Path with a Career Assessment and Counseling" earlier in this chapter)

>> Readjustment counseling (refer to the previous section for more details)

>> Career assessments (check out the section, "Mapping Your Path with a Career Assessment and Counseling," earlier in this chapter)

You may apply through the VA's website, by mail, or in person if you're the dependent of a VR&E-eligible veteran and you're eligible for certain VA education benefits as a result of your sponsor's service.

Exploring Benefits for Children of Vietnam and Korean Service Veterans

If you're the biological child of a veteran with qualifying service in Vietnam, Thailand, or Korea, and if you suffer from spina bifida or another *congenital anomaly* — a problem that arose while you were developing in your mother's body — that resulted in a permanent physical or mental disability, you may be eligible for *Chapter 18* benefits. Chapter 18 benefits include a monthly stipend, free healthcare, and up to two years' worth of vocational or educational training. It doesn't matter how old you are or what level of disability you have; you may still apply if you qualify, and parents may apply for a child regardless of age. These benefits *don't* depend on your parent's character of discharge or length of service, either. The following sections let you explore who qualifies, what's covered, and how to apply.

Identifying who qualifies

You may apply for these benefits if you have spina bifida and your biological mother or father served in

>> The Republic of Vietnam for any length of time between January 9, 1962, and May 7, 1975

>> Thailand for any length of time between January 9, 1962, and May 7, 1975

>> A unit in or near the Korean Demilitarized Zone (DMZ) for any length of time between September 1, 1967, and August 31, 1971

However, you only qualify if you were diagnosed with a form of spina bifida other than spina bifida occulta *and* you were conceived after your parent served in Vietnam, Thailand, or the DMZ during a qualified period.

If you have another congenital anomaly (see Table 21-1), you may also qualify for these benefits. However, in cases such as these, your biological mother must have served in Vietnam between February 28, 1961, and May 7, 1975, and you must have been conceived after your mother first entered Vietnam.

Applying and knowing what's covered

To apply, you need VA Form 21-304, which is available on the VA's website. After you complete the form, mail it to the address listed on the form. (And here's a tip: *Always* use the address listed on the form. If the address on the form doesn't match what's on the VA's website, *default to the address on the form.*)

The VA will evaluate the severity of your disability and put you into a category that determines your monthly payments, which can range from a little more than $100 to more than $2,000, depending on your condition. Level I is least disabling, and Level III is most disabling for spina bifida; Level IV is most disabling for the congenital anomalies listed in Table 21-1.

TABLE 21-1

Covered Anomalies

Achondroplasia	Hip dysplasia	Poland syndrome
Cleft lip and cleft palate	Hirschsprung's disease	Pyloric stenosis
Congenital heart disease	Hydrocephalus	Syndactyly (fused digits)
Congenital talipes equinovarus (clubfoot)	Hypospadias	Tracheoesophageal fistula
Esophageal and intestinal atresia	Imperforate anus	Undescended testicle
Hallermann-Streiff syndrome	Neural tube defects	Williams syndrome

If you're eligible for VA healthcare because of spina bifida or another congenital anomaly, the VA will handle all your medical needs — not just those related to your condition. That means you're eligible for case management, standard healthcare, treatment for your condition, and prescriptions. You may even be eligible for dental services, provided they're necessary for the treatment of a covered medical benefit.

Additionally, you may be entitled to services to improve your vocational potential. (In plain English, that means you may be able to get money to go to school, participate in a training program, and get personal and work adjustment training.) You may also be eligible for employment assistance, including vocational and psychological counseling that helps you find and keep a job as well as transportation assistance.

Accessing Special Caregiver Benefits

The VA defines a *caregiver* as a spouse, son, daughter, parent, stepfamily member, extended family member, or person who lives full time with a disabled veteran to provide care. If you fall into one of those categories, you may be eligible for certain caregiver benefits available through the VA, depending on your sponsor's needs and disability level.

REMEMBER

Some special caregiver benefits relate to general support, such as coaching and skills training, and others are financial benefits that you can get to help offset your living costs. Each of these programs and benefits has its own criteria, and you may be eligible for more than one program at a time. The VA also often changes its eligibility requirements as well, so you can find the most current information on its website or by talking to a caregiver support coordinator (CSC) at your local VA medical center. The VA maintains a CSC directory on its website, and it has a Caregiver Support Line you can reach by calling 855-260-3274. The following sections break down the benefits available to caregivers.

Accessing Comprehensive Assistance for Family Caregivers

The Program of Comprehensive Assistance for Family Caregivers (PCAFC) provides caregiver education and training, mental health counseling, and travel, lodging, and financial assistance when traveling with the veteran to receive care. If you're a primary family caregiver, you may also receive a monthly payment, access to healthcare, access to some services provided by the DOD (such as commissary and exchange privileges) and the Department of Morale, Welfare, and Recreation (MWR), and at least 30 days of respite care per year.

Knowing who's eligible for PCAFC

You're eligible to apply if the veteran you care for has a disability rating of 70 percent or higher, you're at least 18 years old, and are

>> The spouse, adult child, parent, stepfamily member, or extended family member of a disabled veteran

>> A person who lives full time with a qualifying veteran (or who is willing to live with the veteran if designated as a family caregiver)

In addition, the veteran you care for must have been discharged from the military or have a date of medical discharge, and they must need at least six months of continuous, in-person care. The care must involve help to support the vet's health and wellbeing, personal needs related to daily living, or safety, protection, or instruction in their daily living environment.

REMEMBER

To qualify for this program, the veteran must appoint you as a primary caregiver or secondary caregiver. The *primary caregiver* is the main caregiver, and the veteran may only appoint one person to fill this role. The veteran may nominate up to two *secondary caregivers*; these are people who serve as backups to the primary caregiver when necessary. Only primary caregivers are eligible for monthly payments, healthcare services, DOD and MWR privileges, and respite care services.

Applying for PCAFC

You may apply for this program with the veteran; you both need to answer questions and sign the application. If you want to apply, you may do so through the VA's website or by mail using VA Form 10-10CG. When you apply by mail, use the address listed on the form to ensure that it goes to the right place. If you don't want to mail the form, you may bring it to your local VA medical center's CSC.

Receiving General Caregiver Support Services

The Program of General Caregiver Support Services (PGCSS) provides help from peers, skills training, online programs, coaching, and referrals to resources that can help caregivers take care of veterans. It's available to *general caregivers* — those are people who provide personal care services to a veteran who's enrolled in VA healthcare and needs help with one or more activities of daily living. General caregivers are also people who provide supervision or protection to vets who have symptoms related to impairments or injuries, including neurological conditions.

REMEMBER

You don't need to formally apply to enroll in PGCSS. You just need to talk to a CSC and complete an intake process. The veteran must agree to receive care from you; you then can enroll and begin using the available services. Some of these free resources include

>> **Text support:** You can sign up for Annie, the VA's text message service that sends you messages to help you manage stress and care for yourself, manage a veteran's dementia-related behaviors, and cope with bereavement. You get to choose which types of messages you need when you sign up with your CSC.

>> **Skills training:** You're eligible to participate in workshops that help you care for your veteran, including education on suicide prevention and managing your own stress and physical health. You may also take in-person or virtual courses on self-care and resiliency, as well as coping mechanisms you can use when times get tough.

>> **Online and email support:** As a caregiver, you may access resources on the program's website (www.caregiver.va.gov), including self-care journals, tip sheets, and resources specific to your veteran's diagnosis. You may also sign up to receive emails from the VA that help you.

>> **One-on-one coaching:** You may choose to connect with VA coaches who give you a workbook and help you face difficult situations with stress management and self-care, problem-solving, and veteran safety as well as specific guidance on your veteran's diagnosis. You may choose group support and coaching, which are led by trained facilitators to teach you relaxation techniques and other coping methods.

>> **Respite care:** The VA will pay for short periods of respite care when you need a break or can't be there for a few days.

>> **Referrals to other resources:** Your CSC connects you with community resources and other VA benefits you may be entitled to as well as lets you know when there are special events for caregivers.

Getting healthcare for caregivers

Some caregivers qualify for healthcare through the Civilian Health and Medical Program of the Department of Veterans Affairs (CHAMPVA). This benefit is also sometimes available to current and surviving dependents of disabled veterans and servicemembers who died in the line of duty.

The CHAMPVA program covers the cost of some healthcare services and supplies using a cost-sharing model. You may be eligible for this program if you're a family member who's caring for a disabled veteran and you're not entitled to care or services through another health plan, but only if you're the primary caregiver. If you qualify, here's a quick rundown of what CHAMPVA covers:

>> Mental healthcare (up to 23 outpatient visits per year without preauthorization; more with preauthorization)

>> Doctor's office visits

>> Prescriptions

>> Hospital services (inpatient and outpatient, including ER visits)

>> Radiology and lab services

>> Durable medical equipment

You may apply for CHAMPVA through your CSC.

Using the Camp Lejeune Family Member Program

The Camp Lejeune Family Member Program is for dependents of veterans who were stationed at MCAS New River or Camp Lejeune for at least 30 days between August 1953 and December 1987 and didn't receive dishonorable discharges. If you qualify, you're entitled to healthcare benefits. You qualify if you can prove your relationship to the veteran, you have a document that shows you lived at either base (or that your mother was pregnant with you while working or living on base), and medical records that show you have one of the following conditions:

>> Breast, bladder, esophageal, kidney, or lung cancer

>> Female infertility or miscarriage

>> Hepatic steatosis

>> Leukemia

>> Multiple myeloma

>> Myelodysplastic syndromes

>> Neurobehavioral effects

>> Non-Hodgkin's lymphoma

>> Renal toxicity

>> Scleroderma

Though it's not required, you may want to have your doctor fill out VA Form 10-10068b, which can help the VA determine your eligibility. You may file a claim using VA Form 10-10068, which you can fax or mail to the VA for evaluation.

Chapter **22**

Examining Burial and Memorial Benefits

ying is expensive. A 2021 study by the National Funeral Directors Association says that the median cost of viewing, preparation, a small funeral, and burial is just under $8,000. (A funeral with cremation averages just a little less than that.) Those costs typically don't include a wake or celebration of life ceremony, and if you want a fancy casket, it can cost thousands (even *renting* one from a funeral home can cost around $1,000). Then, someone has to foot the bill for your post-life real estate; whether you choose a burial plot or a spot in a mausoleum or columbarium, it may cost between $200 and $25,000, depending on your location. (For the record, a *mausoleum* is designed for an entire body, whereas a *columbarium* is for cremation or aquamation urns).

Whether you qualify for burial in Arlington National Cemetery with some 400,000 of your brothers- and sisters-in-arms, you want to be buried in a VA National Cemetery or a civilian graveyard, you prefer to be cremated or aquamated, or you're looking for something else, there's a good chance that the VA will cover all or some of the costs associated with your death and memorialization. This chapter explains your interment options, all the death and memorial benefits that the VA covers (and doesn't cover), as well as funeral honors and how to arrange a military funeral for someone you care about.

Choosing Your Final Resting Place

As a veteran, you may be eligible for interment or inurnment in Arlington National Cemetery, a VA National Cemetery, a National Park cemetery, or a state or tribal veterans' cemetery. And, of course, you may choose to be interred in a civilian cemetery. Each has its own requirements (including service requirements, in some cases), which you can check out in the following sections.

Arlington National Cemetery

Today, more than 400,000 people are buried in Arlington National Cemetery (ANC). If you make the cut, you're in good company; you'll be in the same neighborhood with military heroes such as Admiral Grace Hopper, General John J. Pershing, Anita Newcomb, Walter Reed, and Audie Murphy; former presidents John F. Kennedy and William Howard Taft; and celebrated icons such as Ruth Bader Ginsburg, Joe Louis Barrow (you know him as boxer Joe Louis), Medgar Evers, and Thurgood Marshall.

ANC is divided into 70 sections, and some are full; others are reserved for specific people, such as those killed during the wars in Iraq and Afghanistan. You may be eligible to choose between inurnment or in-ground burial. Though it's run by the Army, Servicemembers and veterans from all branches may be buried in ANC.

Table 22-1 outlines who's eligible for burial in Arlington, and under which circumstances, but regardless of anything else, you must have an honorable discharge to be laid to rest there.

REMEMBER

Your eligibility for any type of interment at ANC is verified at the time of your death — not before, so there may be a long wait between the time you die and the day you're actually laid to rest at Arlington.

A BRIEF HISTORY OF ARLINGTON NATIONAL CEMETERY

The first person ever buried on Arlington's hallowed grounds was William Christman, a private who served with the 67th Pennsylvania Infantry Regiment; he was buried there on May 13, 1864, when the Civil War filled Washington hospitals with wounded soldiers. The Army didn't have anywhere to put those who died, so they began burying them along the outer perimeter of Confederate General Robert E. Lee's confiscated estate.

TABLE 22-1

Eligibility for Interment at Arlington

Servicemember	Inurnment	In-Ground Burial
Dies on Title 10 federal active duty (other than for training)	Eligible	Eligible
Dies on active duty for training (Title 10)	Eligible	Not eligible
Retired veteran receiving retirement pay	Eligible	Eligible
Veteran with at least one day of active duty other than for training	Eligible	Not eligible
Veteran with a Medal of Honor, Distinguished Service Cross, Distinguished Service Medal, Silver Star, or Purple Heart	Eligible	Eligible
Reservist or Guardsman who dies under honorable conditions while on active duty for training or full-time service	Eligible	Not eligible
Former POW	Eligible	Eligible

Interment or inurnment at ANC doesn't cost your estate anything, but you do have to pay if you choose to use a burial vault to protect your casket or urn. Your alternative is to use a free government grave liner, which is made from reinforced concrete (your casket or urn is then placed inside, and a concrete lid goes on top of everything). ANC uses these liners to prevent your grave from sinking (not to protect your casket or urn).

Your estate must also pay all the costs associated with the preparation of remains, the casket or urn, and transporting the remains to ANC. The only exception is when a servicemember was on active duty at the time of their death. Sometimes the VA and Social Security Administration (SSA) are able to help pick up the tab for some of these costs.

VA national cemeteries

The National Cemetery Administration runs all 155 VA national cemeteries and 34 soldiers' lots and monument sites across 42 states and Puerto Rico. Veterans, servicemembers, and even some family members may qualify for burial in one of these resting places. VA national cemeteries don't charge for the gravesite itself, opening and closing of the grave, a burial liner, a headstone or marker provided by the government, and ongoing care of the gravesite.

You're only eligible for burial in a VA cemetery if one of the following is true about the person who qualifies for benefits:

>> They're a veteran and didn't receive a dishonorable discharge.

>> They died on active duty, active duty for training, or inactive duty for training.

>> They're the spouse or minor child of a veteran, even if the veteran has already passed away.

>> They're the unmarried adult dependent child of a veteran (in some cases).

Some people aren't eligible for burial in a VA national cemetery, such as those who were convicted of treason or subversive activities, former spouses, and veterans with dishonorable discharges.

Unlike ANC, the VA may make an eligibility determination in advance of need (that is, before you die). Though the VA doesn't accept reservations for any of its cemeteries, it will consider your pre-need application if you qualify for burial or inurnment in one of its resting places.

National Park cemeteries

The National Park Service manages 14 national cemeteries, but only one — the Andersonville National Cemetery in Georgia — is still active. The rest are no longer accepting new burials (other than for family members of those already buried there who wish to be buried in the same plot). You may be eligible for park burial if you're a veteran who was discharged under other than dishonorable conditions.

State and tribal veteran cemeteries

Many U.S. states and territories have established their own veterans cemeteries, as have many First Nations tribes. These cemeteries typically receive setup funding from the VA, but they're maintained and run by the state, territory, or tribe. Usually, eligibility requirements in these cemeteries are similar to those for VA national cemeteries, but they sometimes include residency requirements.

You can find your state's vet cemeteries, including tribal cemeteries, on the VA's website (and follow their links to discover eligibility requirements) at www.cem. va.gov/find-cemetery/all-grant-funded.asp. Your costs for burial in one of these cemeteries depends on your state's rules and funding policies.

Burial on a military installation

Lots of veterans qualify for burial on a military installation, and just about all significantly sized bases have them. These cemeteries, which are typically open to veterans with other-than-dishonorable discharges, are maintained and managed by the installation they're on. If you're interested in being buried or inurned on a base that's near-and-dear to your heart, your best bet is to find out what agency runs it and reach out. Often, these cemeteries are run by the Directorate of Public Works or Mortuary Affairs.

Burial at sea

The U.S. Navy may bury you at sea from a naval vessel, but because the *committal service* (the service typically held at a gravesite) takes place while a ship is deployed, family members aren't permitted to attend. If you choose burial at sea, the commanding officer of the ship assigned to the duty notifies your family members of the date, time, and longitude and latitude of your disposition after the service.

REMEMBER

There's typically a waiting period of 12 to 18 months before a burial at sea takes place, which starts after the Navy receives your remains at the port of embarkation. You may be eligible for a sea burial if one of the following is true about you:

>> You're an active-duty member of any branch of the uniformed services.

>> You're a retiree or veteran who was honorably discharged.

>> You work for the Military Sealift Command.

>> You're a dependent family member of an active-duty servicemember, retiree, or veteran of the armed forces.

The Navy can't guarantee you a spot on a ship prior to your death. Instead, the person authorized to direct your disposition (the Navy calls this person a PADD) after your death may contact the Navy and Marine Corps Mortuary Affairs office to request information and provide documentation to request your burial at sea. A burial flag is required at all sea burials for veterans and servicemembers. Your PADD may provide a flag; if they do, the Navy will return it to them after the committal ceremony. If your PADD doesn't provide a burial flag, the Navy will provide one, but it won't send the flag to your PADD following the ceremony.

You can find ports of embarkation in Norfolk, Virginia; Jacksonville, Florida; San Diego, California; Bremerton, Washington; and Honolulu, Hawaii. Each has its own coordinator, and you can get their contact information by searching for the Navy's mortuary affairs officer in each port.

Private cemeteries

Private cemeteries sometimes have sections specifically for veterans and their families, and each comes with its own costs. However, most veterans buried in private cemeteries qualify for some burial benefits, including a free headstone, marker, or medallion; a burial flag; and a Presidential Memorial Certificate. I cover those in the following section.

TIP

Many people choose to pre-purchase burial plots so their families don't have to do it while they're grieving. If you're interested in a particular cemetery, you should contact them to find out how much it costs for an in-ground burial, mausoleum crypt, or inurnment space. You should also look into the cemetery's upkeep policies, who owns it, and the cemetery's policy on headstones, grave markers, and grave decorations (such as flowers and other items).

Asking Uncle Sam to Pick Up the Tab

If you choose to be buried or inurned in a private cemetery, the government may provide a headstone, marker, or medallion; a burial flag as a keepsake; and a Presidential Memorial Certificate. It may also pay some expenses if the person paying for the burial and funeral costs won't be reimbursed by any other organization. The person paying for these costs must be a surviving spouse or partner from a legal union, a surviving child or parent, or the executor of the veteran's estate.

REMEMBER

For an eligible party to get help with burial and funeral costs, at least one of the following must be true about the deceased veteran:

>> They didn't receive a dishonorable discharge.

>> They died as a result of a service-connected disability or while receiving VA care.

>> They died with an original or reopened claim for VA compensation or pension pending at the time of their death.

>> They received a VA pension or compensation, or they were eligible for disability compensation but instead chose to receive full military retirement pay.

These burial benefits are *reimbursed expenses*, which means you must pay for the services first, and then apply for the benefit. You may be reimbursed for the actual burial and funeral costs, the gravesite's cost, and the cost of transporting the veteran's remains to their final resting place. The amount you receive depends on when the veteran died, whether their death was service-connected, and a number of other factors. Check the current amount you may be entitled to receive on the VA's website (the numbers are subject to change).

For a nonservice-connected burial allowance, you must apply for reimbursement within two years of the veteran's burial or cremation. If the veteran received a discharge upgrade after death, you can file an allowance claim within two years of the date of the upgrade. There's no time limit on filing for reimbursement if the veteran died from a service-connected disability. You may apply through the VA's website or by mailing a completed VA Form 21P-530EZ to your nearest VA regional office.

TIP

If you're a surviving spouse, you don't need to file a claim. As long as you're listed on the veteran's profile, the VA will automatically send you money after receiving notice of the veteran's death.

Getting a marker, headstone, or medallion

When a vet is buried in Arlington, a national cemetery, a state or tribal veterans cemetery, or a National Park cemetery, the VA automatically gives them a free grave marker or headstone. The VA also provides free markers, headstones, and medallions for most other veterans, including vets buried in unmarked graves in any cemetery around the world.

REMEMBER

If you order one of these headstones or markers, the government will inscribe the veteran's legal name, branch of service, year of birth, and year of death at no additional charge. You may request additional information, such as birth date and month, death date and month, highest rank, medals earned, war service, emblem of belief, or other inscriptions. You may also ask that the government reserves space for future inscriptions at your own expense (such as a spouse's information).

These memorial items are completely free for those who qualify. The most current qualification requirements are listed on VA Form 40-1330, which you need to file to apply for any of them. The form also includes nearly 80 available emblems of belief, such as the Dharma wheel, many crosses, the atheist and humanist symbols, Thor's hammer, and the Star of David.

Receiving a burial flag

The VA provides burial flags at no cost. These flags are furnished to honor the memory of a veteran's service, and they're usually given to the veteran's next of kin. You're eligible for a free burial flag if the veteran meets any of the following criteria:

>> Served during wartime

>> Died on active duty after May 27, 1941

>> Served after January 31, 1955

>> Served in peacetime and left the military before June 27, 1950, after serving at least one enlistment or because of a service-connected disability

>> Served in the Selected Reserves (in some cases) or served in the Philippines' military forces while in service to the United States, provided they died on or after April 25, 1951

You may apply for a burial flag by filling out VA Form 27-2008 and bringing it to a funeral director, a VA regional office, or a U.S. post office.

Getting a Presidential Memorial Certificate

Presidential Memorial Certificates (PMCs) are engraved paper certificates signed by the current president. You may request one if the veteran is eligible for burial in a national cemetery and you're the veteran's next of kin, a close family member, or close friend. If the veteran is buried in a VA national cemetery, you don't need to apply; if they're buried elsewhere, you may apply by using VA Form 40-0247. Upload the form through AccessVA, turn it in to any VA regional office, or mail it to the address listed on the form.

Knowing what the VA won't pay for

The VA won't (and can't) pay for some services, such as cremation, aquamation, and nontraditional dispositions. It also won't pay for embalming, the casket or urn, or in most cases, transportation to the cemetery. But if a servicemember dies while on active duty, their military branch typically pays most of the costs (including everything listed here, plus the cost of a family member accompanying the remains from the place of death to the funeral home). Additionally, the military pays to transfer the remains of retirees and dependents who die while being treated in a military hospital.

Getting Your VGLI or VALife payments

If a veteran has a form of VA life insurance when they die, which I cover in Chapter 7, their *beneficiaries* (the people they elected to receive payments) may file a claim and choose how they want to receive their payments.

Understanding Military Funeral Honors

The Department of Defense (DOD) and veterans service organizations provide military funeral honors. These honors are part of an extremely long tradition and required by federal law; upon request, the DOD must provide an honor guard consisting of at least two military members to provide funeral honors. At minimum, the honor detail must perform the flag-folding ceremony, present the American flag to the veteran's next of kin, and play "Taps" (but it may play a recording if no bugler is available).

TIP

You can request that the U.S. Air Force, Army, Navy, or Marine Corps do a flyover at a military funeral. However, each branch has its own eligibility requirements, and there's no guarantee that your request will be granted. Keep in mind that these requests are subject to aircraft availability, budgets, and weather conditions.

Families may also request that members of the honor guard act as pallbearers, provided enough personnel are available. Additionally, you may request a rifle volley (which is different from, but commonly mistaken for, a 21-gun salute) performed by a firing party consisting of seven or eight members.

The military funeral honors provided at ANC are different from those performed in other cemeteries. For funerals at Arlington, the U.S. Army's Honor Guard may provide a casket team, a firing party, a bugler, a marching element, a military band, a riderless horse, a caisson team, and a battery cannon salute.

TECHNICAL
STUFF

The rifle volley comes from an old battlefield custom; when warring armies in the 17th and 18th centuries needed to remove the dead from the battlefield, they'd fire three volleys to signal a pause from the fighting. After the deceased were removed and cared for, the side that asked for the pause would fire another three volleys to signal that they were ready to return to the battle. Cannon salutes are related to an old British Navy tradition; when a ship fired a cannon, it was partially disarmed until the cannon was reloaded, so today, a cannon salute symbolizes respect and trust.

A veteran may be eligible for funeral honors if they were on active duty or in the selected reserve at the time of their death, they were discharged from active duty under conditions other than dishonorable, or they served a full term of enlistment in a reserve component and were discharged under conditions other than dishonorable.

DYING ON DUTY: THE DEATH GRATUITY PAYMENT

When an active-duty servicemember dies or is killed in the line of duty, the military pays a death gratuity to the people the servicemember identified as beneficiaries prior to their death. It's a one-time, tax-exempt, lump-sum payment of $100,000, and usually, survivors get it within 72 hours of filing DD Form 397, *Claim Certification and Voucher for Death Gratuity Payment.* However, the servicemember must have died while on active duty, active duty for training, inactive duty for training, or within 120 days of their release from active duty if their death is service-connected. Eligible survivors are also able to get free financial counseling through their military service or Military OneSource. If the servicemember had Servicemembers' Group Life Insurance (SGLI) or if the deceased was a veteran who elected to extend SGLI after leaving the service, survivors need to file Form SGLV 8283, *Claim for Death Benefits.* SGLI is separate from the death gratuity.

Laying Indigent Veterans and Unclaimed Remains to Rest

When someone pays to inter or inurn an *indigent veteran* (a vet who doesn't have enough resources to pay for burial and funeral expenses) or a veteran's unclaimed remains, the VA may be able to reimburse them for the casket, the burial, or the plot (or any combination of the three). In some cases, the VA may also reimburse transportation to the nearest state or tribal cemetery. When the veteran is laid to rest in a private cemetery, they may be entitled to a headstone or marker (see the earlier section, "Asking Uncle Sam to Pick Up the Tab," for more information).

Chapter **23**

Surveying Survivor Benefits

When a veteran passes away, they often leave behind family members; these family members are known as *survivors*. Sometimes survivors are spouses, children, parents, and other dependents, and many of these people qualify for a variety of benefits from the Department of Veterans Affairs, the Department of Defense, and the veteran's service branch. This chapter explains what benefits may be available to you as a survivor and how to get them.

Using Bereavement Counseling Services

Surviving spouses, children, and parents of servicemembers who die while serving on active duty may be eligible for bereavement counseling through the VA. Commonly called *grief counseling* and designed to help you through the loss of your loved one, it's available at community-based Vet Centers, in your home, or in another place you feel comfortable. You can get more information and schedule your counseling appointments by calling your nearest Vet Center or emailing vetcenter.bereavement@va.gov.

Differentiating between the Death Gratuity and the Survivors Pension

When a servicemember or veteran dies, their survivors may be entitled to a death gratuity or death pension. The *death gratuity* comes directly from the DOD when a servicemember dies on active duty (or within 120 days of release from active duty if the death is service connected). It's a lump-sum, tax-exempt payment of $100,000 that the DOD typically pays a beneficiary within 72 hours of receipt of the claim (DD Form 397).

The survivors pension is different from the death gratuity. When a veteran dies, the surviving spouse and some unmarried dependent children may be entitled to the *survivors pension*, which is a monthly stipend to help cover living expenses. However, survivors only qualify if the veteran meets any of the following:

>> Entered active duty on or before September 7, 1980, and served at least 90 days on active military service with at least one day during a covered wartime period

>> Entered active duty after September 7, 1980, and served at least 24 months or the full period for which they were ordered to active duty, with at least one day during a covered wartime period

>> Was an officer and started active duty after October 16, 1981, and hadn't previously served on active duty for at least 24 months

Additionally, the survivor's family income and net worth must fall below certain limits set by Congress, which are subject to change. The benefit is available to unremarried spouses, dependent children younger than 18 (or younger than 23 if attending a VA-approved school), or dependent adult children who are unable to care for themselves due to a disability that occurred before they turned 18.

The eligible wartime periods for the survivors pension include World War II (December 7, 1941 to December 31, 1946), the Korean conflict (June 27, 1950 to January 31, 1955), the Vietnam War era (November 1, 1955 to May 7, 1975, for veterans who went to Vietnam and August 5, 1964 to May 7, 1975, for veterans who served outside Vietnam), and the Gulf War (August 2, 1990 through the present).

You may apply for the survivors pension by filling out and filing VA Form 21P-534EZ, which you can upload through the VA's website (I explain how to set up credentials in Chapter 3), mail to the VA's Pension Intake Center, or submit in person at your nearest regional VA office.

Filing a Life Insurance Claim

If your sponsor was enrolled in a government-sponsored life insurance program, such as VGLI or VALife, head to Chapter 7 for information on making a claim. If your sponsor was enrolled in another life insurance program, you need to file a claim through the company that provides the benefit.

Most servicemembers opt into Servicemembers Group Life Insurance (SGLI). This life insurance, which servicemembers pay for through pay allotments, provides up to $400,000 in coverage to surviving family members in the event of the service-member's death while serving on active duty.

To receive your SGLI benefit, you must file Form SGLV 8283 with the VA. If the servicemember is terminally ill (that is, they have a doctor's diagnosis that says they have nine months or fewer to live), you may be eligible to receive up to 50 percent of your SGLI benefit through the Accelerated Benefit Option. To receive accelerated payments, file Form SGLV 8284 with the VA.

TIP

You may be able to get short-term financial support through your SGLI policy if your sponsor is recovering from a traumatic injury. You may apply for the SGLI Traumatic Injury Protection Program (TSGLI) by working with the servicemember to fill out and file Form SGLV 8600.

Investigating the Survivor Benefit Plan

When a military retiree dies, their retirement pay stops — even if they have a surviving spouse or dependents who rely on that money. But the Survivor Benefit Plan (SBP) is a program that some retirees enroll in at the time they retire; by paying premiums from their gross retired pay, and by staying current on payments, retirees can ensure that their dependents continue to receive up to 55 percent of their retired pay. If your annuity is 55 percent and your sponsor received $1,000 per month in retired pay, you receive $550 per month. This income is taxable. I cover the nuts and bolts of the SBP in Chapter 8.

To make a claim under the SBP, the beneficiary must notify the Defense Finance and Accounting Service at www.dfas.mil/. Typically, it takes a few months for SBP payments to start, but don't worry; they're retroactive to the date of the veteran's death.

Delving into Dependency and Indemnity Compensation

Surviving spouses, children, and parents of servicemembers who die in the line of duty, as well as survivors of veterans who die from service-connected injuries or illnesses, may be eligible for Dependency and Indemnity Compensation (DIC) from the VA. These tax-free monthly payments vary in size depending on your relationship with the veteran and the veteran's circumstances.

REMEMBER

As a surviving spouse, you may be eligible for DIC if you lived with the veteran or servicemember without a break until their death (or, if you were separated, the separation wasn't your fault, such as a deployment) and one of the following is true:

» You married the vet or servicemember within 15 years of their discharge from the period of service during which they acquired their qualifying illness or injury.

» You were married for at least one year.

» You had a child with the veteran or servicemember.

» The veteran was rated 100 percent disabled or had permanent and total disability for at least ten years before their death.

As a surviving child, you may be eligible if you aren't married, you aren't included in the surviving spouse's compensation, and you're younger than 18 (or younger than 23 if you're attending school).

Surviving spouses or children of active-duty servicemembers who die must use VA Form 21P-534a to make a claim. Spouses and children of deceased veterans must fill out and file VA Form 21P-534EZ to make a claim.

As a surviving parent, you may be eligible for DIC if you're the servicemember or veteran's biological, adoptive, or foster parent and your income falls below a certain amount. You can find the current income threshold on the VA's website, where you can also download VA Form 21P-535 to make a claim.

You may file your application on the VA's website, by mailing it to the VA's Pension Intake Center, or by going to a VA regional office.

Talking to a Financial Counselor and Preparing Your Will

When you make a claim under SGLI, TSGLI, or VGLI, you're entitled to free financial planning services through the VA. The Beneficiary Financial Counseling Service (BFCS) gives you free, professional financial advice from a third-party company contracted by the VA, including a customized financial plan and up to 40 hours of individual personal counseling with financial professionals upon request. You're eligible for these services for up to two years following your claim settlement.

You're also entitled to a free online will preparation service where you may create a will without hiring an attorney. You answer a series of questions and the same contractor that provides financial counseling will provide you with a legal will that's valid in all states.

Choosing CHAMPVA or TRICARE

You remain eligible for TRICARE unless you remarry, and children remain eligible until they age out or lose eligibility for other reasons. If you had this health insurance before your sponsor passed away, it's not going anywhere (though you still have to pay your premiums to keep your policy). Refer to Chapter 6 for more on TRICARE.

If you don't have TRICARE and your spouse or parent passes away while serving on active duty or from a service-connected disability or condition, you may be eligible for health insurance through the Civilian Health and Medical Program of the Department of Veterans Affairs (CHAMPVA). You're only eligible for CHAMPVA if you aren't eligible for TRICARE and you meet certain conditions. You can apply for benefits under this health insurance program, which provides coverage similar to TRICARE, by mailing VA Form 10-10d and VA Form 10-7959c to the Veterans Health Association's Office of Community Care at the address listed on the forms.

Buying a Home or Getting Foreclosure Help

As the surviving spouse of a veteran who died while serving in the military or as a result of a service-connected disability (or who was totally disabled, even if their cause of death wasn't service connected), you may qualify for a VA home loan benefit. This benefit allows you to buy a home with no down payment, competitive interest rates, and a number of other perks, which you can find out about in Chapter 15.

You may also qualify if your spouse is missing in action or is a prisoner of war. You need a certificate of eligibility (COE) to apply for a VA loan through a bank, credit union, or other lender, but you may only get a COE under these circumstances if you receive Dependency and Indemnity Compensation. (See the earlier section, "Delving into Dependency and Indemnity Compensation," for more details on how to apply for that benefit.)

Using Career and Educational Benefits

If you're the surviving spouse or child of a servicemember or veteran, you may be eligible for Chapter 35 benefits that help you find your career path or attend school. The following sections give you an overview of each.

Utilizing the Survivors' and Dependents' Education Assistance Program

The Survivors' and Dependents' Education Assistance (DEA) program provides monthly payments for career training programs, college and graduate degree programs, apprenticeships, on-the-job training, and educational and career counseling. You may be eligible for this program if you're the spouse or eligible child of a veteran who died while on active duty or as a result of a service-connected disability (as well as under some other circumstances). I cover the DEA program extensively in Chapter 21 because that chapter is designed for both survivors and the eligible dependents of permanently and totally disabled veterans.

Note: You're not allowed to use DEA benefits and the Fry Scholarship at the same time, which I explain in the following section. However, you may use one after the other.

Getting the Fry Scholarship

The Marine Gunnery Sergeant John David Fry Scholarship — just called the Fry Scholarship for short — is available to the children and spouses of a member of the armed forces who died in the line of duty on or after September 11, 2001, a member of the armed forces who died in the line of duty while not on active duty on or after September 11, 2001, or a member of the Selected Reserve who died from a service-connected disability on or after September 11, 2001.

The Fry Scholarship provides money for tuition, housing, and books and supplies for school. It covers full in-state tuition costs at public schools and up to a certain amount (which is subject to change, but current rates are available on the VA's website) for training at private or out-of-state schools.

As the child of a qualifying servicemember, you may apply for the Fry Scholarship under these conditions:

>> If you turned 18 or graduated from high school before January 1, 2013, you can get a Fry Scholarship until you're 33 years old.

>> If you turn 18 or graduate from high school after January 1, 2013, you may get this scholarship at any age over 18 or after you graduate.

>> If your parent was in the Selected Reserve and passed away from a service-connected disability, you can get this scholarship regardless of your age.

>> If your parent died in the line of duty before August 1, 2011, you could qualify for this scholarship *and* the DEA program, which I cover in Chapter 14.

WARNING

Surviving children aren't allowed to use the Fry Scholarship and receive DIC at the same time. You may only use one or the other. However, surviving spouses *are* allowed to receive DIC while using a Fry Scholarship as long as they don't remarry.

To get a Fry Scholarship, you must first choose a school and ensure that it's approved for VA benefits. You may apply online through the VA's website or by filling out a VA Form 22-5490 and mailing it to the VA regional office where you want to go to school. You may also apply in person at a VA regional office. And if you've already started a program, that's okay; simply ask a certifying official at your school to fill out a VA enrollment certification (VA Form 22-1999).

TIP

Although you can't use the DEA program at the same time you use a Fry Scholarship, you can use them back-to-back, so when one runs out, you may apply for and use the other. The VA caps combined benefits at 81 months of full-time training if you meet certain requirements.

Extending your benefits with the Edith Nourse Rogers STEM Scholarship

If you receive the Fry Scholarship, you may be eligible to extend your benefits for an additional 9 months or $30,000 in additional benefits through the Edith Nourse Rogers STEM Scholarship. It's available to people who meet the following:

» They're currently enrolled in an undergraduate STEM degree program or qualifying dual-degree program.

» They've earned a post-secondary degree or graduate degree in an approved STEM degree field and are enrolled in a covered clinical training program for healthcare professionals.

» They've earned a post-secondary degree in an approved STEM degree field and are working toward a teaching certification.

However, you must be enrolled in a program that requires at least 120 standard semester hours or 180 quarter credit hours, have already completed at least 60 standard credit hours or 90 quarter credit hours, and have fewer than 6 months left on your Fry Scholarship. Find out more about this scholarship in Chapter 14.

Getting the Iraq and Afghanistan Service Grant

If your parent or guardian died due to their military service in Iraq or Afghanistan after September 11, 2001, you may be eligible for the Iraq and Afghanistan Service Grant from the U.S. Department of Education. This grant is equal to the maximum Pell Grant award.

To qualify, you must not be eligible for a Pell Grant based on your financial situation (but still meet the other Pell Grant requirements). Your parent or guardian must have died as a result of military service performed in Iraq or Afghanistan after 9/11, and you must have been less than 24 years old or enrolled at least part time in a college or career school at the time of your parent or guardian's death. You apply for this benefit after filling out the Free Application for Federal Student Aid (FAFSA).

Chapter **24**

Shopping 'til You Drop: Benefits for Retirees and Other ID Cardholders

When you retire from the military, you receive a shiny, new identification card that tells the world that you did your time; that ID card is your golden ticket to shopping, dining, and entertainment on military installations (as well as a bunch of other perks that I cover in this chapter and Chapter 25). Your retiree ID, as well as your spouse's and dependents' ID cards, entitle you and your loved ones to use the commissaries, exchange stores, MWR facilities, restaurants, gas stations, and even thrift shops on your favorite military installations. Many of these benefits are also available to Medal of Honor and Purple Heart recipients, former prisoners or war, and disabled veterans' caregivers, even if they don't have retiree ID cards. This chapter is your guide to all the on–installation benefits that are yours for the taking.

Exploring the Exchange

Four military exchange systems operate on military installations worldwide (I've even shopped at exchanges on the large installations downrange). These systems include the following:

» Army and Air Force Exchange (AAFES)

» Navy Exchange Service Command (NEXCOM)

» Marine Corps Exchange (MCX)

» Coast Guard Exchange (CGX)

They all fund themselves through the sale of products, food, and services — no taxpayer money is involved. And even better, about two-thirds of the proceeds the exchanges earn go back into the military communities they serve through Morale, Welfare, and Recreation (MWR) programs, such as community swimming pools, golf courses, recreation centers, and other quality-of-life programs. The rest of the earnings go into building new facilities and making improvements on old ones.

These exchange systems are responsible for most of the shopping (PXs, BXs, NEXs, MCXs, CGXs, and shoppettes), movie theaters, restaurants, gas stations, liquor stores, and uniform sales you find on military installations. They also offer online shopping, which you can access by proving your retiree status.

On average, you save between 15 and 20 percent when you shop at an exchange — and you don't pay sales tax. Exchanges do price-matching, too. If you find something cheaper at another store or online, you simply have to show your cashier proof, and the exchange will match the lower price. The exchange services typically make billions of dollars in sales each year, and they'll be happy to take some of your retired pay and turn it into services for current servicemembers and their families.

Commandeering Commissary Benefits

The commissary on your nearest installation is most likely run by the Defense Commissary Agency (DECA), and it's there to save you some cash on your grocery bill. Most food and household items at the commissary are sold at discounted prices. According to DECA, you save between 20 and 30 percent at the checkout register when compared to local grocery stores. (The agency is required by law to save shoppers 23.7 percent against local market averages.)

TIP

If you want to save even more, you can sign up for the DECA rewards card and the digital coupons it offers. And here's a pro tip: If you shop at a commissary overseas, they'll take coupons that expired up to six months prior to your shopping trip (no such luck when you're stateside, though).

You can stroll the aisles at your leisure, shopping for produce, meats, and other items, as well as order custom cakes and other goodies from the bakery section. Most commissaries have delis, and some have sushi bars and other quick-pick-up items. Some commissaries have even adopted a click-to-go program that enables you to shop online and pick up your items at the store.

TIP

Tip your baggers! The people who bag your groceries and help you load them in your car don't receive hourly pay; they work only for tips because DECA considers them self-employed. A good tip is between 5 and 10 percent of your total purchase. If you don't want to tip them, you have the option of heading to a self-checkout or bag-your-own lane. Otherwise, they're working for you for free, and that's not cool.

TECHNICAL
STUFF

When you shop at a DECA commissary, you pay a surcharge that goes toward construction, equipment, and maintenance. DECA pays its employees with taxpayer subsidies, which enables the agency to keep prices down.

Handling Personal Maintenance (and a Few Other Things)

Nearly every military installation has, at minimum, a barber shop where you can get a cheap haircut. (But you've been warned: You usually get what you pay for!) Most also have laundromats and dry cleaners, tailors, and other essential services. Some have one-hour photo shops, mail and shipping alternatives to the U.S. Postal Service, florists, specialty shops, and nutrition stores. And when you make your way through the sliding glass doors of any major exchange, you typically have to zigzag around kiosks from major retailers, local business owners, and a variety of other companies.

Although subcontractors operate all these services, shops, and activities, the exchange system manages them. (Personally, I think *For Dummies* kiosks would be awesome, so if anyone from an exchange service is reading this, give me a call!)

Diving into Perks for Families and Kids

Many military installations have plenty of fun places for families and friends to hang out, such as golf courses, community swimming pools, and even disc golf courses, and if you have base and MWR privileges, you can use them. Even better, you may be able to enroll your appropriately aged kids in child and youth services, such as sports, clubs, and fitness programs. You may even be eligible to enroll your children in the childcare facilities on your nearest installation. Just keep in mind that sometimes active-duty kids get priority and retirees' children are only accepted on a space-available basis.

REMEMBER

Your family isn't just your spouse and kids, though. Retirees and qualifying ID cardholders may also use military veterinary treatment facilities for their four-, two-, and no-legged family members. You may even save some money by visiting a military veterinarian.

TIP

If you're traveling overseas with a pet, the best place to get titer tests and other services required for intra- and intercontinental travel is a military veterinarian's office because the vets there can often provide you with the documentation you need (rather than sending it off to the USDA).

Having a Night on the Town on Your Local Installation

Who says you need to go to the city for an evening out? If you have the right type of ID card, you can patronize the restaurants, movie theaters, and bowling alleys (and any other attractions available) on your nearest military installation.

Although some installations have only a small food court with bad dietary choices, many larger installations feature big-name chain restaurants (and even a few local favorites). You won't save much money while dining on a military installation, because the prices are generally the same as they are outside the gates, but these places are usually within walking distance of other attractions, such as the movie theater and bowling alley.

TIP

Speaking of movie theaters and bowling alleys on military posts and bases, they're usually run by the exchange services and the MWR, respectively. That means your costs probably *are* lower when you use these facilities as compared to the corporate facilities off-installation — and who doesn't want to save a little cash?

Visiting On-Installation Museums

Many military installations feature charming little museums, such as the Army Intelligence Museum on Fort Huachuca, the U.S. Army Chemical Corps Museum at Fort Leonard Wood, and the Marine Corps Mechanized Museum at Camp Pendleton. Admission to many on-installation museums is free, and though they're not typically huge places to explore, they're great spots to visit a time or two to get your history fix. Some installations are starting to incorporate other types of museums, such as the Children's Museum at Joint Base Lewis-McChord, that may charge admission.

Snagging Cheap Tickets

Whether you've been itching to go to a major theme park or you've been waiting for your favorite sports season to start back up so you can catch a game, your retiree ID card gives you the green light to use the MWR's services, including ticket purchases for all kinds of attractions, events, and tours (including Disney, SeaWorld, and other theme parks). You can even book discounted cruises through the MWR.

Playing Around with the MWR

On many installations, the MWR runs fun attractions such as obstacle courses, laser tag, and karaoke rooms. They also plan social events, hold crafting classes, and put together group trips to local off-installation attractions. You may also use your nearest MWR to rent party supplies (like grills, tables, and chairs), bounce houses, dunk tanks, and costumes (such as Santa and the Easter Bunny).

Breaking a Sweat at Fitness Centers

Your retired-military ID card gets you into the MWR's fitness centers, located on military installations worldwide. After you're registered with your installation's fitness center, you can use all the equipment, tracks, saunas, locker rooms, and other amenities. Some fitness centers also hold group fitness classes for a small fee. It's a free gym membership, which can save you hundreds of dollars every year.

Lawyering Up

If you're a military retiree, you're most likely eligible to use your nearest installation's legal services office. Though military lawyers can't represent you in court, they can give you legal advice — and they can provide a full suite of other great services, including will preparation and estate planning, as well as notary service.

Figuring Out Former Spouse Access

Usually, when a veteran divorces, their spouse (if the spouse is nonmilitary) loses their ID card and all the privileges associated with it. However, one notable exception is the 20/20/20 rule from the Uniformed Services Former Spouse Protection Act.

This rule says that an unremarried former spouse gets to keep full benefits (including medical, shopping, and all the rest) if all the following apply:

>> The couple was married for at least 20 years.

>> The veteran performed at least 20 years of military service leading to retirement.

>> There's at least a 20-year overlap of marriage and military service.

However, if the former spouse remarries, they lose their benefits.

Cashing In on Civilian Discounts for Vets

You don't have to be a retiree to qualify for all kinds of veteran discounts. In fact, a simple veteran ID card from the VA or a veteran designation on your driver's license can net you significant savings in several places. Many local and national retailers, restaurants, and service providers have significant discounts for vets; you just have to ask.

» Taking R&R at military lodging and Armed Forces Resorts

» Finding fabulous travel discounts only for vets

» Touring the National Parks for free

Chapter **25**

Seeing the World with Travel Benefits

Whether you spent a few decades zipping all over the globe in the military's service or you served a few years and decided to move on, you may be eligible to take advantage of travel benefits only available to certain veterans and their families. These benefits include tagging along on military flights, staying at military lodging and special resorts, and getting steep discounts on airfare, hotels, rental cars, and more. I take you on a quick tour of these benefits (and how to take advantage of them) in this chapter.

Getting around with American Forces Travel

You have plenty of affordable ways to get from Point A to Point B when you're eligible to use American Forces Travel (www.americanforcestravel.com). The DOD's Morale, Welfare, and Recreation (MWR) runs this full-service website offering discounted rates on car rentals, hotels, flights, and cruises. You can even book an entire trip package using its website if you're one of (or the spouse of) the following:

>> A veteran with an honorable discharge (or general under honorable conditions)

>> A military retiree

>> A Medal of Honor or Purple Heart recipient

>> A veteran with a service-connected disability

>> A primary caregiver of an eligible veteran

Because the service is an MWR project, your military and veteran discounts are built in. And like all other MWR programs, proceeds go toward bettering life for servicemembers and their families.

Snagging a Spot on Space-A

The United States Air Force's Air Mobility Command (AMC) keeps the military on the move by scheduling flights to and from just about every installation with an airfield (and then some). That's great news for retirees and their dependents, veterans with a permanent 100 percent disability rating, and surviving spouses because they're eligible to grab a seat on the thousands of aircraft that are already heading somewhere each week.

This type of travel, commonly called *Space-A* (short for *space-available*), is typically free — but you may have to pay taxes and, in some cases, federal inspection fees. If you're charged a fee, the terminal may accept cash or credit cards, so be prepared for both.

One day you may take a trip on a C-130, and another you might be on a Patriot Express flight (a commercial airliner commissioned by the military for travel to a specific destination), depending on where the good people working at the AMC can squeeze you in. The following sections explain how to get one of these coveted spots (and what to do with it after you get it).

Checking your priority level

The AMC assigns priority levels to those eligible to fly. That doesn't mean you get to sit in first class (or that you'll have to fit into an overhead luggage bin). It just means that there are people who have more important trips than you do, and they get to call dibs on seats first. Categories I, II, III, IV, and V are for active-duty servicemembers and their families, DOD teachers and their families, and some others. Category VI is your jam, but unfortunately, it puts you at the back of the line.

REMEMBER

The good news is that after you have a confirmed seat, you can't be bumped from your flight; the bad news is that empty Space-A seats are normally identified sometime between four hours and a half-hour (yes, that's 30 minutes) before a flight departs.

Finding a terminal and getting on the list

You can find a complete list of all military passenger terminals in the United States and overseas on the Air Force's AMC website at www.amc.af.mil/, including contact information and web addresses for each terminal. When you find a terminal you want to leave from, check its website or Facebook page for a 72-hour flight schedule. These schedules include destinations, the number of available Space-A seats, and the time that terminal staff plans to announce those who were selected for the flight; they call that time *roll call*.

REMEMBER

When you find a flight you want, fill out a Space-Available Travel Request and email it to the appropriate address to get on the waiting list. Priority within your category depends on when you signed up for the waiting list. For example, if you and I are both Category VI and we both sign up for a flight out of Baltimore to Honolulu, but you signed up first and there's only one Space-A seat available by the time they get to our category on the list, your butt is in the seat — not mine.

Packing accordingly

Usually when you fly Space-A, you're allowed to check two 70-pound bags per person. However, different aircraft have different baggage allowances, so check before you show up at the terminal. All AMC terminals follow the same baggage and screening guidelines that the Transportation Security Administration (TSA) does, so that means limited liquids in your carry-on.

TIP

When you check bags, you also pay for meals on the flight (if they're available and you want them). Military cargo flights typically offer you the option of a box lunch, whereas Patriot Express flights sometimes serve hot food and alcohol.

Getting ready for roll call

If you're on a waiting list, mark yourself present at the terminal up to 24 hours before the scheduled roll call. That way, AMC staff knows you're still interested in the seat and will be there for the flight. During the actual roll call, a staff member will announce how many seats are available and call out names of selected passengers; they list the names in order of priority, so you'll be toward the end.

When a staff member calls your name, go to the desk and confirm (again) that you're present. Show them your military ID card (and ID cards for dependents older than 10 who are traveling with you), as well as other documents that may be required (such as your passport).

Some terminals offer virtual roll call (VRC), which means you can wait anywhere you want. If your terminal offers VRC, you receive an email that asks you to check in; you must answer that email within 30 minutes or so. If you don't, you're booted from the list. After you check in, AMC staff will email you again to let you know whether you made the cut for a seat. If you made it, head directly to the terminal — do not pass Go, do not collect $200.

TIP

Don't leave right away if AMC staff doesn't call your name; stick around until people start boarding. Sometimes new seats become available at the last minute thanks to no-shows.

Hopping on your flight

Stay in the terminal with all your baggage until it's time to board the plane. AMC staff will let you know when to check your bags, which may occur right after roll call or much later. After everyone's bags are checked, AMC staff will announce boarding. Then, you go through a security check and wait. Typically, you choose your seat after you board unless you're flying on a chartered Patriot Express flight; those come with assigned seats listed on a boarding pass.

Catching Your Zs at Military Lodging

Many decent-sized military installations have a hotel of their very own, and you can often book a stay there if you have an ID card that lets you on the installation or you meet other special requirements (such as visiting a family member in a military hospital). Installations that don't have name-brand hotels may still have transient billeting options. Though your savings may vary by staying on a military installation, you'll be close to all the on-base amenities you're used to. Use the following numbers and websites to find out what's available at your destination:

>> **Air Force Lodging:** 888-AF-LODGE; https://af.dodlodging.net/

>> **Army Lodging:** 800-GO-ARMY-1; https://army.dodlodging.net/

- >> **Navy Lodge:** 800-NAVY-INN; www.navy-lodge.com/

- >> **Marine Corps Transient Billeting:** https://usmc-mccs.org/index.cfm/services/lodging/temporary-lodging-facilities/

- >> **Coast Guard Lodging:** www.dcms.uscg.mil/Our-Organization/Assistant-Commandant-for-Human-Resources-CG-1/Community-Services-Command-CSC/MWR/Coast-Guard-Lodging/

Getting R&R at Recreation Centers

The military isn't all work and no play. In fact, the DOD owns five Armed Forces Recreation Centers (AFRCs) that are open to servicemembers, retirees, and honorably discharged vets with a 100 percent service-connected disability, plus their families. Veterans covered under the Purple Heart and Disabled Veterans Equal Access Act of 2018 (such as Medal of Honor and Purple Heart recipients, former POWs, and some caregivers) are eligible to stay at the Hale Koa and Shades of Green, though that may change in the future; the best way to find out if you fall into one of those categories is to call the recreation center directly. Here's a quick peek at each of these resorts:

- >> **Dragon Hill Lodge in Seoul, South Korea:** Dragon Hill Lodge in downtown Seoul is operated by the Army and features American-style resort rooms, three sit-down restaurants (I'm partial to Greenstreet), and a small food court with a few fast-food options. You can also use the on-site shoppette, swimming pool, or workout room, and get discounted tours and attraction tickets from the Discover Seoul desk.

  You can walk to the famed Itaewon area from DHL, so after you shop, dine, and drink to your heart's content, you can catch a ride on the Seoul Metro and get anywhere you need to be. (And take it from me: The subway is clean, easy to use, and fast — and there are single-use ticket kiosks with English instructions. I don't travel around Seoul any other way!) Find out more at www.dragonhilllodge.com/.

- >> **Edelweiss in Garmisch, Germany:** Edelweiss Lodge and Resort is a vacation retreat nestled in the Bavarian Alps, where every season is spectacular. Located in Garmisch, Edelweiss offers special packages just for retirees that include tours where you can immerse yourself in the culture, scenery, and history. Of course, local tours are available for all guests, and if you're there during winter, you get to enjoy more than 70 kilometers of ski and snowboard runs (or work with an instructor if you don't have your snow legs just yet).

Edelweiss has a café, a buffet, a mountain-style alehouse bistro, an outdoor hot tub, indoor pool, and fitness center. It also has a spa where you can get massages, sugar scrubs, foot wraps, and more. Check it out at www. edelweisslodgeandresort.com/.

» **The Hale Koa in Honolulu, Hawaii:** The Hale Koa Hotel in Honolulu, just steps from Waikiki (and the beach), is a high-rise hotel featuring two more-upscale restaurants, a few cafes and smaller restaurants, and a handful of bars. You can enjoy authentic island experiences, take tours, attend a luau, and relax on the beach all in one trip. The Hale Koa also has a small Exchange store, a day spa, barber and beauty salon, and a well-equipped tour desk so you can get tickets for everything you want to see and do while you're on the island — including making a trip to Pearl Harbor. You can discover more and plan your trip at www.halekoa.com/.

» **Shades of Green in Orlando, Florida:** The Shades of Green Resort is right in Walt Disney World, giving you a fun (and affordable) alternative to staying in an Orlando hotel and purchasing separate theme park tickets. At Shades of Green, you can purchase military- and veteran-discounted tickets to all the parks and attractions in Orlando, and they're tax-free. You can enjoy all the area amusement parks.

Plenty of restaurants are within Shades of Green, as well as a pair of swimming pools, a hot tub, a three-level water slide, a splash park for kids of all ages, a spa, and a fitness center. The resort frequently features package deals for veterans. Check it out at www.shadesofgreen.org/.

» **The New Sanno Hotel in Tokyo, Japan:** The New Sanno Hotel in the heart of Tokyo is run by the Navy, and it's packed with all the amenities you'd expect from any specialty resort. Featuring American-style rooms, a wide range of restaurants, and a free family movie theater, this hotel is just a seven-minute walk from the nearest subway station, which makes it easy to get out and check attractions off your bucket list.

The resort also has an indoor swimming pool and hot tub, saunas, and a well-equipped fitness center. You can find out more about the New Sanno and check your eligibility at www.thenewsanno.com/.

Using the MWR for Tickets and More

If you're eligible to use MWR services as a qualifying veteran, you can take advantage of all the great deals it offers. Head to your nearest MWR Information, Tickets, and Travel (ITT) office for discounts on special events, attractions, hotel reservations, and cruise bookings. The virtual version of the ITT office is the American Forces Travel website (www.americanforcestravel.com/).

TIP

Museums all over the United States offer free admission to eligible veterans with ID cards during the summer months. They're part of the Blue Star Museum Initiative, which you can explore at www.arts.gov/initiatives/blue-star-museums.

Joining the Armed Forces Vacation Club

The Armed Forces Vacation Club (www.afvclub.com/), part of Wyndham Worldwide, connects eligible members with affordable vacations in destinations all over the world. You can find weeklong trips for just a few hundred dollars if you sign up for its free membership; you qualify if you're a current or former member of the U.S. military. Membership is also open to Gold Star families, civilian DOD employees, and Association of the U.S. Army (AUSA) members as well as immediate family members of someone who qualifies.

When you join the AFVC, you can browse vacation and resort rentals by destination, the dates you want to travel, and $379 R&R vacations at golf, beach, and city resorts. You may also purchase certificates for friends and family members to use at the resorts. The deals they offer aren't available to the public, but there's a small catch: Most of them are timeshare properties. According to the AFVC, you *may* be given an opportunity to attend a timeshare presentation in exchange for a gift or premium service — but you're never obligated to do so. (If you're skilled at firmly saying, "No, thanks," you should be fine.)

CHECKING IN ON GREAT MILITARY TRAVEL DEALS

If you're itching to hit the slopes, check out the Epic Pass (www.epicpass.com/pass-results/military.aspx), which gives you steep discounts on ski resort stays and lift tickets. If you're a theme park aficionado, ask about veteran discounts at SeaWorld, Busch Gardens, Walt Disney World, Universal Studios, LEGOLAND, and others. Even better, check out the ID.me shop (https://shop.id.me/military) to get exclusive deals on travel destinations and other goodies.

Stamping Your National Park Passport

Veterans and their family members can get an America the Beautiful Military Pass for free admission to National Parks. You can flash this credit card-sized piece of plastic at the people collecting admission fees at more than 2,000 federal recreation sites (including Grand Canyon National Park, which famously charges quite a bit per car) to get in for free.

Your pass is good for a lifetime; all you need is a valid DOD identification card, a Veteran Health Identification Card (VHIC), veteran ID card, or a veteran designation on your state-issued driver's license or identification card. Show one of these items at your favorite parks and recreation areas to get this free perk.

REMEMBER

You can buy a National Park Passport book (they have small and large versions) at nearly any Ranger Station or park gift shop. It comes with a complete list of all the parks and a map, and it's divided into regions. Each region features space for cancellation stamps, which you can get at Ranger Stations in the parks you visit.

TIP

If you have children or grandchildren, look into the National Park Service's Junior Ranger Program. Kids can earn Junior Ranger badges by completing a series of age-appropriate activities within the park, including filling out a Junior Ranger booklet with questions, mazes, and fun games related to each park (you can get a park-specific booklet at any Ranger Station). When your child completes the booklet, bring it to a park ranger together; the ranger swears them in as an official Junior Ranger and gives them a plastic or wood badge featuring the park's name. I tell you this for the most solid reason ever: On dozens of trips, the Junior Ranger program stopped my son from letting us know that he was hot, bored, or tired every five minutes, and it got him interested in the wealth of information around him.

Chapter **26**

Sidling up to State Veterans Benefits

A lot of states have huge rosters of perks reserved for people who have served honorably in the U.S. Armed Forces — and even in those states that only have a handful of benefits, they're pretty good. This chapter covers some of the most common state benefits for veterans and how to access them.

Moving in on State Veterans Homes

Every state in the union has at least one veterans home. These homes are facilities that can provide veterans with the care they need, and they're owned, operated, and managed by state governments. In order for one of these facilities to qualify as a veterans home, it must be certified by the Department of Veterans Affairs and meet VA standards; these facilities have to maintain certain standards to keep their certification. Every state has its own eligibility and admission criteria for veterans homes.

Though some only admit vets, others are more family friendly and admit nonveteran spouses, Gold Star parents, and others. You can find a list of federal VA-certified veterans homes at `www.va.gov/GERIATRICS/pages/State_Veterans_Homes.asp`, or you can check out state-certified veterans homes by searching your state's name plus "veterans home" online. For example, a search for "Michigan veterans home" brings up facilities affiliated with the Michigan Department of Military and Veterans Affairs.

Taking Advantage of Financial Perks

States are proud of their returning veterans, and sometimes they share financial perks. Here are a few you may enjoy thanks to your military service:

>> **Tax breaks:** Some states don't require disabled veterans to pay property taxes at all, and some offer reductions of homes' assessed values for property tax purposes. Some states even offer homestead tax exemptions that are only available to vets.

>> **Licensing discounts:** Some states give you reduced cost (or free) driver's licenses, hunting and fishing licenses, and even business licenses.

>> **Admission to state parks and recreational areas:** Most states offer free or discounted state park passes, camping passes, and admission tickets to state historical sites to honorably discharged veterans. Some are dependent on disability, whereas others are more of a free-for-all.

>> **Educational benefits:** Several states have special tuition grants, fee waivers, scholarship programs, and other benefits for veterans. Some even extend benefits to vets' spouses and kids. However, these benefits vary widely between states — and so do qualification requirements.

TIP

Looking for other park perks? Admission to more than 2,000 national parks, national monuments, wildlife refuges, and national forests is completely free to most veterans (though you may still have to pay for special recreation permits or to camp). The America the Beautiful Military Pass is yours if you have a DOD ID card, a Veteran Health ID card, or veteran ID card, or you have a veteran designation on your state-issued driver's license or ID card; it's a free lifetime pass that never expires. Considering that admission fees at some national parks are pretty high (I'm looking at you, Grand Canyon), this is a great deal you shouldn't pass up.

Using State Veteran Preference for Jobs

Forty-six states and Washington, D.C., use the federal government's point system to offer veterans preference in hiring (I explain how all that works in Chapter 11). That means if you're interested in working for your state government, you may have an edge over all the other applicants. The four remaining states use *absolute preference* for veterans, which puts your resume at the top of the pile — even if other job candidates are more qualified. (In case you were wondering, Massachusetts, New Jersey, Pennsylvania, and South Dakota are those four states.)

Exploring Burial Benefits

If you're not interested in (or don't qualify for) burial at Arlington National Cemetery, which I cover in Chapter 22, you most likely qualify for burial in one of your state's veterans cemeteries or a VA national cemetery. State veterans cemeteries are operated and maintained by the state, whereas the VA is responsible for all VA national cemeteries. Every state has veterans cemeteries, but only 42 states and Puerto Rico have VA national cemeteries. Either way, you may be eligible for a plot in one or the other based on your service record. Some states offer grants to help with burial costs, as well.

REMEMBER

Indigent vets who have no next of kin are entitled to a casket or cremation urn from the VA for interment in a national, state, or tribal veterans cemetery.

Focusing on Your State's Benefits

Though state benefits are subject to change and the best way to get current information on each type of benefit is to connect with your state government, Table 26-1 gives you a quick rundown on the perks that may be available in your state. Some benefits are only available to disabled vets. Your local VA office or your state can give you the most current information on qualifying and applying for these benefits. U.S. territories have their own sets of benefits, which you can find on each territory's website.

TABLE 26-1   ## State Veterans Benefits

State	Financial Benefits	Educational Benefits	Recreation Benefits
Alabama	Property tax reductions and exemptions*	Free tuition for Purple Heart recipients; discounted tuition for some military dependents	Free admission to state parks; discounted fishing and hunting licenses for disabled vets; free pistol permits for retirees
Alaska	Property tax exemptions	Free and reduced tuition for some veterans; CDL test waivers	Alaska Railroad discounts; reduced fares on the Alaska Marine Highway System; discounted hunting and fishing licenses; free camping passes
Arizona	No state income tax on federal retirement pay; Arizona Military Relief Fund for emergency assistance; free vehicle license tax or registration fees*	Free tuition for veterans and dependents*; CDL test waivers; reduced real estate licensing requirements*	Free or discounted hunting and fishing licenses; free or discounted state park entrance fees
Arkansas	Personal property tax exemption*; no state income tax on retired pay	Free tuition for dependents*	Discounted hunting and fishing licenses; half-price camping in state parks*
California	Special loan programs; property tax exemptions; no motor vehicle registration fees*; waived business license fees and taxes; veterans preference on state contracts*	Free tuition for dependents*; CDL test waivers	Reduced annual fees for hunting and fishing licenses*; free passes to state parks*
Colorado	Property tax exemptions*; discounted income tax on retired pay	N/A	Free hunting and fishing licenses*; free state park admission in August each year (and on Veterans Day)
Connecticut	Property tax exemptions; no income tax on retired pay; sales and use tax exemptions in commercial agricultural production	Free tuition and fees for veterans and some survivors; CDL test waivers	Free lifetime passes to state parks*
Delaware	Pension benefits for paraplegic veterans; discounted income tax on retired pay; some school district property tax exemptions*	Free tuition and fees (even for out-of-state schools) for some children of deceased veterans	Discounted state park admission; free hunting and fishing licenses*

State	Financial Benefits	Educational Benefits	Recreation Benefits
Florida	Property tax exemptions*; homestead exemptions*; free driver's licenses*; free, paid training fellowship in the Veterans Florida Agriculture Program	Tuition waivers*	Discounted state park admission; discounted or free county and municipal park admission; discounted hunting and fishing licenses
Georgia	Homestead tax exemptions*; vehicle tax exemptions*; free business licenses*; free driver's licenses	N/A	Free and discounted hunting and fishing licenses; discounted state park admissions*
Hawaii	No income tax on retired pay; property tax exemptions*; discounted vehicle registration*	N/A	N/A
Idaho	Discounted income tax on retired pay; discounted property tax*; grocery tax credit*; financial assistance to veterans*	N/A	Free access and camping at state parks*; discounted hunting and fishing licenses
Illinois	No income tax on retired pay; "bonus" payments for wartime service; compensation to survivors of Vietnam veterans*; POW compensation; homestead exemptions; waived state license and credential fees for some jobs	Waived educational requirements for police and firefighters; financial aid for survivors; free tuition and fees for some veterans	Free admission and camping at state parks for the time period equal to your military service; free and discounted hunting and fishing licenses
Indiana	No income tax on retired pay; property tax deductions*; free vending licenses	Free tuition*; CDL test waivers	Free and reduced admission to state parks; free hunting and fishing licenses*
Iowa	No income tax on retired pay; home ownership assistance grants; property tax reductions; homestead exemptions*; grants to injured veterans*	Reduced tuition for children of those killed in action	Discounted hunting and fishing licenses*
Kansas	No income tax on retired pay; homestead exemptions*	Free tuition for children of those killed in action; free tuition for some veterans	Free hunting and fishing licenses*; discounted state park admission*
Kentucky	Reduced income tax on retired pay; property tax deductions*	Tuition waivers for survivors	Discounted hunting, trapping, and fishing licenses*

(continued)

TABLE 26-1 *(continued)*

State	Financial Benefits	Educational Benefits	Recreation Benefits
Louisiana	No income tax on retired pay; property tax exemptions*; Military Family Assistance Fund	Dependent educational assistance*	Free hunting and fishing licenses*; free and discounted admission to state parks*
Maine	Discounted mortgages; no income tax on retired pay; property tax exemptions*; free vehicle registration*; free driver's licenses*; veterans emergency financial assistance	Free tuition for dependents*	Free hunting, trapping, and fishing licenses*; free admission to state parks and recreation areas
Maryland	Property tax exemption*; discounted income tax on retired pay; pension tax exclusion*;	CDL test waivers	Free hunting and fishing licenses*; free admission to state parks
Massachusetts	No income tax on retired pay; property tax exemptions*; motor vehicle tax exemptions*; disabled veterans annuities*; compensation for families of those killed in action; bonus payments to returning servicemembers	Free tuition	Free parking at state parks*
Michigan	No income tax on retired pay; property tax waivers*; free vehicle registration*; emergency funding for veterans; burial allowance	Tuition assistance for children*	Free hunting and fishing licenses*; free admission to state parks*
Minnesota	No income tax on retired pay; property tax exemptions*; short-term financial assistance; special needs grants; free dental and vision care (income-based); exemption from some requirements of firearms safety courses	Minnesota GI Bill tuition payments; surviving spouse and dependent education benefits*	Free hunting and fishing licenses*; free admission to state parks*
Mississippi	No income tax on retired pay; low-interest mortgage loans	N/A	Hunting and fishing licenses not required*
Missouri	No income tax on retired pay; property tax credits*	Caps on tuition amounts; survivor's grants*; CDL test waivers	Free hunting and fishing licenses*

State	Financial Benefits	Educational Benefits	Recreation Benefits
Montana	Property tax exemptions*	Tuition waivers for veterans and orphans	Discounted hunting and fishing licenses*; discounted camping and amenities at state parks
Nebraska	No income tax on retired pay; emergency financial assistance; homestead exemption*; expedited occupational licensing; military experience–based occupational licensing	Tuition waivers for children*	Free or discounted hunting and fishing licenses
Nevada	Annual tax exemptions*	Tuition waivers*	Discounted hunting and fishing licenses*; free entrance to state parks*
New Hampshire	Property tax exemptions*; Global War on Terror bonuses; support for indigent veterans; free peddler's licenses*	Free tuition for surviving children*	Free hunting and fishing licenses*; free admission to day-use state parks*
New Jersey	Veteran income tax deductions; property tax deductions*; catastrophic entitlement payments*	Tuition assistance for orphans*; CDL test waivers	Free hunting and fishing licenses
New Mexico	Total property tax exemption*; discounted property tax; vehicle excise tax exemption*; reduced vehicle registration fees	Tuition waivers for orphans; scholarships for Vietnam vets; wartime veteran scholarships	Free hunting and fishing licenses*; free admission to state parks*
New York	No income tax on retired pay; burial allowance*; gold star annuities; free E-Z passes for the Thruway*; death benefits*; free peddler's license*	Free tuition; tuition grants for children	Discounted hunting and fishing licenses*; free access to state parks and golf courses*
North Carolina	No income tax on retired pay; property tax exemption*; vehicle highway tax exemption*	Scholarships for children of wartime veterans	Discounted hunting and fishing licenses*
North Dakota	No income tax on retired pay; property tax deductions*; hardship grants for veterans; PTSD grants	Free vocational training; dependent tuition waivers*	Discounted hunting and fishing licenses*; free admission to state parks*

(continued)

TABLE 26-1 *(continued)*

State	Financial Benefits	Educational Benefits	Recreation Benefits
Ohio	No income tax on retired pay; veteran bonus payments; homestead exemptions*; injured veteran grants*; home loan programs; financial assistance; free educator licenses; free registration for personal watercraft	Scholarships for orphans	Free hunting and fishing licenses*; free or discounted camping at state parks
Oklahoma	Discounted income tax on retired pay; sales tax exemption*	N/A	Discounted hunting and fishing licenses*; free admission to state parks
Oregon	Property tax exemptions*; veterans emergency assistance payments	N/A	Free hunting and fishing licenses*; free parking and camping at state parks*
Pennsylvania	No income tax on retired pay; emergency financial assistance; real estate tax exemption*; blind veterans pension*; paralyzed veterans pension*	Tuition grants for orphans*	Free or discounted hunting, trapping, and fishing licenses*
Rhode Island	Discounted tax on retirement pay; property tax exemptions; free vehicle registration*	Free tuition*	Free hunting and fishing licenses*; free admission to state parks*
South Carolina	Property tax exemptions*; homestead tax deduction*	Free tuition for children*	Free hunting and fishing licenses*; discounted admission to state parks*
South Dakota	Property tax exemption*; returning veterans bonus	Free tuition*	Free hunting and fishing licenses*; free admission to state parks*
Tennessee	Motor vehicle privilege tax exemption*; property tax deductions*	Free tuition for orphans; CDL test waivers	Free hunting and fishing licenses*; discounted camping in state parks
Texas	Property tax exemption*; homestead tax exemptions; free driver's licenses*; veterans home loans; veterans home improvement programs	Free tuition (Hazlewood Act)	Free hunting and fishing licenses*; free admission to state parks*
Utah	No income tax on retired pay; property tax abatement*; free vehicle license and registration fees*	Tuition waivers*; CDL test waivers	Discounted fishing licenses*; free access to state parks
Vermont	Property tax reductions	CDL test waivers	Free hunting and fishing licenses*

State	Financial Benefits	Educational Benefits	Recreation Benefits
Virginia	Property tax exemptions*	Tuition waivers; CDL test waivers	Free and discounted hunting and fishing licenses*; free admission and parking to state parks*
Washington	Property tax exemptions*	Free tuition for dependents*; civilian healthcare profession credentialing waivers; CDL test waivers	Discounted hunting and fishing licenses*; free admission to state parks*
West Virginia	No income tax on retired pay; homestead tax exemptions; veterans cash bonuses*	Free tuition for veterans and orphans	Free hunting and fishing licenses*; discounted lodge rooms, cabins, and campsites at state parks
Wisconsin	No income tax on retired pay; property tax credits; needy veterans grants	Free tuition	Discounted hunting, trapping, and fishing licenses*; free admission to state parks*
Wyoming	Property tax exemptions*; hunter safety class exemptions	N/A	Free hunting and fishing licenses*; free admission to state parks*
Washington, D.C.	Age-based property tax discounts	N/A	N/A

*This benefit may only be available to disabled veterans, Medal of Honor recipients, ex-POWs, overseas or combat veterans, survivors, or spouses.

5

The Part of Tens

IN THIS PART . . .

Discover the easiest ways to get the VA to deny your disability claim.

Find out how to get the most from the benefits you're entitled to receive.

Head to the Cheat Sheet at www.dummies.com by searching for "Veterans Benefits For Dummies Cheat Sheet" to scout out the best places to get help making a VA claim.

Chapter 27

Ten Ways to Get Your Disability Claim Denied

If you love filling out extra paperwork, listening to the beautiful music the VA plays while you're on hold, and waiting months (or longer) for money to show up in your bank account, this chapter's for you. Check out the ten easiest ways to get your disability claim denied so you can apply (and reapply) to your heart's content.

Skipping the Medical Diagnosis

The VA requires you to prove that you have a service-connected disability before it will give you a dime in disability pay. That means you may need a medical diagnosis from a qualified healthcare provider, which you can learn about in Chapter 9. Without a diagnosis, the VA won't approve your disability claim, and you get a free stack of denial letters.

Failing to Prove a Service Connection

The VA wants to know that your disabilities were caused or made worse by your time in the military. If you can't prove either of those things, the VA is going to deny your claim. The good news is (if you want the VA to approve your claim, that is) that the VA automatically presumes some disabilities are connected to service, such as Type 2 diabetes in Vietnam vets who were exposed to Agent Orange or irritable bowel syndrome in Gulf War vets who served in Southwest Asia. Chapters 9 and 20 cover presumptive service connections and how you may be eligible for disability compensation without connecting the dots between your condition and your service.

Failing to Show a Disability

If you have a quarter-inch scar in your left armpit from a rucksack strap, the only way the VA is going to approve your claim is if you prove that it's preventing you from working or functioning in your day-to-day life. In this case, you'll probably never find work as an armpit model and you need to explain how it's disabling. Otherwise, claim: denied. Refer to Chapter 9 for more information on painting that picture for the VA.

Handing in Shoddy Evidence

The VA needs to see real evidence that relates to your condition or disability before it agrees to pay you for a disability. That means you need to furnish medical records, letters from people who witnessed your injury, or other proof. Chapter 9 identifies the types of documentation the VA finds acceptable.

REMEMBER

If you don't have a lot of documentation because you didn't hang on to your medical records or your disability appeared after you left the service, don't worry too much. The VA has a *duty to assist*; that means it must do what it can to help you get your hands on military medical records that support your claim.

Being Late

When you were in the military, you learned that 10 minutes early was 5 minutes late. The same principle applies with the VA; when it asks for documentation, you need to file it right away. Although your VA rep isn't going to make you do a hundred pushups, they'll slam the brakes on your application if you don't respond in a timely manner.

REMEMBER

If you drop the ball, the VA will deny your request for disability pay — and then you have to start all over with a new claim. Check out Chapter 3 for more information on submitting your application the right way, with or without help from a veterans service organization (VSO).

Missing the Window of Opportunity

The VA only pays you for disabilities you're currently suffering. If you hurt your back on duty and have been working toward recovery in the years since you left the military, you can't file a claim after you're all patched up. You need to file while you're still disabled. The VA won't pay you for disabilities you used to have (though it will pay you for secondary disabilities that arise as a result of a service-connected disability, which you can read all about in Chapter 9).

Letting Your Healthcare Provider be Vague

Your healthcare provider's recommendation on your disability compensation only counts if they do it right. It must be detailed and specific, so "it might be related to an old war injury" isn't good enough. Your provider should say why they believe your disability is service-connected and back it up with evidence. Chapter 9 touches on how your healthcare provider can establish a service connection for a primary, secondary, or subsequent disability.

Dodging the C&P Exam

If you're a vet applying for disability benefits, you may have to go to a Compensation and Pension (C&P) exam at your nearest VA medical facility. During this exam, a VA healthcare provider will evaluate you for symptoms of the disability (or disabilities) you say you have as a result of your military service.

The provider will also talk to you about how your disability is connected to your service. The VA automatically presumes some illnesses and injuries are tied to your service, but you have to back up others with documentation (such as military medical records). But if you don't show up to your C&P exam, you won't get benefits. Chapter 9 has the details on these exams.

Getting a Low Rating

You don't have a ton of control over the disability rating the VA gives you, and if your rating is less than 10 percent, you don't qualify for compensation. You need to proactively try to increase your rating if you want a claim for payment to go through. Chapter 9 explains how you can increase your rating.

Flying Solo

VSOs provide free help in filing disability claims. They'll fill out forms for you, tell you what kind of documentation to provide, and walk you through the process. If you want to suffer through the paperwork on your own (and risk denial for doing something the wrong way), fly solo. Otherwise, find a VSO to give you a hand. See Chapter 3 for more information on getting free help from one of these organizations.

Chapter 28

Ten Tips to Maximize Your Benefits

Whether you apply for disability, education, housing, or any other type of benefit, keep in mind that you earned them all through your own blood, sweat, and tears. But with that said, check out these ten tips to get the most out of your VA and other benefits.

Have a Sit-Down with Your Provider

Tell your healthcare provider the whole truth about *every* issue that's ailing you, including medication side effects, especially if those issues arose during or after you spent time in the military. Even if you weren't injured while you were in the military, consider how today's aches, pains, and other issues may be connected to your service. If you think the symptoms you're experiencing may be service related, hunt around online to find out whether others have had similar experiences (and head to Chapter 20 to take a closer look at what the VA presumes is connected to military service). Raise all your concerns with your healthcare provider.

TIP

If you can't afford a visit to a civilian healthcare provider to get a diagnosis but you believe your issues are tied to your service, start a claim. You can ask the VA to examine you to help find a link.

File Claims as Early as Possible

The VA can only retroactively pay you so much, so as soon as you recognize a disability-related issue, document it and file a claim. Every day you wait is another day without financial compensation for your condition. That's true even if you already have a disability rating; new conditions can raise your rating and increase your compensation.

REMEMBER

If you file a claim online, the date you begin your claim is your *effective date*; you don't have to finish it all in one sitting. If the VA approves your claim, you receive back pay from your effective date until approval. If you plan to file by mail, submit an *Intent to File* form if you're not quite ready to submit your claim; that's how you set an effective date while you prepare your evidence and get your application ready. You have up to a year after filing this form (or opening a claim online) to submit your claim. Get more information on filing a claim in Chapter 9.

Provide Documentation on Time

When the VA or any other agency asks you for documentation to prove your eligibility for benefits, provide it quickly (ideally *with* your application). Otherwise, you're wasting time that could literally cost you. Remember that if you can't find documentation you need, the VA has a *duty to assist* you; that means it's required to help you dig up whatever information you need, such as military treatment records.

Don't Be Afraid to Appeal

Sometimes the VA issues unfavorable decisions, but you generally have the right to appeal. Use it! Otherwise, you could be leaving benefits on the table. Just be sure to meet appeal deadlines. If you miss them, you may have to start a new application — and that will cost you back pay.

Apply for a Discharge Upgrade

If you don't qualify for benefits because of your discharge status, apply for an upgrade or ask the VA to recharacterize your service. A discharge upgrade can qualify you for benefits offered outside the VA, while a VA discharge characterization only applies to VA benefits. I explain exactly how to do both these things in Chapter 2.

Get a Veteran ID Card

If you're eligible for one, get a veteran ID card from the VA. You can show it at civilian establishments to get special discounts designed just for you. You may also choose to get a veteran designation on your state-issued driver's license or ID card, which many establishments accept as proof of your past service. Check out the book's Cheat Sheet at www.dummies.com and search for "Veterans Benefits Guide For Dummies" for more information.

Take Advantage of Life Insurance

Some vets are eligible for low-cost life insurance, which I cover in Chapter 7. You can get VA life insurance whether or not you're disabled (and whether or not your disabilities are service-connected). Though these programs cost money each month, opting in may be worth the peace of mind you can give your loved ones.

Get All the Health Exams

As a veteran, you're most likely entitled to one or more free health exams related to your exposure to something in the military. Even if you don't have any symptoms, it's worth signing up for the exams you qualify for, because they can help you if you need to make a future claim. Check out Chapter 20 to see what you may have been exposed to (including burn pits) and what qualifies you for a free exam.

Leave Your TSP Money Alone

If you have money in the Thrift Savings Plan (TSP — see Chapter 8) when you leave the military, don't touch it unless you absolutely need to. That money can continue to earn interest as long as it's in the account. And if you get a government job in the future, you can start stashing more money in it to grow your retirement fund faster.

Use This Book until the Pages Fall Out

This book is your one-stop shop for all the benefits you're entitled to, so comb through every chapter. Leave no page unturned! Check the eligibility requirements for each benefit to see if you're entitled to receive it:

>> Part 2 covers compensation programs, such as medical care, life insurance, retired pay, and disability pay.

>> Part 3 explores how you can enter the civilian workforce, head back to school, and buy a home using your VA loan benefit.

>> Part 4 covers special benefits for vets of certain wars, burial and memorial benefits, and survivor benefits, plus all the fun perks for vets and retirees (such as Space-A travel, discount attraction tickets, and shopping on military installations).

Index

I

T

About the Author

Angie Papple Johnston joined the U.S. Army in 2006. During her second deployment as part of Operation Iraqi Freedom, Angie served as her battalion's public affairs representative, covering breaking news from Tikrit to Kirkuk. She has earned a Combat Action Badge, several Army Commendation medals and Army Achievement medals, and numerous accolades for her work in Iraq. She also served as the Lead Cadre for the Texas Army National Guard's Recruit Sustainment Program (RSP) in El Paso before becoming the CBRN noncommissioned officer-in-charge in an aviation battalion in Washington, D.C. She currently resides in Asan, Korea, with her husband (another noncommissioned officer in the U.S. Army), their awesome son, and two super-cute dogs.

Dedication

This book is dedicated to every servicemember who once handed the military a blank check. From one veteran to another, I sincerely thank you for your service and strongly encourage you to cash the check the military has now given you. And for Sadie; I hope you can use this when it's your turn.

This book was written in loving memory of the best-ever aunt, Kathleen Bienenstein. *Ti amo.*

Author's Acknowledgments

Lindsay Lefevere, thank you for all the opportunities you've given me to help servicemembers and veterans throughout the years. I appreciate you more than you know!

Chad Sievers, I'm so grateful for all your hard work to ensure that this is the best possible resource. Also, sorry I write such long chapters, and thanks for keeping everything (and me) on-track. Thank you for all the guidance and fixes you've made. I appreciate it more than you know!

Attorney Rebecca Deming, your tremendous expertise and knowledge of VA disability claims has been an exceptional help. Thank you for making such valuable contributions and ensuring vets get the best information.

Bonnie Swadling, thanks for always being in my corner. I love you and can't wait for our road trip.

The Davids: Thank you both for entertaining each other while I work, going to TKD and getting kicked in your tummies, and supporting me in everything I do. I love you guys so much.

Mom, Dad, Darl, Tina, and Jesse: I love you guys. Jesse, I think it's time to throw in the towel. You've had 26 years to become mom's favorite child, but at this point, it's probably not going to happen. Chin up, though — fourth place isn't bad.

Publisher's Acknowledgments

Executive Editor: Lindsay Lefevere

Project Manager and Editor: Chad R. Sievers

Technical Editor: Rebecca Deming

Production Editor: Magesh Elangovan

Cover Photo: © Rawpixel.com/Shutterstock

Take dummies with you everywhere you go!

Whether you are excited about e-books, want more from the web, must have your mobile apps, or are swept up in social media, dummies makes everything easier.

Find us online!

dummies.com

dummies
A Wiley Brand

Leverage the power

Dummies is the global leader in the reference category and one of the most trusted and highly regarded brands in the world. No longer just focused on books, customers now have access to the dummies content they need in the format they want. Together we'll craft a solution that engages your customers, stands out from the competition, and helps you meet your goals.

Advertising & Sponsorships

Connect with an engaged audience on a powerful multimedia site, and position your message alongside expert how-to content. Dummies.com is a one-stop shop for free, online information and know-how curated by a team of experts.

- Targeted ads
- Video
- Email Marketing

- Microsites
- Sweepstakes sponsorship

20 MILLION
PAGE VIEWS
EVERY SINGLE MONTH

15 MILLION
UNIQUE
VISITORS PER MONTH

43%
OF ALL VISITORS
ACCESS THE SITE
VIA THEIR MOBILE DEVICES

700,000 NEWSLETTER
SUBSCRIPTIONS
TO THE INBOXES OF
300,000 UNIQUE INDIVIDUALS EVERY WEEK

# of dummies

Custom Publishing

Reach a global audience in any language by creating a solution that will differentiate you from competitors, amplify your message, and encourage customers to make a buying decision.

- Apps
- Books
- eBooks
- Video
- Audio
- Webinars

Brand Licensing & Content

Leverage the strength of the world's most popular reference brand to reach new audiences and channels of distribution.

For more information, visit dummies.com/biz

PERSONAL ENRICHMENT

Staying Sharp	Facebook	Guitar	Investing	Beekeeping	Digital Photography
9781119187790	9781119179030	9781119293354	9781119293347	9781119310068	9781119235606
USA $26.00	USA $21.99	USA $24.99	USA $22.99	USA $22.99	USA $24.99
CAN $31.99	CAN $25.99	CAN $29.99	CAN $27.99	CAN $27.99	CAN $29.99
UK £19.99	UK £16.99	UK £17.99	UK £16.99	UK £16.99	UK £17.99

Meditation	Pregnancy	Samsung Galaxy S7	iPhone	Crocheting	Nutrition
9781119251163	9781119235491	9781119279952	9781119283133	9781119287117	9781119130246
USA $24.99	USA $26.99	USA $24.99	USA $24.99	USA $24.99	USA $22.99
CAN $29.99	CAN $31.99	CAN $29.99	CAN $29.99	CAN $29.99	CAN $27.99
UK £17.99	UK £19.99	UK £17.99	UK £17.99	UK £16.99	UK £16.99

PROFESSIONAL DEVELOPMENT

Windows 10	AutoCAD	Excel 2016	QuickBooks 2017	macOS Sierra	LinkedIn	Windows 10
9781119311041	9781119255796	9781119293439	9781119281467	9781119280651	9781119251132	9781119310563
USA $24.99	USA $39.99	USA $26.99	USA $26.99	USA $29.99	USA $24.99	USA $34.00
CAN $29.99	CAN $47.99	CAN $31.99	CAN $31.99	CAN $35.99	CAN $29.99	CAN $41.99
UK £17.99	UK £27.99	UK £19.99	UK £19.99	UK £21.99	UK £17.99	UK £24.99

SharePoint 2016	Fundamental Analysis	Networking	Office 2016	Office 365	Salesforce.com	Coding
9781119181705	9781119263593	9781119257769	9781119293477	9781119265313	9781119239314	9781119293323
USA $29.99	USA $26.99	USA $29.99	USA $26.99	USA $24.99	USA $29.99	USA $29.99
CAN $35.99	CAN $31.99	CAN $35.99	CAN $31.99	CAN $29.99	CAN $35.99	CAN $35.99
UK £21.99	UK £19.99	UK £21.99	UK £19.99	UK £17.99	UK £21.99	UK £21.99

dummies.com

dummies®
A Wiley Brand